BILLIONAIRE

I Am Single; I Am One

*Paradigm-Shifting Perspective
from the King's Son*

KAREEM AINSLEY

WESTBOW
PRESS®
A DIVISION OF THOMAS NELSON
& ZONDERVAN

WestBow Press books may be ordered through booksellers or by contacting:

WestBow Press
A Division of Thomas Nelson & Zondervan
1663 Liberty Drive
Bloomington, IN 47403
www.westbowpress.com
1 (866) 928-1240

All Scripture quotations are taken from the King James Version.

ISBN: 978-1-9736-9174-7 (sc)
ISBN: 978-1-9736-9176-1 (hc)
ISBN: 978-1-9736-9175-4 (e)

Library of Congress Control Number: 2020908803

Print information available on the last page.

WestBow Press rev. date: 05/20/2020

To the male who will become a gentleman, realizing he is a king.

To the female who will become a lady, realizing she is a queen.

To the parent who loves his or her child and was willing to invest in the past, that is now present, while securing the future today.

Inyembezi zakho zizwakele kepha impendulo nayo isobala.

CONTENTS

FIFTH GEAR

SIXTH GEAR

SEVENTH GEAR

INTRODUCTION

Humans have been entrusted with singleness. Each individual is packaged with the end at the beginning. Embracing, unpacking, maximizing, and optimizing this fact will guide us in unveiling wholeness, oneness, and completion as a single individual. This transformative insight is built from the architectural constitution framework, which will guide in the examination and exploration of the blueprint. It is expected that a structure built on these foundations will be impenetrable, providing that there are no breaches. While you are being guided in the process of determining your purpose, a celestial transcendence will occur as scales are removed from your eyes, allowing you to visualize your true reflection in the true mirror.

A systematic and principled approach to becoming the person you are intended to be and not being the person someone else desires you to become will be engaged. This will allow the actual work execution and allow the individual to function as initially designed. The work that will be done in development will prepare you not only for a job but also for the work intended. It will prepare you not only for skill employment but also for skill deployment and sharing of the gifting which is developed as it is your gift that makes room for you.

Your birth was your introduction into this system in which, if not timely understood, you will be trapped in a time loop, dampening your potential as you remain stuck in the revolving servitude door until you become no more. Nothing in the system functions the way it is purported to function, and everything has a tendency not to do what is expected. It may seem like chaos, but it is organized in that manner to drain your energy while keeping you distracted from reality as you are lured towards the occult orchestral fantasy. In embracing your freedom, you, it must be noted, cannot be simultaneously free and ignorant; so you must choose. Ecclesiastes 11:6 tells us, "In the morning sow thy seed, and in the evening withhold not thine hand:

for thou knowest not whether shall prosper, either this or that, or whether they both shall be alike good. The time has come for the eyes to be open, allowing that which is within to become."

The process is commensurate with social engineering, bombarding you with propaganda and separating you from your identity while presenting the idea that you are someone you were not created to be. The system will try to impose who you are, what you should become, where you are going, and how you should live in between, creating massive dependence and simultaneously altering your thinking inclination. If you should conceive in the thought, you will be able to put the pieces together, but they will not allow such.

The social construct surrounding education is a tool that has been weaponized and has been converted into miseducation in an effort to impede human beings and misdirect them away from their intended focus, making them slaves to error. The slow learner who fails to grasp the miseducation concepts is provided the special education system, uniquely designed and constructed to create mass destruction, annihilation, demonizing unorthodox thinking, and revolutionary behaviour. When the sabotage methodology does not work in accordance with the plan or is proven to be in error, it is referred to as an academic miscalculation. This is similar to a research team presenting claims which are proven unfounded and irreproducible, but to retain the institution's prestige the gaffe is considered academic miscalculation, even though the information can be deemed to have been intended to utilize misdirection while clouding truth from the innocent.

In keeping with the objective, you are kept sedated with lullabies. Quietly and gently, you are kept asleep, allowing mystification to penetrate. When you do decide to awake from that slumber, you are confronted with the pretentious social media override, flooding your system with a social dopamine validation feedback loop, modifying the norms of interaction. Created are tools which rip apart the natural societal fabric and present a programmed state of pretentiously and innocuously passing the time your intellectual independence is surrendered, making your psychological vulnerability subject to exploitation. As the loop continues, there is a numbing of rationality as inhibitions are mind-jacked.

People naturally tend to support that in which they are interested, and it has been proven that most people don't want to hear the truth, as they are more comfortable in believing fictions presented as fact and not actual fact. With this overwhelming information bombardment, and with underdeveloped filters, the mind is allowed to operate automatically without constraints, finding comfort in clicking, liking, texting, sharing, and engaging in impulsive actions without calculating the repercussions, which eventually leads to an individual's demise without any taking of responsibility or aiding in the rescue.

Multiple individuals' minds have been hijacked by the surreptitiously subjoined reality interlocking with fantasy with the delusive intent to give over control. In fact, these victims become the marionettes subjected to the subconscious direction. Mechanistically in the modern era, chauvinism has blinded the actions imposed by separatism, promoting habitual inferiority and activating a self-destructive time bomb in the name of commercialism, which encourages cooperate cannibalism. The process is designed to insinuate that you are inadequate and that a new item will resolve your problem. This is where scepticism must step in for a while, allowing cynicism prominence, as you are more than the projection.

Amidst the unwelcome offerings, the world presents mental castration, physical massacre, and soul mutilation. Preparation is critical for the best navigation as growth and development occur. In growing, you must be willing to reject the wrong exhibited with boorishness assassination, incongruity calibration, prioritization rearrangement, critical thinking, and embracement of innovation while developing and exercising competence that indicates growth. People who don't grow are unwilling to dissociate from that which has become their accepted dysfunctional normal in knowledge and practice. The unwillingness to admit wrong makes it impossible for them to discover that which is right. Their clinging facilitates their lives' turning out unexpectedly wrong, which is their right. In finding the right, that which is wrong must be surrendered.

In functioning appropriately, integrity is fundamental to trust as character is fundamental to power. Without character, power will destroy the potential holder. The root word for *holy* means "one." It speaks to integrity. To say that the Lord our God is one means the Lord is holy. Because this is so, we should each seek to be one person, existing on principle and not necessarily popularity. Character is unchanging, and it is not a chameleon. Morality facilitates the development of values; it is these values which will protect the individual once aligned with character despite the societal supply of neurosis. Humankind's fall caused a loss of character, but as we grow, we will regain that which was lost. We need to think of ourselves as being the people we were intended to be, amidst the generational atrophy, and we must live as we are important to this universe, because we are.

Unexplored power, unused ability, and dormant strength are called potential. On this journey, that potential will be unleashed, as within our creation there is embedded great power and authority. Many will never explore this reservoir and, because of this, will never become who they were intended to become. Having potential means that you have not yet become all you could be. When you become something that you intend to be, it is not potential but the actualization of that potential, as potential is never that which you have done; it is more that which you are yet to contribute. This indicates that potential is never-ending, as it is all you can be that you have not yet become. You are more than you think you are, but until you believe this, you will be only the person you are and not the person you could become. Opinions do not change potential; knowledge of the truth will set you free from the bondage of incompetence. Being delivered does not mean that you are free; leaving Egypt does not mean that Egypt has left your system. The mentality is more important than your location. Today it is time that you are introduced to yourself.

The social lobotomy has severed the frontal lobe, eradicating inhibition-control mechanisms and subjecting the associates to underdeveloped consciousness, thereby forcing the choice between the low road and, at best, the middle road. Though what we go through is chosen on our behalf, how we go through it is dependent on the action we take. It is our mandate to elevate consciousness and become the solution, understanding that time is more valuable than money and that fear can create monsters where none exist. We need people who will hold their heads high with pride in walking the unconventional high road.

Low road—treating other people worse than they treat us.

Middle road—treating other people as they treat us.

High road—treating other people better than they treat us.

Inherently trapped within is a leader who reflects the *leadership spirit* awaiting release by way of how we think to form the *spirit of leadership*. The ability needs to collide with the mentality to make manifest that which is within, bringing that which is without. The source of vision is purpose; vision is the visualization of your purpose, which is then shared, making disciples. Leadership is about service, not controlling by way of oppressive manipulation; its power is parallel to empowerment, inspiring people with a purpose worthy of pursuit while they become that which has been discovered, moving from potential to actual. It is crucial to have politics with principles, pleasure with a conscience, wealth with work, knowledge with character, business with morality, science with humanity, and worship with sacrifice; this is the leadership quality to be desired as we become one with ourselves.

It is the intent of this work to cultivate a unique generation equipped and capable to systematically pivot their trajectory amidst the chasm of orthodoxy, discerning the illusions disguising actual truth and reality. A mechanistic approach in foundational principles and concepts will allow for the dissection in arriving from whence we were to where we are going to where we should arrive. We will, during the development, cover the exploratory terrain of the origin, sustenance, virtue, kingdom concepts, relationships, integration, leadership, sexuality, purpose, health, success, financial abundance, and love, all amalgamating in producing the whole. The revelatory experience is destined to appropriately recognize the misconceptions imposed, allowing the realization that life is more than surviving and striving, as we were designed to thrive and live fully. In becoming one, we will embrace sustenance and survival, and evade the systematic trap. There will be unity during the mental/psychological, physical, and spiritual fusion restoring as one the mind, body, and soul. The sleeping consciousness will be awakened. You will realize that though you endure an ephemeral *loneliness*, you are complete and whole, especially knowing very well you are never *alone*. Be one, be single, be awake, develop, and become as together we cover *Billionaire: I Am Single; I Am One*!

As we read in Proverbs 25:11, "A word fitly spoken is like apples of gold in pictures of silver."

FIRST GEAR

Time Initiation

The Originator

Your Origin

TIME INITIATION

Time takes only as much as you give it.
—Prince Kareef Ainsley

Prelude

Once there was a little child who could not seem to determine where it all began. On the quest for knowledge, the child engaged in a consultation with the parents. During that sitting, the child asked, "When did this all begin?"

The mother asked, "What is it that you speak of?"

The child said, "Life, the world, you know. All that is around us. How did it all come together?"

This enquiry initiated a vast investigation.

"My child, we can help you with that," the father replied.

"Do you want us to go on an adventure?" Mother asked.

The child responded with a resounding, "Yes, let us have some fun facts."

The family huddled together in the central room, which had lime-green walls and blue skirting. The ceiling window was wide open, allowing sun to reach the white floor and reflect its radiant, blinding light. The view was immaculately encapsulating—enticing as the natural desire for paradise.

The father said, "Do you see the light reflecting from the ball of gas above onto us?"

The child said, "Yes, Father, I do. It is most lovely. And the sound of the rushing waters presents a beautiful experience to us."

"Indeed. That is it. That is exactly how it all began. So what will we do with what we know?" said Father calmly.

"It is story time. There is a being who thought and spoke, and it was so!" said Mother.

The Creation of Time

> And God said, "Let there be lights in the firmament of the heaven to divide the day from the night; and let them be for signs, and for seasons, and for days, and years: And let them be for lights in the firmament of the heaven to give light upon the earth: and it was so." And God made two great lights; the greater light to rule the day, and the lesser light to rule the night he made the stars also. (Genesis 1:14–16)

This illustration marks the implementation of time as we know it—with days, years, and seasons. The beginning of time does not mark the beginning of life, as life forms existed before the calculated approach to time. *Homo sapiens* have been given time as a blessing for the protection, preservation, and refinement of the race. As we journey in time, we can prepare to marvel at the intricacy of its structural arrangement. The approach causes us to realize that what we have been taught traditionally about the beginning may not have been an unadulterated form.

It is important to note the following:

- God created time.
- Humanity was then placed in it (to allow them to be protected from eternity).
- God is not confined by time, and He does not live in it.
- God lives perpetually in eternity.

Had we lived in eternity, we would have been experiencing all the bad things forever, an idea that is similar to torture. It is not His will that any should perish; hence the gift of time for the remission of sin. Everything in eternity remains. God took us out of eternity so we could enjoy the benefit of time. Had we lived in eternity, we would've failed to survive because we need to prepare to live in eternity. When the preparation is complete, a gradual embrace of eternity will be inevitable. It is imperative that we understand that existence of life should not be treated casually, as the enemy's desire for humanity is that we become a casualty. In order to make it to the intended future, you must develop faithfulness, as unfaithfulness will lead you on the path of damnation. Life is a calculated privilege given as a gift from God. It is expected that each moment be handled with care. As wisdom is increased, it should be remembered that counsel is essential. When wisdom is elevated, it is God positioning your life so that you may influence others and change the course of events. As a plant needs to be planted in the appropriate environment to reach its full potential, you are to select the appropriate environment to develop yourself and keep you in line with your destiny. The quality of your choice makes the change permanent. Decide for yourself what your legacy and societal contribution will be.

Time Application

God exists in both time and eternity. "I am that I am" references His eternal nature.

> And God said unto Moses, I AM THAT I AM: and he said, Thus shalt thou say unto the children of Israel, I AM hath sent me unto you. (Exodus 3:14–16)

> I am Alpha and Omega, the beginning and the end, the first and the last, in this revelation we see where he is the encapsulation of that which He created, *time*. (Revelation 22:13; emphasis added)

Time can be thought of as a set piece of eternity cut out for the preparation of a people to reach eternity. Out of the goodness of the nature of God, humanity was placed in a spot to experience beginnings, ends, changes, and seasons. Our position in time was divinely designed to allow us the opportunity *to live life in seasons* and to enable us to manage destiny in days. As a people, we are not expected to live all our existence in one moment. We are allowed the privilege to live our lives in milliseconds, seconds, minutes, hours, days, weeks, months, years, generations, centuries, and so on. With time, we are afforded the opportunity to manage choice and regulate change. You can decide to do something different this period in comparison to another. So whatever was done last season that was not beneficial, release yourself from it in this season.

One of the luxuries we have been taught is that time allows us to divide our lives into three dimensions: past, present, and future. In the past, one can say, "I used to be a certain way." In the present, the same individual can declare, "I am now this way." And in the future, one can desire to be another way. All the challenges that one experiences are facilitated by time. It gives humanity the assurance that these confines will not last forever. Time allows you to push things away from you, allowing you some distance on the journey.

> Brethren, I count not myself to have apprehended: but this one thing I do, forgetting those things which are behind, and reaching forth unto those things which are before, I press toward the mark for the prize of the high calling of God in Christ Jesus. Let us therefore, as many as be perfect, be thus minded: and if in any thing ye be otherwise minded, God shall reveal even this unto you. (Philippians 3:13–15)

So as we move in time, we should not live in our past. We should actually live in the present and make plans for the future so we can enjoy a full and fruitful life.

Ecclesiastes 3:1 reminds us, "To everything there is a season, and a time to every purpose under the heaven." This indicates to us that time has meaning, value, and purpose; it speaks to the observation that seasons are natural in order to have diversity and eradicate the mundane. The seasons help with the training and preparation for eternity. In that same chapter, verses 10 and 11 give us the compass to understanding that the hearts of humans are burdened with eternity. There is a natural desire that exists in humans to reach such a realm. Even though the burden exists, we are reminded that everything is beautiful in its time—an individual is a baby and then a child, an adult, and a geriatric. Change happens as a person goes through the process. Humans have a purpose to fulfil in the time that has been given. The destiny and purpose of humanity is engrained in the created by the Creator. The responsibility for the appropriate use of time is individualistic.

Taking things out of seasons creates an aberration, which will not yield the true potential, as would have been the case had the appropriate moment been waited for. It can be compared to a fruit tree that brings forth fruit in its season. What if we desire a ripe fruit at the blossoming of the tree and then take the blossom ourselves? Will we, at that moment in time, receive the fruit that we anticipated? The answer is no. We took the fruit in an immature state, so it was not yet ready for consumption. So too is time and timing. The moments given to us at each stage should be enjoyed until that stage has passed. As children, we do childish things; however, when adulthood is embraced, it is expected that we fit in to the form accordingly. Seasons have inherent blessings assigned to them. When the right season is capitalized, things will naturally fall into place like clockwork. If you desired financial support for a particular project, you will receive it in the season. In the right seasons, your enemies will submit to your will and command. Things that were difficult will become more manageable.

No matter how diligently we try to outsmart the Creator, it will not be so; if our hearts' spirits are connected to the Lord's will, all will be as we expect. Humans must purpose in their hearts to serve and please the Lord. "But I am like a green olive tree in the house of God: I trust in the mercy of God for ever and ever" (Psalm 52:8).

If we submit to God's mercies, then our needs will be met. What we must seek after is to be rooted in the ways of the Master. There is an invested interest in humanity; it is the desire of the Lord that each fulfil his or her destiny for which he or she was created.

Before we were, we were without knowing we were. We won't know until we are after we have been. Ecclesiastes 3:15 tells us, "That which hath been is now; and that which is to be hath already been; and God requireth that which is past."

1. God created the substance from which we came.
2. He made us.
3. Within us was implanted a purposeful mandate.
4. After such a time, life was given unto us.
5. He commits to helping us to accomplish that purpose within us.
6. If anyone tries to stop you from fulfilling in accordance with His will, He will stop that person.
7. Your purpose will be fulfilled only if you desire it to be.

The assurance is given that the Lord will do that which is His perfect will concerning your life; just remember that no one will force you into doing that which you have no desire to do. No failure can stop God's plan for your life; only *you* can stop it. We read in Ephesians 1:11, "In whom also we have obtained an inheritance, being predestined according to the purpose of him who worketh *all* things after the counsel of his own will" (emphasis added).

You have made many miscalculations, and those have been conformed to aid in the formation of your purpose. We have been robbed by ourselves. With this realization comes an acceptance of the situation of depravity, which is paramount in a cyclic shutdown. It takes a commitment, halting the tides and saying, "No more will this be allowed to persist." It must be purposed in the heart. These moments of slippage and leakage are pivotal opportunities to exercise the franchise of methodological recalibration; these are occasions for reset and restoration.

The past, present, and future are occurring concurrently right before your eyes without you even realizing it. A second ago you were reading the paragraph above, now you are reading this writing of explanation, and you will continue to read without realizing that you have entered the future, which became the present and now is the past. This concept may take some time to grasp logically; however, it becomes more intense when we examine the manual of the Creator.

Note with attention:

- ✓ God does not start what is not ended. Your beginning is the past of God.
- ✓ When it is finished, it is started. When it becomes the past for God, it becomes your present when you embrace it. It is clear now that we understand how it is that we can have an expected end.
- ✓ He always begins with the end before He starts, so when it becomes, it is complete.
- ✓ When God begins something, that is proof that it is finished.
- ✓ You should not forget that your end has already been determined, so seek not to become weary in well-doing; just encourage yourself in the Lord if you need a little strength to hold firm.
- ✓ You are complete and legitimate, not an occurrence of chancery, coincidence, or random probability, notwithstanding any other incomplete explanatory concept or ideas of serendipity.

We read in Isaiah 46:9, "Remember the former things of old: for I am God, and there is none else; I am God, and there is none like me."

- • You were not begun until you were complete.
- • You are not an experiment.
- • You are a result of divine selectivity.
- • God is not worried about your future, as your future is God's past.

- You were created to fulfil a purpose that only you are capable of executing.
- You were never a homunculus, so you have been given an equal privilege to live in the fullness of time.
- Enjoy time as the Lord makes it available.

Your destiny is established and finished, as you were born to begin your end.

1. What God has finished, you were born to start.
2. Your conception is proof that you are at the beginning of your end. And existence is proof.
3. God will never cancel what He has committed to do, but are you committed to it?

During the discovery process, we will examine characters who were predestined as you have been. Being predestined is one thing; the next step is to fulfil that destiny. One of the highest powers that has been afforded to humans is that of choice. All human beings need to choose for themselves their destiny; the best option is to select the chosen destination. Our destinies are established, but there is no guarantee. We will need to decide if this is what we desire for our lives, as the Lord will only knock at the door gently and will not impose upon us.

You have been geared for the best end; however, you need to choose the path for that end. "Not because we were destined for greatness" means that indeed we will become that which we were created to be. What you accomplish is not up to God; it is actually determined by you. Your destiny is determined by the decisions you make, and that destiny determines the course of your life based on your choices. Once you have a plan and a sense of direction, you will choose the path in accordance. The things incubated within will manifest eventually. Seek to incubate and develop only healthy habits. Your course is chosen by your destiny, and your choices determine the course you are on.

When the heavens and earth were created, the earth was without form and void, and darkness was upon the face of the deep. This was observed, and in preparation, the presence of God created the photons to illuminate so that which was unseen could be seen. The account reveals the Spirit of God moving upon the face of the waters. A division of light was spoken, and it was so. The dividing of light marked the beginning of time for the man as we see in Genesis 1:5: "And God called the light Day, and the darkness he called Night. And the evening and the morning were the first day."

THE ORIGINATOR

The world and the universe are complexly organized with calculation measures showing that one cannot exist without realizing that one's existence was predetermined for a specific time. Is it possible that such a calculation could have come from uncontrolled explosive energy, or was it a controlled situation that created that which is? In order to examine and determine the roots of the Originator, it is imperative that we briefly delve into the principle of energy. The reason for doing so is that all theories of the Originator have this universal basic principle of thought. If quantum physics and astrophysics were to be examined, we would find a direct correlation with the biblical literature of many religious sects. This could be considered a simplified version of the universe's complexity allowing for ease of understanding while stimulating theories of exploration. The predication of the Originator would indicate that there is an energy form that created all and is in all while being everywhere and nowhere (places the mind is yet to conceive) simultaneously. Energy lives outside us, within us, and through us and is us. A few theories that exist are the dimensional theory, vibration frequency, photonic light, matter, gravity, and time, all coming together to indicate that there is the need for a specific sequential order of operation. This demonstrates that we need someone or something to amalgamate all within his or her set proportion for full functionality.

It has been noted that in specific parts of the Bible, if the letters are converted to numbers, the Fibonacci sequence will be observed. In other aspects, you will observe numbers which appear random but which are actually frequencies of resonance, which aligns with the Fibonacci spiral. These spirals align themselves with the created, such as spiral galaxies, the thumbprint, and the ear, pointing us back to the Originator. There is an infinite number of numbers, which indicates that there are infinite numbers of frequencies. With this unlimited number of frequencies, it means mass can take any of the countless forms. Scientifically, it directs our attention to the fact that there are different universes that exist outside Orion.

Quantum Revelation

It is with this same appreciation, foundational principle, and concept that the quantum computing system is being built, unifying mathematics and physics and validating the expressed biblical reality of time, space, origin, and existence. This future presented exists in quantum computing with the computer being a sensitive machine responsive to noise, environmental interference, and perturbations. The concept of incoherence is still baffling to the developers whose intentions are to solve problems whose solutions are already available; however, they still desire to prove and understand them scientifically. The system is based on quantum bit processors as qubits; in this state, calculations can be made of small isolated outcomes based on superposition. A coin can exist as heads or tails as we are traditionally taught; however, the reality is that a coin can exist as a head, as a tail, and also on its side (being heads and/or tails). The same principle has existed since the inception of time. The Spirit of God is able to see the end at the beginning. During any given moment before it occurs, the exact calculations would have already been made. Quantum mechanics proves that it is possible, likened to the way of escape made in advance of the occurrence, as is a promise by the Creator. Instead of following the traditional binary approach, quantum processing can be more than 0 and more than 1. It can be both at the same time, considered superposition, revealing that it is possible for a Creator to be at two places at the same time, being everywhere and nowhere simultaneously.

Entanglement is a principle with a scientific basis. It presents the idea that two or more related or unrelated entities can be joined as one and can be either at the same time or both at the same time. This was already displayed when God became a man to offer salvation to humanity. It was God being divine in the human state, classically called divinity clothed in humanity. However, before that, it was displayed in the creation of humankind when it was stated, "Let us make man in our own image." At the end there was one man created. The more that science examines reality, the more it reveals the Originator's need for the existence, functioning, and substance of the world, galaxy, and universe. Humanity has gone to the atomic level in order to enjoy the fact of origin with scientific evidence. The world was created in symphonic harmony with a unified vibration frequency intertwined with an inexact computation proportion reflecting the Originator's perfection.

Psalm 14:1 reads, "The fool hath said in his heart, There is no God. They are corrupt, they have done abominable works, there is none that doeth good." If you are uncertain about your Originator, then it means there is a probability that you don't exist. The question is, are you in existence? Within the human being, the natural desire exists to worship. While on a quest to fulfil, some resort to worshipping gods, people, and things. Many fail to realize that the things they crave to worship were created for them by a Source. The logic of the matter indicates that the Originator is more supreme than the created. In simple terms, the watch is not greater than the watchmaker. The Originator who creates should be worshipped, not what is created.

Science Desires God

We read in Hebrews 11:6, "But without faith it is impossible to please him: for he that cometh to God must believe that he is, and that he is a rewarder of them that diligently seek him." Let us not base our judgement on hope, feelings, or assumptions but on the understanding of an Originator and on the irrefutably undisputable facts. For life to exist as we know it, there are some fundamental parameters that need to be achieved. Over two hundred have been listed. These must be perfectly met or else the whole thing falls apart. Without a massive planet like Jupiter nearby whose gravity will draw away asteroids, a thousand times as many asteroids would hit earth's surface. The odds against life in the universe are simply astonishing.[1]

Could it be possible that all such parameters are in place by chance? Based on the complexity of accuracy, the most probable understanding is that the universe was created perfectly by intelligent energy. Astrophysicists now know that the value of the four fundamental forces include gravity, the electromagnetic force, and the "strong" and "weak" nuclear forces; had they occurred less than one-millionth of a second after the energy surge, had any one value be altered, the universe could not have existed. The thought that the universe just happened can be compared to the probability of having a coin and tossing it and having it come up heads ten quintillion times consecutively. Even the thought of even such odds by mere chancery is irrational. Oxford professor John Lennox has stated, "The more we get to know about our universe, the more the hypothesis that there is a Creator ... gains in credibility as the best explanation of why we are here."

Timepieces are essential, as without one we would be in disarray and unable to keep track of everything, especially being on time. We should note that some timepieces are more accurate than others. How accurate is the one that we rely on? Where did the inventor derive the information with which to build the one that we rely on in an effort to make the information reproducible? Oftentimes we readjust the time as it needs to be synchronized with the Time Master's master time when it loses a second or two. It was only about 1967 when naval astronomers observed the motion of the earth in relation to the heavens to accurately measure time. The most precise clocks were set by this accurate measurement. What type of energy could have made this master clock as the blueprint, which we now use as the standard of all standards?

God's Time

We read in Genesis 1:1, "In the beginning God created the heaven and the earth." It was in the year 1968 when the atomic clock that

---

[1] "Science Increasingly Makes the Case for God", *Wall Street Journal* (1966).

uses caesium-133 atoms as they vibrate at the rate of over nine billion times per second, the accuracy of which is allegedly within one second of thirty million years, was built. It was an optical clock built by scientists at the National Institute of Standards and Technology in Colorado. This clock is even more accurate than the other clocks on which time was based, as its measuring principle of time is carried out with the use of light in a quantity called femtoseconds (one million-billionth/one-quadrillionth of a second). The optical frequencies consistently oscillate at one-quadrillionth. These clocks are said to drop one second every thirty billion years. These earthly clocks have been derived from what was created, the heaven and the earth. Humankind has only harnessed in part the potential of the vastness of that which has been given by the Originator. "For by him were all things created, that are in heaven, and that are in earth, visible and invisible, whether they be thrones, or dominions, or principalities, or powers: all things were created by him, and for him" (Colossians 1:16).

Some believe that there was a time when all matter just miraculously came into existence. This belief is scientifically unfounded. The first law of thermodynamics indicates that matter and energy cannot be created or destroyed, but transformed from one form to another. This is saying that no new matter or energy is being brought into existence and that nothing is passing out of existence. The thought that the universe came from nothing violates the first law of thermodynamics established by the scientific community, who are willing to ignore it. This indicates that the origin has to be divine, the universe's having been created by a Being greater than us. The specific moment during the Creation needed someone all-powerful to exhibit such energy.

With the discovery of radium, a radioactive element, it was realized that it continually gives off radiation. Uranium has an atomic weight of 238; it decomposes and releases three helium atoms. Each of these atoms has a weight of four. Uranium becomes radium with an atomic weight of 226. The process of decomposition continues until we eventually end with the inert element lead. The operation of decomposition takes time. This means that there was a time when uranium could not have existed, because it always decomposed in a controlled, systematic way. The radioactive element has not existed forever. This proves that matter came into existence, and it never always existed. Things did not gradually become something else; something cannot slowly be derived from nothing by itself. Matter could not have existed by accident. Humans are incapable of building something from nothing, even with our God-given creative genius. The exquisite detail of the universe could not have been self-derived.

Entropy, the second law of thermodynamics, indicates that everything moves towards disorder. The universe is currently in a state of winding down, moving towards disorder. When an explosion occurs, it only creates disorder, chaos, and destruction; it never once constructs anything. An explosion which never creates could not have created a life form, perfectly ordered in a systematic approach. Impossible! Our universe is slowing down. So this would seem to indicate that the universe once had been wound up, and some energy had to do the winding. That is God!

Did You Know …?

- ✓ A blood precipitation test indicates that the chimpanzee is the closest relative to the human.
- ✓ Milk chemistry indicates that the donkey is the closest relative to the human.
- ✓ A cholesterol level test suggests that the garter snake is the closest relative to the human.
- ✓ Tear enzyme chemistry indicates that the chicken is the closest relative to the human.

We need to realize that just being close to something does not make us the thing that we are in proximity with. Proximity does not become; it is about and not necessarily within or merged with. Just because a shepherd cares for sheep and is close to the sheep does not mean that the shepherd will become a sheep. You are unique, defined, and an original. There is no one like you, there is no one comparable to you, and there will never be any after you that is you. Remind yourself that you are an original as you are authentically human.

Irreducible Complexity

Which part of the mousetrap can be removed and leave the mousetrap still working? The answer: no part. Though ingenious, the mousetrap is a simple mechanism. The mousetrap cannot be made any simpler or more functional; it is in a state of irreducible complexity. So too is it with some organisms which cannot exist with any of their parts removed.

These types of creatures cannot be produced gradually from a slight modification of one part as they would never be able to reproduce to continue the process of their existence. They need to exist as a whole and be complete, or else they will fail to exist. It is simple all-or-nothing. That is how it must be with molecular machines or nanomachines. Advanced research done in Japan and Germany has explored the F1 with an engine block, a driveshaft, and three pistons running at speeds between 0.5 and 4 revolutions per second. In Germany the yeast 26S proteasome has been under investigation, which contains more than two million protons and neutrons, considered to be the largest nonsymmetrical molecule mapped currently; it serves as an intracellular waste disposal and recycling system. A cilium is an example of an irreducibly complex machine. Cilia are hairlike organelles on the surface of many animals and lower plant cells, serving to move fluid over the cell's surface or to "row" single cells through a fluid.

There are millions of animals and insects which have been created. They possess varying functions and purposes and are distinguishable from all others. They could not have been derived from a randomized occurrence to create such a systematic design. Within each of these organisms there exist molecules which aid in the formation of protein, which combines in a specific sequence to produce amino acids. This is determined by the genetic preembedded nature of the organism and the specific form it will possess. Each organism differs at such a high level that it appears a need to be developed by the design of an Intelligent Being.

When a human being creates, that which is produced is inferior to the human, no matter the level of complexity. The created is never greater than the Creator. Humankind is intelligent and creates marvels, but nothing created by humankind is more marvellous than the human. Such is the case with the world that has been created. It is a marvel designed and generated by an intelligent life form much superior to a human.

The eye of a human remains the same size from birth, unlike our ears, nose, limbs, and other body parts. The ingenious nature of the design of this feature, being complete at the onset, is remarkable. It has been approximated that over ten billion calculations occur in the retina every second. The eye is responsible for its complicated processes of irrigation, lubrication, cleaning, and protection, all happening concurrently each time we blink, which happens approximately 4,200,000 times a year. We achieve image stabilization by way of the vestibulo-ocular reflex (VOR), which allows us to walk and to read the words on a screen while observing minuscule details with rapid variable eye direction movement.

The glory of the earth is that it is just a tiny stage in the cosmic arena, a lonely speck in the enveloping cosmos whose Saviour has to be a God. Imagine any one human being having all the power; would anyone without being taught or under instruction be able to create this majestic world in all its beauty within an instant without precedence in the appropriate, size, shape, texture, and form and with all the elements of precise engineering? To put things into perspective, it takes us a lifetime to understand simple computations which are limited, so how would it be possible for us to design one trillion galaxies, each approximately one hundred billion stars away? Could we think to create light and have it travel at one hundred and eighty-six thousand (186,000) miles per second, not forgetting sound, which moves at about six hundred and sixty miles per hour? Interesting. So if humans, beings which are conscious, are contemplating if they could do this, could a force just happen to do it without any thought?! There would also need to be manipulation of the rudimentary atoms to facilitate the combination and production of particles and create subatomic entities within them. Millions of plants would need to be designed that are interdependent—thirteen million animals and insects that are dependently interdependent on the entire plant life previously created. It is daring to tender a request: please remember to generate enough food and water for all creatures so they will be able to be sustained for the duration of time allotted to them. This is less than the minimum requirement for life to exist, yet no human could create it. We could have never done all of this on our own, even with intellectual superiority. Someone did all these calculations effortlessly, knowing the ends from the beginning, as this One was the Originator of it all. This could not have been a coincidence.

Originator Presents Insight

The God of the universe can be seen calling out the snow to be upon the earth and the rain in due season. It is He who is able to speak to the animate and inanimate, and they obey. He is the One who commands the beast to go into its den or remain in its place. It is vital that each individual who is capable of reasoning to dialogue with self and enquire. The question that we will be left with is: how much do we really know and understand about the world and its origination? Nothing has been added to the earth since its creation, yet only now are we able to explore some dimensions on which a full grasp is yet to be determined. In realizing this, we should allow ourselves to be taught the ways of the wise. However, there is one essential requirement of human beings as they sojourn in this time period, and that is that they fear Him, which is the ultimate expression of love, respect, and reverence to the Creator.

To the many questions in mind, relevant answers exist to bring us comfort as our eyes become illuminated through divine wisdom. Job received the answer he was looking for when he was afflicted; he was placed in a state where he questioned God, and indeed answers were presented to him by God. As God revealed who He was and some of His accomplishments during the creation process, Job was humbled in reverence. We read in Job 38:1, "Then the Lord answered Job out of the whirlwind, and said, Who is this that darkeneth counsel by words without knowledge?" The answers given were in the form of questions but were based on the context. You can realize God's self-reference, which was eventually revealed. First it was established that God is the One who has all the knowledge and that whatever was done was purposed to be done.

During this revelation, an understanding of creation, which has not yet been fully scientifically grasped, was presented. God revealed that He is the One who laid the foundations of the earth. This indicates that He is the One who measured it, built it, laid stones upon it, and fastened it in place. It is continually being displayed that the whole process was one that is celebrated by other beings, meaning that there are other creations existing in other galaxies. Control of the sea was in His hands as the waters were kept together in their place.

Moses, in later years, would exercise God's authority in parting the Red Sea, after which time Jesus would be revealed commanding the waves to be calm, and it was so. The clouds were clothed, the mornings were commanded, and the formation of the earth was an artwork which possessed only God's signature. It was He who created the light directing to the Source of all light. This revelatory experience of communion with God solidifies that only God, the Creator, the Originator, could have created all that we are able to experience, just as Orion's belt is under God's guidance. In those moments of the creation process, art, science, and stewardship united in a kingdom sequence, presenting magnificence, enthralling resplendence, beheld by the stewards of the created. It was presented as a gift. Indeed all things come from God.

In these accounts, we see that a Being takes responsibility for the creation of the universe that many have come to enjoy. We have been instructed of the meaning of things God desires for humankind to be illuminated with, precisely, so we can reflect His truth in intent and purpose. So how then is it that people still fail to express a belief or even the understanding that there is a Being more excellent than what they are able to perceive in the created? They have been fed the illusion that there is no God without facts or justification and only speculative deception to stimulate doubt in their hearts. This stimulation of doubt causes humankind to be at odds with their own existence, as the identity of humankind is lost in this disconnection from the Source and the severing of righteousness. This causes individuals to be in conflict with themselves and more prone to transgression of the law. The world was never intended to be as we now observe it. Just like we can see good expressed by a loving God, in the absence of the presence of God, there is evil. This is the thing which causes one to question righteous instructions in one's own self-interest, blinding one to the landscape of consequences. Those caught the snare of such consequences finding themselves in an immediate pickle. If we can admit to ourselves that good exists, we must think it fair to say that God exists. If we can say that evil can be distinguished from good, then this means there must be a manipulator of such works. This brings us to the final analysis, accepting that there is an Originator, and that is God, the One who informs us of things before they occur, who allows us to see them unfold before our eyes, and who declares His power and strength so that we may embrace Him.

Originator's Infallibility in Plain Sight

Remember what Hebrews 11:6 says: "But without faith it is impossible to please him: for he that cometh to God must believe that he is, and that he is a rewarder of them that diligently seek him." Could it be possible that there is a Being who is willing to prove all things and present all things and yet who creates doubt of His existence? Could it be that we are unwilling to know because this would mean that we must go through a transformation process? Is it that we would ideally desire to be whole, but because we have become so comfortable in being a fraction, we deviate from the Originator's plan?

If we desire to understand the origins of it all, we must revisit the foundation of what was divinely given as instructions for us to follow—the Bible. Let us not deceive ourselves into believing that things appeared by chance; that is what the greatest deceiver of all time would have us believe. The images of him being the boogeyman, a handsome man with horns on his head, a man wearing a red suit with a pitchfork in his hand portraying the epitome of evil and causing all things wrong, are a misrepresentation of this spirit. Most often, humans attribute their doings that are evil to the Devil, saying, "The Devil made me do it." Though Satan may influence, he has no authority to force the hand; it is the impregnated desire that manifests by way of the enticed appetite. The beast in Revelation which gets its power from Satan is not the Devil but an expression of the energy that is possessed. It is intended that the confusion, ignorance, misconception, mystery, myth, and superstition will be made transparent by shrouding the truth about his identity and origin.

We learn from 1 Corinthians 14:33, "For God is not the author of confusion, but of peace." For all churches of the saints, this indicates that it is not the intention of the Lord that we have misconceptions about the universe, the world, and the created things. For this reason, the reference book has been made available so the pieces can be glued together in an orderly fashion to present to us with the collage of the sequence of events. Let's seek to heed the words in 1 Thessalonians 5:21: "Prove all things; hold fast that which is good." The creation of doubt was never a part of the intended plan of perfect harmony with God. It came into existence with the manifestation of sin. This subject has perplexed scholars in their quest to understand how it is that one who is sovereign and infinite in wisdom, power, and love would have allowed such occurrence as they see the expression of woe, gloom, doom, destruction, and desolation, which creates a mystifying effect, prompting doubt and blinding them to the truth revealed in God's Word, which indicates with absolute certainty that His character, governance, and principles are unquestionable. Sin is an intruder, which means that there is truly no place for it to dwell. It should not be hoarded, justified, defended, or supported. The most accurate account of this is found in 1 John 3:4: "Whosoever committeth sin transgresseth also the law: for sin is the transgression of the law." The foundation on which the world was constructed is based on the principle of love. Love created a harmonious relationship among all beings in existence. There was the perpetuation of peace, joy, and oneness as all at one time was perfect. There was always freedom of the will and of expression.

This expression was misused by the one who was next to Christ, the one who perverted freedom. In him (Lucifer) did sin originate. Prior to his fostering of this intruder-sin, Lucifer stood highest in power and glory among the inhabitants of heaven. He was first of the covering cherubs, holy, in glory, and undefiled. Iniquity was manifested in the heart of Lucifer. This being was given power, command, and authority over angels; however, his pride, overwhelmed with misguided motives, corrupted the perception of the intended purpose of such an influence. Heaven enjoyed and rejoiced in reflecting the Creator's glory. During the time of righteous honouring, all heaven was at peace, and the Creator was the only focus. Lucifer could have remained in the position of nobility had he a swift realization of the iniquity being observed and eradicated it. Gradually there was the growth of the intruder within, which caused the focus, goal, and purpose to be blurred as self-exaltation took precedence. As we read in Ezekiel 28:17, "Thine heart was lifted up because of thy beauty, thou hast corrupted thy wisdom by reason of thy brightness: I will cast thee to the ground, I will lay thee before kings, that they may behold thee."

Principle Deviation

The intended direction of operation was for Lucifer to seek God's supremacy, exercising his loyalty while pledging his allegiance solely to his Creator. When comparison manifested in his imagination and Lucifer had a desire to move outside the specified role he was created for and into the role of another, for which he was given no authority, he became jealous of Christ. Instead of directing all the glory and praise to the Master, Lucifer subtly diverted it towards himself. This creature's desire for power, which was the prerogative of Christ alone to wield, created a divide. This discord, once planted, marred the celestial equilibrium. Observation of this occurrence led to the heavenly council's pleading with Lucifer, and all was laid down as a reminder of what had been expected of him, reminding him of the nature, supremacy, goodness, justice, and glory of the Creator in relation to the law of God. The warnings given in love and mercy generated the growth of the spirit of resistance. The glory and honour placed on Lucifer were not regarded as gifts from God; gratitude was not expressed towards his Creator. In his brilliance, he desired to be equal to God. Though already loved by all the heavenly beings and clothed more extravagantly in relation to his role, his satisfaction was even farther away. He desired for more while his contentment faded. Angels, under his authority, delighted in the execution of the commands given. These they carried without question or hesitation as wisdom and glory was his clothing.

The Son of God (Christ) was the acknowledged sovereign in heaven. In the councils of God, Christ was present, while Lucifer was not permitted to partake in such a divine purpose. Then the question arose: Why should Christ alone be allowed to have such supremacy? Why should Lucifer not be equal? In a bid to defuse the concern, Lucifer departed from the immediate presence of God. Working on the matter with a hidden agenda, he presented the appearance of unadulterated reverence for God. He stimulated some of the angels to see the unacceptability of their situation, urging them to seek to act on their free will while seeking sympathy for himself, insinuating that God had dealt unjustly in excluding Lucifer from God's divine council. He presented the argument that the intention of purpose was to create holy liberty for the heavenly inhabitant. In the mercy of God, Lucifer was allowed an opportunity to rectify the matter and display the loyalty expected;

however, it was not to be so. He was allowed to remain in heaven with the intent that the full realization of his error would be revealed. He was offered pardon on the condition of pretence and submission; however, he did not accept the pardon as he could not see the drifting from glory through his eyes. He forfeited his position as covering cherub as he was unwilling to return to God, accept the Creator's wisdom, and be satisfied with the place carved out specifically for him.

The time for toleration of this ludicrous behaviour had come to its end. There was no getting through to Lucifer as the distillation presented to the others was that his actions were done in an effort to safeguard God's integrity and that he had done nothing in conflict with God that would otherwise require repentance. The Word of God was being misrepresented, and falsification of evidence was presented in an effort to have the laws of heaven changed to suit the needs of Lucifer. In the final moments of the enquiry, it was decided that Lucifer could no longer remain in heaven and that those who sympathized with him would need to leave in like manner for the stabilization of heaven. Even though Lucifer did not accept the actions as a rebellion, in the end he blamed the rebellion on Christ.

A third of the angelic host had fallen with Lucifer as they believed that there should be no laws to govern their action as they can rely on their free will to guide them on such a path. Though they could have been destroyed for their rebellion and their disruption of the harmony in heaven, they were allowed to live in an effort to display the constant love and mercy of God and to reduce the likelihood of worship out of the spirit of fear. This rebellion is a lesson to the universe. It indicates the consequences of transgression, and it displays the immutability of the law of God, which will remain unquestioned. Lucifer is not a man, but a fallen angel referred to as the Devil or Satan. "And they had a king over them, which is the angel of the bottomless pit, whose name in the Hebrew tongue is Abaddon, but in the Greek tongue hath his name Apollyon" (Revelation 9:11).

The Originator Originates

As a people, the caution is that we not be conformed to this world but embrace the transformation of the mind, allowing the right and perfect will of God. This is the state of purity required for us to enjoy glory's fullness. This world was created for humankind to occupy and experience, and that can only be accomplished if we accept and follow the wisdom the Originator presents. We have no excuse to remain in darkness as we know how the world came into existence.

YOUR ORIGIN

So God created man in his own image, in the image of
God created he him; male and female created he them.
—Genesis 1:27

Critical Questions

- ✓ Are you asleep or awake? Maybe you are the manifestation of the thoughts of another?
- ✓ You could be only a dream. How do you know for sure that you are real?
- ✓ You think that you are feeling. What if these are pseudo feelings and you are not really thinking or feeling at all?
- ✓ Maybe you are just carrying out that which you have been preprogrammed to do?
- ✓ What if you are connected to a machine in virtual reality or even in augmented reality?
- ✓ Who is truly in control of the outcomes? Are you sure that you are here?
- ✓ Are you seeing yourself or only the perspective allowed?
- ✓ Is that truly your view, or is it the view that has been shared with you?
- ✓ When did your clock actually start? Was it when they told you, or was it actually before that?
- ✓ Will your clock need a new power source?

Whatever it may be, may God be with you through it all.

For us to fully grasp the importance of our existence, we first need to understand that in order for us to be, there must have been some occasion before us. That speaks to a time that to many is unaccounted for. Science dictates that it is easier for a system to fall into disorder than into order. The scientific community indicates that breaking a glass takes less work compared to putting the pieces back together; to get it in its original state, we need for it to be recreated. In order for it to be recreated or even created in the first instance, there needs to be a glassblower or some other creator.

Deriving from the Substance

Genesis 2:7 reads, "And the Lord God formed man of the dust of the ground, and breathed into his nostrils the breath of life; and man became a living soul." It should be known that a human being is a spirit living within a body. Humankind is like the Originator, who is a Spirit. During the creation process, God stopped and formed a human being from the ground in His image, according to His likeness. Though the body was formed and complete, the creation of humankind was not yet, as only the frame giving authority for existence on earth was present. It was not until God gave the first man his spirit, by God's breathing into his nostril, that the man became a living soul. So the man was not a man until both the physical and spiritual were one and in unison. Then he became a living soul.

The word *create*, derived from the Greek word *bara*, means "to form from nothing"; however, we see the use of another term in the book called *Made or Make*, which in Hebrew is Asad/Asha, which means to form from something that already has existed or been created. Note, everything was created before it was made as this is the logical sequence of occurrence. Creation can be considered to be the catalyst that started the process of that which is now presented. We read in Genesis 1:1, "In the beginning God created the heaven and the earth." This verse indicates that before time began, God, a sovereign being who displays deity, established the beginning from nothing and, during that process of nothingness, formed the heaven and the earth without question. So this reveals to us that creation can only be authenticated by God, and it forms a part of His character.

No other creature that exists, or no other creation, can be higher than Him who created. John 1:3 tells us, "All things were made by him; and without him was not any thing made that was made." Before anything could have been created, it needed authorization, and that authorization came from God. Everything that is created came from God. Before God created anything, there was only God. In His infinite wisdom, God commissioned creation, and He began to do what came naturally to Him. This is why everything we have become or will ever become is because God allowed it to occur. This is also the reason God despises idolatry, because worshipping of the things God created is an insult to the Creator. That is why Jesus answered and said unto him (the Devil), "Get thee behind me, Satan: for it is written, Thou shalt worship the Lord thy God, and him only shalt thou serve" (Luke 4:8), as Jesus knew there was no need to worship the created when there is the Originator/Creator.

Preparation Process

The emphatic declaration of God shows His process in the creation of things. The biblical account reveals concerns for the state of affairs on earth prior to the placement of humankind on the planet. Genesis 1:2 reads, "And the earth was without form, and void; and darkness was upon the face of the deep. And the Spirit of God moved upon the face of the waters." We observe that the state of affairs on earth was outside the nature of God, which was revealed to us in His Word. The first thing we find is that the earth was without form. This means that things were out of order, in disorder. But we know that God is a god of order as expressed in 1 Corinthians 14:40: "Let all things be done decently and in order." It goes further to state the second thing that the earth was void of was meaning, taken from the Hebrew, which would indicate chaos or confusion. We are reminded in 1 Corinthians 14:33: "For God is not the author of confusion, but of peace, as in all churches of the saints." This is again outside the character of God. The third thing was darkness (absence of knowledge or ignorance) as the account indicates that darkness covered the whole earth, whereas God is a god of illumination, as seen in 1 John 1:5: "This then is the message which we have heard of him, and declare unto you, that God is light, and in him is no darkness at all." It is essential that each individual allows God to enter into his or her life as there is no unexpected end in such a case. If He is in your life, then your state of ignorance and expression of arrogance will be neutralized. Consider John 1:4: "In him was life; and the life was the light of men."

We read in Ezekiel 28:12, "Son of man, take up a lamentation upon the king of Tyrus [the prince of demons. The spirit that controlled the leader of Tyre was Satan], and say unto him, Thus saith the Lord God; Thou sealest up the sum, full of wisdom, and perfect in beauty." This is God speaking to Lucifer as he is responsible for the chaos, void, and disorder. Lucifer was created, and he is not a man; he is an angel who had fallen because iniquity, a quality of sin, was allowed room for development and manifestation.

In the subsequent verses, we see that God started to prepare the earth for the inhabitation of humankind as His Spirit moved upon the earth's face. So God decided that it was time to expand the kingdom of heaven to earth. Earth was created for humankind specifically. The first created man was placed in the garden with a mandate. It is interesting to note in the Genesis 1:26 account the use of the word *us* in the process of making humankind. This indicates that the process of humankind's existence was a singular, plural, unanimous, collective, and collaborative effort by God. Humankind's existence was a process thoroughly thought out. We can rest assured that God is the only one who can create humanity. A human is basically the spirit that comes from God living inside the body to make the creature a human. This state of creation was perfect and complete. From the man were all others likened unto him created. God took the man and placed him in the Garden of Eden, but before the place was prepared for humankind's existence, five days prior, as on the sixth day, a man was created according to the Genesis account of the process.

It is seen that the spoken words were of the Originator's pen in the process of the glorious creation; however, when it reached the special moment for the formation of humankind, there was a pause in the use of words. Humanity, the crowning jewel of the world's creation, was a gift suited for the being to inhabit in its expression of beauty and magnificence. The epitome of perfection was the splendour of his hands, health, stature, structure, and clothing of righteousness. There is not an infinitesimal decimal or fraction or diminutive variable the Lord has not accounted for in the creation of the world.

Back to Eden

The Hebrew translation of *Eden* refers to a spot or a delightful spot. Let's examine five things for humankind's delight.

The first thing was God's presence. Hence, a woman must meet the man in the presence of God. Remember, Eve met Adam in Eden. It should be noted that the woman, too, must have been in the presence of God in order to be equipped to make the appropriate selection. Adam was formed from the earth. During that period he was in the presence of God, even after his activation (becoming a living soul) and responsibility entrusting. During this process, he was carrying out duties as spiritually directed. This displays a synchronicity with God. Deep sleep was allowed upon him so that the woman who was in him could be extracted. After the process of extraction/delivery, she was allowed to commune in the presence of God before her presentation to the man. It should be noted that it was never the woman who went and woke the man; it was God who made the presentation. In following Eve's example, the woman should not be overcome with the desire to wake up Adam (man) prematurely. The man does not become a man outside the presence of God.

The second thing was work. "And the Lord God took the man, and put him into the garden of Eden to dress it and to keep it" (Genesis 2:15). While the male develops, good work ethics should be encouraged. The man was designed to work. If the man disregards work, then questions of concern need be raised. The woman must have the necessary skills in nurturing for the duties to be expressed as intended.

The third thing was to cultivate. Cultivation refers to extracting the best from that which is around by presenting a suitable environment for maximizing the potential, making things fruitful. Hence the woman is not a finished product but a revolutionizing amorphous base under the cultivation of the man. It is the man's duty to extract the best from the woman and the woman's duty to extract the best from the man. God has given both the raw material. It is for them to unite and produce the best representation. As Ephesians 5:25–29 tells us, "Husbands, love your wives, even as Christ also loved the church, and gave himself for it."

The process of cultivation goes further in indicating what needs to be done:

- If the woman is not eating well, then start cooking for her.
- If she has a challenge in taste, expose her to that which is more desirable and acceptable while elevating her level of consciousness.
- If she doesn't speak a proper language and that is your desire, facilitate schooling so she may develop eloquence and decorum.
- The reciprocal is expected from the complementary party.

For no man ever yet hated his own flesh; but nourisheth and cherisheth it, even as the Lord the church.

The fourth thing was to guard the garden. The male is the protector of everything under his care. Note that protection does not mean abuse. As Genesis 1:28 reads, "Replenish the earth, and subdue it: and have dominion over the fish of the sea, and over the fowl of the air, and over every living thing that moveth upon the earth."

The fifth thing was His Word. We read in Genesis 2:16–17, "And the Lord God commanded the man, saying, Of every tree of the garden thou mayest freely eat: But of the tree of the knowledge of good and evil, thou shalt not eat of it: for in the day that thou eatest thereof thou shalt surely die." The male must be equipped to study and teach the Word to the woman and their family. The man got the Word from God; hence, he should teach it to his wife! The man was positioned to give the woman knowledge, tapping into the wisdom directed from the Originator. As Genesis 2:18 reads, "And the Lord God said, it is not good that the man should be alone; I will make him a help meet for him." The reason for this is that the man has qualified and has accepted his responsibilities.

Men and women need to be able to accomplish these five prerequisites independently prior to enjoying the Garden of Eden:

1. Be in God's presence.
2. Work.
3. Be willing to cultivate.
4. Guard the garden.
5. Have God's Word.

You Were Predestined

Before you were, you were without knowing you were, until you are, after you have been. Prior to your creation, you were predestined to achieve a purpose; it is up to each individual to consciously decide if it will be completed. Isaiah 44:24 reads, "Thus saith the Lord, thy redeemer, and he that formed thee from the womb, I am the Lord that maketh all things; that stretcheth forth the heavens alone; that spreadeth abroad the earth by myself." We read in Jeremiah 1:5, "Before I formed thee in the belly I knew thee; and before thou camest forth out of the womb I sanctified thee, and I ordained thee a prophet unto the nations." Every human being created came from God, who created the first man. From this man came that which we now observe as the world's population. It should be known that without Adam (man), there would have been no Eve (woman). The creation of Adam was the foundation of the human race (*Homo sapiens*) as within that man was the population of this world in this dimension (earth).

The man was the first to give birth in the unadulterated form. Through this process Eve was presented, though not as a baby exhibited to a mother after the process of birthing. Genesis 2:22 tells us, "And the rib, which the Lord God had taken from man, made he a woman, and brought her unto the man." So the woman was derived from the man as the man had been pregnant with the woman and the Originator performed the delivery—a genetically engineered stem cell perfect delivery, comparable to a C-section, just more excellent. As Genesis 2:21 reads, "And the Lord God caused a deep sleep to fall upon Adam, and he slept: and he took one of his ribs, and closed up the flesh instead thereof." In this process is a glimpse into the future of anaesthesia and the possibilities that would exist. God in his glory indicated that He is the Originator of all things and that He is within His time so we can appreciate our role. The process of birth would then be passed on to the woman in time, to come after the grasping of the knowledge of good and evil.

SECOND GEAR

Don't Touch What You Don't Want

The Vine Is Divine

Bad Company Corrupts Good Character

DON'T TOUCH WHAT YOU DON'T WANT

It is impossible to unsee what we have seen, so, too, it is impossible to undo what we have done within the same unilateral, unidirectional continuum/timeline. In this life, there are some experiences that we can certainly live fuller lives without knowing it. It is not true that everything is worthy of our digestion, indulgence, or validation. Ideally it proves prudent to make decisions from an informed position, but there are times when we need to make the decisions based on our conviction from One who is infallible and has left specific instructions for us to be guided.

Indiscretion's Cost

Alex was an aspiring grandfather; however, his health had been gradually deteriorating to the point his body was unable to filter his blood adequately. This caused toxins to become concentrated in his body to a lethal dosage, which eventually had the potential to take his life. Based on his rapid deterioration, his attending care providers gave him only nine months before his organs would expire and cause the demise of the rest of his body. During that time, he was also placed on a kidney transplant list, of which he made it to the top.

His daughter had just graduated from an institution of higher learning, and they decided to celebrate as a family. In the moment of celebration, Alex consumed an alcoholic beverage. Three days later, he was scheduled to report to the hospital as an organ had become available. He went in and did the routine preliminary screening to verify his health status and suitability for accepting the transplant. The questions asked were specifically geared to ascertain if he had adhered to the guidelines for transplant eligibility. He verbally indicated that he had adhered to them. The results of a blood test showed alcohol in Alex's system. One of the conditions to retain his eligibility was to abstain from the consumption of alcohol in any of its forms. This miscalculation cost him the chance which had been provided to him to receive the kidney. That is, his failure to abstain in accordance with the predetermined agreement caused him to lose his chance. This action also caused him to be moved from the top of the list to the bottom. That one choice, that one compromise he'd made, prevented him from actualizing the state of perfect function that had once been possible. The healthcare providers soon realized that it was not a valuable choice, knowing what was now known, to transplant the organ into Alex's body. Alex was later informed that he only had three months to exist in the physical form, and eventually he was no more, sooner than necessary. The family then paid the ultimate price for the indiscretion; Alex never became a grandfather as he smothered his aspiration under the influence.

The Originator was quite specific and meticulous about the process, purpose, and scope of the things He created and made. Each item, thing, and being He created/made was explicitly unique according to the intent for which it was created. In order to maintain transparency and clarity, interpersonal dialogue and communication was of paramount importance to ensure adequate understanding and disclosure of consequences. This process of information dissemination allows those being entrusted with the power of choice to make logical and informed decisions. It also allows them to exercise their faith in their Originator, who gave the manual of all things beforehand. But being empowered with information and direction for a specific decision does not negate the fact that freedom of choice allows for the probability of operating on principle or under beguilement. In the final analysis, it is the decision which is chosen that determines the end. Specific instruction was given in the Garden of Eden, indicating that everything was for the creatures to enjoy; however, there was a but. The fruit of the tree of knowledge of good and evil needed to be abstained from, and if not, then death would be the consequence.

The association that was made with the serpent/Lucifer/Satan/

the Devil caused the created beings to have more confidence in the words of another of the created than in the words of the Originator. This doubt facilitated the beguilement of the woman in the execution of the misguided conception of the truth. The serpent, knowing the truth, misrepresented the Originator and appealed to the self-interest of the man while creating a shadow over the authority of the Originator and His words of instruction. We read in Genesis 3:5–6, "For God doth know that in the day ye eat thereof, then your eyes shall be opened, and ye shall be as gods, knowing good and evil. And when the woman saw that the tree was good for food, and that it was pleasant to the eyes, and a tree to be desired to make one wise, she took of the fruit thereof, and did eat, and gave also unto her husband with her; and he did eat."

In order to move forward, one must realize the need to make it to the future. It will not be in a sprint but like unto a marathon, which you must endure in order to be the one you have been potentiated to become. In this process, you need to appreciate the experience of resting with the surety of the near end.

1. You start the course with freedom and relaxation of the joints, overwhelmed with excitement, having confidence in the training/preparation that has taken place.
2. Next you may move into a state of denial, realizing that your pace is not as it was expected to have been and you are experiencing slight fatigue.
3. You start going into shock, realizing that this race is more challenging than anticipated.
4. You now reach a stage of isolation in which you are looking around to see those around you, only to realize that the persons around cannot complete the course on your behalf.
5. This is good. You are now closer to the finish line than when you first began; however, despair is setting in. You are tempted to lose hope, momentum, and traction, but you are still holding on to the energy that you have left, though your

feet are in an extreme state of fatigue and you feel as though you are on the verge of collapse.

6. You are about to give up because your entire body is tired with fatigue; only the hope of the finish line prevents you from hitting the wall.

7. You are now affirming yourself as you press on, only a little further, putting one foot in front of the other.

8. Finally you are elated when the journey has been completed.

Upon the realization that the beginning is important, not the end, an individual seeks to complete the race as anything short is a display of mediocrity. Your faithfulness is measured by your ability to complete the race. If you are not committed, then it is going to be difficult for you to be your most productive self. The Lord has already created an end for you, and it is His desire that you will seek to choose such an end; however, you will not be forced onto that path. He desires that you succeed as your success is His success. All that you are being asked to do is to be loyal to your future, not your present or past. You were created to succeed—there are warranties and guarantees—but in order for it to work, you need to follow the intended instructions. If the world falls out of order, all that needs to be done is to put the person back together, and then the world will become one. No one is a biological experiment, accident, or coincidence or even a glitch. It is an illusion. That idea was created to deceive you from seeing the truth. You are a concept of destiny that needed to come to the earth for a purpose which only you can fulfil.

In our process of development, it is imperative that harmonious synergy be attained in mind, body, and soul. There should be delicately balanced cultivation of the intellect, cultivation of morals, and spiritual enlightenment and not the divisive compromising of any of these with an imbalance to create questionable motive and judgement. Failure does not cancel your assignments, nor can your problems be more overwhelming than your purpose; never allow your shame to rob you. Whatever you were born to do, you were built with the ability to do, and your ability is determined by your responsibility.

Whatever the reason for your birthing is already invested within you. God's instruction is equal to His spiritual injection. Knowing this, we appreciate the inevitable collision of life for *all* at the intersection of time and change.

A little time after the vastness of the world's creation with all exactness of gravitational pull, axis rotation, quantum mechanics, metaphysical data, and solvable equations all solved and balanced to the precise degree of infinite accuracy, after the laws and theories that would be discovered and those which are still incomprehensible to humankind in our current state of mortality, *all* was *perfect*. The Architect of it all, after bestowing magnanimity upon the Creation, explicitly stated, "It was very good" (Genesis 1:31). In the vast expanse of exemplary perfection, two individuals were set in charge to tend to it and ensure that their stewardship was reflective of the character of the Originator. They had dominion and specific instruction as to all that was acceptable, justifiable, right, and righteous. These two individuals were Adam and Eve, male and female respectively, who received the instruction in Genesis 2:16–17: "And the Lord God commanded the man, saying, Of every tree of the garden thou mayest freely eat: But of the tree of the knowledge of good and evil, thou shalt not eat of it: for in the day that thou eatest thereof thou shalt surely die." The consequence for disobedience was stated clearly in the specific instruction; the account indicates that the Originator had a conversation with the man explicitly pointing to that which should not be done.

Indulgence

In life there will be moments considered to be satisfactory or even states of contentment; however, even in those moments when there is a lack nothing (i.e. no need or want), our curiosity is provoked. This provocation is not on all occasions self-induced; it is more often induced based on the channelling of thoughts on the border of doubt and on "what if", which forms external seedlings which result in an internal manifestation that will eventually cause the fortress to collapse. The fastest and easiest way to destroy is from the inside. Just remember that things are not at all as they appear. Deception and indulgence cause a malignancy that deludes the participants of their satisfaction. Conformity to sin will result in the eternal ruin of humankind. The systematic operation or ruin seeks to capture one who is unaware or who is aware and believes that he or she is smarter than the snares and can free himself or herself with time to spare. A grand illusion is created, presenting the concept that the one under duress is in control and can terminate at any time, typically when the illusion would have been revealed. If revealed, it would have been too late for a pivotal turn of magnitudinal significance. Lurking in our surroundings and based on our interactions, even in the essence of the atmosphere, which is created to fulfil a purpose, is the clandestine operation, maturing plans, skilled movements, blinding us to the end. Generally after this occurrence, the steps and the sequence of events that lead to the developing of trust, regard, and confidence in the abominable would be evident too late. Repulsiveness is generally one of the overwhelming emotions that can sink a person into an abyss of depression; for whatever your involvement in things within your control, your consent is required. You may be perplexed by your failure not to consent. Remain firm in purpose, never allowing willing defilement, and be gallant; then you will have dominion as intended.

Indulgence Process

While the dominators were in the garden enjoying the niceties thereof, a friendship was forged between the woman and the serpent. This creature was described as "more subtil than any beast of the field which the Lord God had made" (Genesis 3:1). The word *serpent* in the Bible speaks to a wonderfully glorious creature of magnificence and beauty; however, after the first manifestation of trickery with the use of subtilty, the perception has long changed and now is associated with that which is evil and presents chaos. The serpent did not act on its own accord; it was infiltrated by the spirit of the fallen angel who had been evicted from his original dwelling because of iniquity. Not all beings are qualified to be more than an acquaintance; friendship should be an esteemed reservation. Further in the verse of Genesis 3:1, the serpent says unto the woman, "Yea, hath God said, Ye shall not eat of every tree of the garden?" The first thing that occurred was the acknowledgement of presence; the serpent ensured that his presence was acknowledged by the woman. The second move was to establish a conversation, and the serpent did this in an effort to allow the woman to become comfortable with and accepting of the essence of its presence. The third, dangerous thing was the establishment of friendship; the serpent with uncensored subtilty ensured that the woman would find comfort in his proximity, to the point of allowing the sharing of thoughts, ideas, and reasoning. As innocent as it may appear to do so, you should not share all your thoughts, especially with those who are not with you and have questionable motives. The sharing of thoughts in Eden was like the opening of a door, and once this door is open, two things frequently occur: things come out, and there is the allowance for things to go in with or without notice.

Not everyone's opinion matters; some headspaces are better avoided. The serpent, later revealed as the Devil, was not about the preservation of the woman's dignity, chastity, or purity. He was all about destroying and creating misery as iniquity had long set in, and he had no remorse for his actions. The fourth stage was to create doubt, questions, uncertainty, and scepticism. This was masterfully done like a well-rehearsed theatrical performance, where the serpent asked what he knew the woman already had knowledge of. In this process of empowering, he was also creating an opening to turn the tables and regain the control and dominance that had been denied from whence he originally came. The woman, not restraining herself, dignified the question with a response. The final phase/fifth stage of the deception was to facilitate the exploration of the doubt from the seed previously planted to complete the mission. After the woman stated that the fruit would cause one to die, the serpent, in verse

4, said to the woman, "You will *not* surely die" (emphasis added). Doubt has now overtaken her understanding as there is now a focus on things which are physical, along with an ignoring of the things which are spiritual, examples of which are faith and confidence in the Word of God. The addition of one word, *not*, in the equation created a destabilization for the woman in that period of vulnerability, and her husband was not at her side to exercise the duty as God intended.

The play and the mental destabilization of the woman occurred when she explored against her better judgement the idea of doing that which was indicated by God that she should not do. Under the beguilement of the serpent, she developed an appetite over which she should have had dominion. Still in shock, she believed that she now saw clearly, when there was never anything wrong with her vision; however, now there was something wrong after the fact. The subsequent statements all were the revelation of the real intent of the serpent, to deceive the woman and cause the transference of iniquity by the transgression of the law. The mixture of truth and error equates to error; right and wrong equates to wrong; and good and bad equates to bad. This was the strategy that overthrew the human race. The woman was enticed to be like a god, knowing good and evil. She moved up to the fruit. When nothing happened, she touched it. Again nothing seemed to happen, so she took it from the tree, and all was still well in her mind. After the fruit was consumed, her and Adam's eyes were opened, and they from that moment began to die in the mortal form. They knew right and wrong, and the glory of their Creator, which once covered them, removed itself from them, allowing them to realize their nakedness. They were escorted to the exit of the garden which was created for them. Just because of that one disobedient act there remains a separation of human beings from their Creator.

When we seek to do a thing, after it is done we should be cognizant of the fact that it cannot be undone. In brief, when you have done something, it remains done until done becomes undone. This principle remains constant in every aspect of our lives. For this reason we should seek to ensure that our doing counts in the direction of establishing, building, renovating, and propagating that which is excellent and commendable. One should live knowing that the best decisions are made under the appropriate circumstances. The failure to remember that they were created in the image of God caused Adam and Eve to crave after that which they already were without their realizing it.

The question that would naturally come to mind is, how do I know that what will be done and that which is being done or has been done is in accordance with the principle of doing? The answer is simple, and it speaks to revisiting our existential origins. There needs to be a constant consultation with the Originator to understand the principles outlined and an expression of faith to believe and do that which is presented in the manual even if the culture we live in negates the direction of the prescribed operation.

Touching speaks to the arousal of feeling, making a connection, leaving a trace of self with that which was contacted. To a great degree, touching plays on our sensuality, the need to connect, become a part or one with something else. Basing a high degree of our contact on feelings is a practice which should be discontinued; connection, bonding, and detaching should be done strictly on the basis of principle and mutually beneficial outcomes. Never should it be used to exploit the naivety of others to accomplish selfish motives or intents.

As demonstrated in the garden, we would have been privileged to enjoy the ambience within the atmosphere with the perfect temperature, surrounded by an impeccable flow of order. The lush beauty of the environment and its inheritance were all in accordance with the proportion extended by the Creator of it all. Peace reigned with tranquillity as the perfect state of humankind, which has never after been reached because we touched that which we did not want. Evident was the glory of the One who was higher than the created, the Creator of all that ever existed, exists, and is to be called into existence. That whole atmosphere was marred by the subtle deception of the old rascal the Devil in one moment of unsuspecting influence, which caused the cascade of terror that exists in the world today.

The eyes of the man and the woman became open, and they knew good and evil. And indeed they would be like gods, just not exactly as it was packaged. The opening of their eyes was the result of the infiltration of iniquity, which had transferred from the serpent to humanity. Prior to this occurrence, the first inhabitants were covered in the glory of God, preventing their exposure to the evil. Had they remained in favour with the Lord, they would have been in the perfect bliss of harmony in the arms of their Originator. Just one touch was all it took, one contact, one moment too close—the simple embrace of acceptance of the grey caused the catastrophe.

As we venture on our quest in developing relationships, we may be enticed or even tempted to touch something that we have no authority to enjoy and which is illegal. As much as things may be within reach, it will take great self-assurance and self-control to avoid the sways that may shift the course from righteousness. It is better to be righteous than right, as doing what is right for the wrong reason is equal to doing bad for the wrong reason. Our motives and intentions should be noble, pure, and true. Only that which we desire should we seek to give to another, but first we must gain an appreciation for the principle of love. If we go back to the original architectural design that was outlined at the moment of humankind's reaching the state of self-actualization, we can foster an attitude which will prevent the perversion of ourselves and others we come in contact with or who contact us. The discipline to do this is rooted in connection with the Vine that is divine.

It is a privilege to be allowed the opportunity to make decisions on our own behalf. The utilization of this privilege will determine the overall quality of your life. The life lived outside the parameters of the original concepts as intended by the Originator is one which will produce less than the desired outcome, reduce your fulfilment, and leave you lacking in relation to the actualization of your full potential.

When you look at the world, you may desire to see differences, which will lead you to segregation, discrimination, and other forms of exclusivity and diverse selectiveness. Now imagine a world where we actually view with clear eyes. You will realize that there are no lines, no divides, as we are all human beings, *Homo sapiens*, all deriving from the same Source. In this actual world, when the lines are removed there will be no separation. If we could envision this grand unification of the people, then the trivial conflicts would lose their place and become irrelevant. The creation of unnecessary conflict and tension is caused by the lack of control to compensate for the variables based on each individual moving in a direction which is antagonistic to the result projected. As we move along the course of life for optimal efficiency, faster recovery, and absolute transparency, it is ideal to calculate the end point before setting out while compensating for the process.

Before relationships are cemented or solidified, the actual intention should be indicated. The motives and purposes need to be determined; the end should be mutually beneficial and should promote impeccable morality. Proving there are questionable motives or unhealthy indicators, the fruit presented appears to be seasonal. Acceptance or consumption of such fruit should be avoided at all costs, and if possible, you should not touch that which you have no desire for in the future or will have no desire for you in the same collision of time and space. Humans should not under any circumstances be used as a commodity for exchange, leverage, or barter. You must remember that we are all created from the same elements and are designed similarly dissimilar. Our appreciation of humankind will only increase when we are purposed to be connected to the Divine.

THE VINE IS DIVINE

The Disconnect

The human being is a spirit that dwells in a body, not a body which has a spirit. In order for you to function correctly, you must be in the presence of your Originator, the One who is God, the Creator of the universe. Outside of this environment, you will become as a battery, filled with power but lacking the connection to express the power that is within, and if connected to another source, there is the high likelihood of electrical short-circuiting, breaker overloading, and even becoming consumed with fire. Outside the presence of God is nothing but death. Humankind will die. In the initial design, we were privileged to have uninterrupted communion with the Maker and King as in the garden we see His voice walking in the midst of Adam and Even in the cool of the day. In that instance, there was a more intimate connection, not the one we now experience. "But of the tree of the knowledge of good and evil, thou shalt not eat of it: for in the day that thou eatest thereof thou shalt surely die" (Genesis 2:17). Precisely what was recorded was what happened in the instance of consumption of the fruit. It was evident, but the two humans did not yet realize the fast succession of events until they were banished from the garden created for them.

1. First, the glory of God left them as they had become soiled by iniquity.
2. Second, they realized that their eyes were open, and they knew they were naked.
3. Third, their conscience became activated, and they went to hide and sewed fig leaves.

4. Fourth, they realized their unworthiness to be in the presence of God, so they stayed away when God was walking in the garden.

5. Fifth, the cycle of blame games began, everyone involved in the process trying to justify why they were not the ones to *bear* the burden of the doing.

6. Sixth, the man, the woman, and the serpent were cursed for their direct and indirect involvement in the process.

7. Seventh, the first understanding of death was demonstrated when God killed an animal for its skin to make clothing for Adam and Eve.

8. Eight, There was a self-induced eviction from the garden.

It was never the plan that we should exist outside the presence of God. When we were cut off from the garden, we began the process of "devolution" as the state of degradation manifested as a consequence of the miscalculation in making that one choice. The estrangement of humankind from God has caused a need for worship, which is often misdirected. We see where humankind has been attempting to reconnect with the Creator through various means; there is the constant lingering of a void, hollow emptiness which needs to be filled, whether or not the reason for this is understood. It will be recognized that no carnality can compensate for or stabilize the need for belonging. This distance created can only be satisfactorily filled with the gifts generously bestowed upon humanity, including praise, worship, and prayer. These acts do not in actuality put us in the presence of God; however, they facilitate the presence of God in coming to us as these are avenues for connecting and communicating with Him. It is the intention of the Originator to reunite humankind with His presence to restore life to what was written in the blueprint. Hence the lifeline of salvation was made available through the Son of God, who died for humanity.

While you travel on this journey of life, remember that your life and your reality are now in your state of consciousness. You should seek every moment to liberate yourself from making plans for the moments that are to come. Life should be lived from the end to the beginning. We have a limited number of hours to exist. Let us fill our state of consciousness with exceptional content so that we may embrace a fulfilled experience amidst life's brevity. We are all going to die; despite that, you are fearfully and wonderfully made as a reflection of the intentionality of the Creator.

To protect the complexity and unlimited capability of the human mind, there needed to be a manual in order to understand its sacred uses. Other organisms have brains, but none have a mind to any degree comparable to the human's. There is none else who exist here on earth in the physical state who can coordinate, plan, think, or even create to the most minute degree of the essential human operation. The mind has designed and produced all that we have on this earth we so enjoy with the elements that were already here. The separator of humans from other animals is the operation of the mind and the process of development; animals operate primarily based on instinct, whereas humans operate on a power far more complicated than just embedded data. We have been afforded the privilege to think and develop, coordinating logic based on the spirit within. Despite our discovery of the subatomic particle, DNA, outer space, and inner space, among the other marvels, none of this would have been possible if we were equal to the other animals that we are commanded to have dominion over. These represent a tip of the wonders of God's works through humankind. We read in Job 32:8, "But there is a spirit in man: and the inspiration of the Almighty giveth them understanding." This reminds us plainly that humankind possesses a spirit called the spirit in humankind. It does not mean that the spirit is immortal. The spirit in the first place does not belong to humankind as it is for the Creator, so when a person dies, his or her spirit returns to Him, while the person sleeps, knowing not and able to do nothing.

Romans 6:23 reads, "For the wages of sin is death; but the gift of God is eternal life through Jesus Christ our Lord." This passage indicates that the every human being has a scheduled date of death because of sin as was established in the garden with our predecessors. Ecclesiastes 12:7 tells us, "Then shall the dust return to the earth as it was: and the spirit shall return unto God who gave it." Putting it simply, we realize that upon being dead, the spirit of a human being rests and does not wander the earth or exist in turmoil. Humans do not possess a soul; they are souls.

For God to have had an intimate connection with His creation, there needed to be a line of connection, a line on which information could be uploaded and downloaded without adulteration. This exists in the Spirit of God, connecting with the spirit of humankind. For this reason, the creation of humankind was precisely engineered. It was the Lord who gave the spirit of humanity to humankind. The Creator has envisioned His created as having a direct mode of connection and communication; however, the intervention of sin marred such an outlook. The Lord is the one who designs, fashions, creates, and presents the spirit of humankind to each individual human being. As humans, we communicate by way of two realms of our being, the physical (feelings) and the spiritual (principles) realms. Many will fail to comprehend things of the spirit and will only seek to stay exclusively in their physical mould. The gap of the spiritual needs to be bridged if humankind is to be elevated to a higher state of consciousness. It takes a spiritual individual to discern things of the spirit. "For what man knoweth the things of a man, save the spirit of man which is in him? even so, the things of God knoweth no man, but the Spirit of God" (1 Corinthians 2:11). So we see as clear as day that the Spirit of God and the spirit of humankind are separate entities, understanding that each performs a different function in knowledge acquisition.

Human knowledge is synonymous with the things of humanity and is acquired because God has given humanity a spirit. Things of God can only be acquired by the Spirit of God; this is only manifested by the indwelling of the Spirit of God in converted minds, a capacity that animals lack. This spirit of humanity was given from conception to allow humans to acquire, retain, and execute learning. The spirit of humankind does not exist in the animal. Without the expression of this spirit in humankind, we would be considered to be like the animals of the field, the fish of the sea, and the fowl of the air. The

Spirit of God comes to humankind by way of acceptance, repentance, and baptism; without this Spirit, the person remains incomplete. When you were converted, you agreed to surrender your total being into the hands of your Maker, and your spirit as well, which is God's. There is a character-building process at work in a converted mind which involves the human spirit. We are admonished to have the fruit of the Spirit, for without it there is no law. Galatians 5:22–23 tells us, "But the fruit of the Spirit is love, joy, peace, longsuffering, gentleness, goodness, faith, Meekness, temperance: against such there is no law." At the end of life, the spirit of humankind is preserved in its complete state with a detailed transcript of the life experience. Your character and morality will be a matter of permanent record. Hence we need to ensure that our spirits remain blameless and are circumspect. Our eyes should be enlightened as our minds are cognizant of another lurking spirit that exists: the spirit of the Devil. The Devil is a spirit who possesses the power to influence humanity to disobey God.

It is more long-lasting and important to influence than to control. Control is momentary and demands constant supervision and micromanagement, whereas influence is perpetual and is evident in the presence or absence of the influencer. Influence is likened to yeast. The yeast we speak of is not the one of *Candida* infection; it is the one which raises the dough, called *Saccharomyces cerevisiae*. When the dough realizes that it has been infiltrated, it is already evident by the transformation which has been taking place. Upon the dough's awakening, it is already yeasted, similar to salt. It is important to note that during the process there is seldom sound. When salt is added to food, it sits there and extracts the flavour by the concentration gradient created while working its way down into the food quietly, affecting the whole meal. The Bible reminds you that you are the light; if the light is absent, then darkness will overtake immediately, and when the light returns, the darkness will vanish, running for cover. This is an expression and admonition of the process of influence. There is no need for light to fight the darkness; all light needs to do is to be present. The reason light is not needed to fight darkness is that to darkness, light is incomprehensible. One never give a permanent response to a temporary situation. It is our responsibility to let our light shine as we uncover the darkness and clear the way for those who encounter us.

Give That which Is Required and Not That which You Want

Documented in the Genesis story, authored by Moses, an inspired man of God, we see where humankind displays piety when a sacrificial system was introduced. The display is evident with two sons of Adam, Cain and Abel. We learn from Genesis 4:2–5, "And Abel was a keeper of sheep, but Cain was a tiller of the ground. And in process of time it came to pass, that Cain brought of the fruit of the ground an offering unto the Lord. And Abel, he also brought of the firstlings of his flock and of the fat thereof. And the Lord had respect unto Abel and to his offering: But unto Cain and to his offering he had not respect. And Cain was very wroth, and his countenance fell."

The example of a sacrifice that was made in the Garden of Eden after the Fall of Humankind is recounted in Genesis 3:21: "Unto Adam also and to his wife did the Lord God make coats of skins, and clothed them." The first sacrifice made was to cover the human beings as the Originator's glory had been removed from them. This is an example of things that were to follow. When the eyes of our foreparents were open and they discerned it, they used fig leaves to cover themselves, sewing them together to create aprons. God, in wisdom, realized the indiscretion demanded a greater sacrifice: blood was required.

The reason God accepted Abel's sacrifice over that of Cain was not because God was displaying favour. It was because He was reminding them of the commitment to be restored to obedience in the following instruction. It is not about what you so eagerly feel or what you have available at the moment to be given. One's actions speak volumes when one decides to offer sacrifice in ways which are unacceptable to the Creator. It does not matter what you think or how you feel; the thing of greatest importance is giving a display of obedience, what the Lord desires, requires, and expects of you as you display faithfulness to Him.

The Regeneration

Another example of worship was displayed by Noah after he built the ark, in which only eight persons were saved. The earth was consumed with water and humankind was wiped from its face, excepting those who were in the ark. In the Flood account, there is societal decadence, depravity, and moral decay which overwhelmed humankind, a willing participant, which grieved the Creator. The divergence in relationship selection disrupted the intended multiplication process, initiating a shift in humanity's restoration sequence. Genesis 6:2 reads, "The sons of God saw the daughters of men that they were fair; and they took them wives of all which they chose. And the Lord said, My spirit shall not always strive with man, for that he also is flesh: yet his days shall be an hundred and twenty years." The boggling cloud that may linger is, why would this multiplication process impede the restoration of humanity in line with the destiny intended? What would have been so inappropriate about the sons of God marrying the daughters of men? It all started after the Fall. We were made aware of the death of Abel by Cain. Abel had brought an offering to God as required, while Cain offered to God that which he saw fitting and convenient but not that which was required. God in His wisdom accepted the sacrifice of Abel because it met the standard required, and He rejected the gift that was given by Cain as it was not within the established parameters.

This infuriated Cain, who, with a kindled spirit, slew his brother. The spirit of humankind is the spirit of disobedience, such as with the sons and daughters of humankind, and the Spirit of God is the spirit of obedience, such as with the sons and daughters of God. During the time the decision to partake in that which was not to have been was being made, there was a divide and conflict in the spirit, which was transferred by Eve to her children. Now that Abel had died, a pure replacement needed to be birthed from the womb of the woman. The third child of Adam and Eve was Seth (meaning "son of God"). The lineage association of Cain and Seth was a reflection of a rebellion. Human beings were beginning to spiral out of control and were destroying themselves in the process. The combination of pure and impure was creating that which was impure, deviating from the path of restoration. In order to restore the balance, a cleansing would need to be initiated. Hence the Lord outlined the plan of action necessary. In the midst of all the chaos, eating and drinking, merrymaking, and having and giving unto marriage, there was one who was in favour with the Lord who had contributed to the purification of humanity without desecration, allowing the restoration of order. This was the generation of Noah, who walked with God. Selecting this man, God indicated to him what needed to be done to secure the future of humanity. Noah was an exception in his generation as his lineage was untainted. Something great was going to happen, something which had not before been seen. The instruction was given to create an ark. It was to be built of gopher wood. It was to be pitch within and without, with a length of three hundred cubits, a breadth of fifty cubits, and a height of thirty cubits. A window for ventilation should be made in it, and a door should be on its side. Within this ark should be three stories (lower, second, and third) as the Lord would "bring a flood of waters upon the earth, to destroy all flesh, wherein is the breath of life, from under heaven; and every thing that is in the earth shall die." Though this was to be done, a covenant was established with this righteous man who would continue humanity with his sons and their wives and his wife. The day fast approached when it would be time to enter into the ark as construction was completed to the specification and the animals were entering as the Lord had commanded. After all was done as it should have been done, it began just as was promised with rain. It rained for forty days and forty nights, destroying every living substance upon the face of the ground except Noah and those in the ark.

In the wake of the flood, catastrophically, because of the water-deposited sedimentary layers, the majority of the world saw the displacement of various layers of mud, which caused the Pangea-like breaking away of the supercontinent into fragments. The first day of the surge began in the six hundredth year of Noah's life, the seventeenth day of the second month. It was at this juncture that all the fountains of the deep opened up with the simultaneous outpouring from the heavens, creating earth's resurfacing process while destroying everything that moved on land. The ground burst at its seams with supernova magma mixed with steam (varying gases in combination), piercing the crust. An ordeal of this magnitude would cause giant rifts and tears to run across the planet. Massive amounts of water rocketed into the atmosphere, falling back to earth as intense global and torrential rain in a symphony. The intensity and the rapid nature of occurrence would cause multiple mega sequences in the reshaping of the earth as it is now known. Similar to a tsunami, the earth was experiencing multiple shocks and cycles with the stretching of subduction zones simultaneously while entombing the shallow marine creatures, followed by land creatures and vegetation. The vegetation would eventually be converted into coal, with what remained being preserved as fossils. The water had peaked above the highest level of the pre-Flood world, and now it was time for the reordering process, which would erode and rework the previous deposits given a reversal in the direction of flow as the water drained from the inner part of the earth to the outer. This flow reversal also removed the residual human remains buried in earlier deposits as they were totally destroyed by the erosive retreating floodwaters. As it was stated, so it was: humankind was indeed wiped from the face of the earth.

The forty-day flood experience now over, the ark was resting upon Mount Ararat while the water decreased and the surface cooling and sinking continued as the water sheeted off the land into the ocean basin. During this process, mountains were being formed as the waters receded while vegetation was springing into action in anticipation of the animals that would come from the ark. We read in Genesis 8:14, "And in the second month, on the seven and twentieth day of the month, was the earth dried." God then spoke to

Noah and informed him that it was time to go forward from the ark after spending approximately a year on the inside. He was also told to allow the animals to make their exit. The door was opened, and out they went. At this time in history there were only eight people in the world, from whom all now are derived. It goes to the root of our origin, indicating that human beings are all related.

This being true indicates that there is a low genetic diversity within the population, one Y (male) ancestor, one mtDNA (female) ancestor, and two versions of each gene as the woman was taken out of the man. From Adam and Eve's lineage came Noah's generation, meaning then that all people are closely related, and only a few mtDNA lines should exist, which may have come from Shem's, Ham's, and Japheth's wives and one Y chromosome line as all Noah's sons came from his loins. All these combinations would set the stage for a rapid population growth, which is evident.

Now there came another hurdle to overcome, the Tower of Babel experience. The people decided it was favourable to build a tower just in case waters should once again overtake the earth. Diversity entered the equation when the Lord confounded their language and the people dispersed in small groups to uninhabited territories throughout what is now known as the Middle East. Territorial mobility was possible as there was the cooling of the earth after the Flood, which caused ice to join with the different land masses.

Rainbow

Noah's first agenda item after alighting from the ark was to offer a sacrifice. As we read in Genesis 8:20–21, "And Noah builded an altar unto the Lord; and took of every clean beast, and of every clean fowl, and offered burnt offerings on the altar." The act of appreciation pleased the Lord and was received with a sweet savour. God blessed Noah and his sons and said unto them, "Be fruitful, multiply and replenish the earth" as was done in the Garden of Eden. The covenant established with God was acknowledged as stated in communication with Noah and his sons. Genesis 9:11–14 indicates, "Neither shall all flesh be cut off any more by the waters of a flood; neither shall there any more be a flood to destroy the earth," reminding them that this covenant would stand, giving them a token between Him, them, and every living creature that exists for perpetual generations. They were assured that their Creator would set His bow in the clouds as a token reminder of this covenant. It is from this experience with the Flood that we ended up having the meteorological phenomenon that is caused by the reflection, refraction, and dispersion of light in water droplets, resulting in a spectrum of light appearing in the sky in a multicoloured circular arc formation known as the bow (rainbow), a glorious reminder that the earth will never again be purified with water, as the next purification will be done with fire.

The bow that served as the reminder of the covenant is represented in many forms. It could be in the optical atmospheric, a phenomenon caused by light from the sun, but also produced from the moon, referred to as a lunar bow or moonbow. There also exists the fogbow variation, formed by smaller clouds and droplets that diffract light extensively, and occasionally it may happen at sunrise or sunset when shorter wavelengths like blue and green are removed from the spectrum, creating a dramatic monochrome red bow. The high-order rainbow also exists, in which there are different gradations based on the number of light reflections inside the water droplets that create it; in theory, this type can go on into infinity. The double bow exists, in which both the primary and secondary bows are visible with the secondary caused by a double reflection of sunlight inside the water droplets. The twinned bow is similar but different from the double bow in that it consists of two separate and concentric bow arcs. The rear bow appears as two rainbow arcs that split from a single base. "And he that sat was to look upon like a jasper and a sardine stone: and there was a rainbow round about the throne, in sight like unto an emerald" (Revelation 4:3). Covenant made, covenant kept. Let us not betray our intellect, but embrace and believe.

Prayer's Purpose

The hand of God is revealed by His acts; however, the mind of God indicates His ways. Understanding the ways of God aids in intimacy development. Many are the plans in a human being's life, but despite humanity's plan, God's purpose will prevail. Everything that we have been given has a purpose; if the purpose for something is unknown, the likelihood that it will be abused increases. There is also a purpose for prayer. First Thessalonians 5:17 tells us, "Pray without ceasing," which means that everyone has been given access to prayer, and it should be utilized accordingly.

Matthew 6:5 reads, "And when thou prayest, thou shalt not be as the hypocrites are: for they love to pray standing in the synagogues and in the corners of the streets, that they may be seen of men. Verily I say unto you, They have their reward." The use of the word *when* indicates that it is expected that the occurrence is imminent and is on the horizon; it will happen. Appreciating that God is as sovereign as His Word, is limited by His Word, and will never violate His Word directs us to have an exuberance and enthusiasm towards prayer. The recorded accounts of Jesus's relationship with His disciples reveals that prayer was a pivotal component in their leader's life. Every morning, independently/alone, He would go away and pray. It was the hours invested in communion with His Father that gave Him power and authority over the physical realm. The time in prayer is not wasted but invested. It is so intimate a duty that it was done alone. This example was more significant than the miracles that were performed by Jesus, to the point that the one thing the disciples asked for themselves was that their Lord teach them to pray. "And it came to pass, that, as he was praying in a certain place, when he ceased, one of his disciples said unto him, Lord, teach us to pray, as John also taught his disciples" (Luke 11:1). This display was one of respect and reverence as the disciples waited until the prayer was completed before seeking to engage in communication; it would suggest that they were watching Him while in the course of prayer. The disciples asking to learn how to pray indicates that Jesus *never* prayed with His disciples. He always prayed *alone*. Prayer was so personal that it was done independently, just as relationships and intimacy are personal and need to be developed on an individual basis.

The disciples of Jesus were tasked with the releasing of a dumb spirit, but they could not do it. The reason is that they were not prepared (with prayer) and they lacked the faith to accomplish the task. When the same task was brought to their Lord, He investigated the belief of the Father, who indicated that He believed His child could be released after the expression of faith. Mark 9:25–26 reads, "He rebuked the foul spirit, saying unto him, Thou dumb and deaf spirit, I charge thee, come out of him, and enter no more into him. And the spirit cried, and rent him sore, and came out of him: and he was as one dead; insomuch that many said, He is dead." The disciples were concerned about why they were not able to do the exorcism. The requirements were revealed: one needs to be prepared for that which one has the intention; without the adequate invested time in preparing, the inevitable, unexpected result will be the outcome. And He said unto them, "This kind can come forth by nothing, but by prayer and fasting."

Prayer's Birth

We read in Genesis 1:26, "And God said, Let us make man in our image, after our likeness: and let them have dominion over the fish of the sea, and over the fowl of the air, and over the cattle, and over all the earth, and over every creeping thing that creepeth upon the earth." God's Words became law when spoken. It is important to note that humankind was made to have dominion ("let them have dominion"). The word *them* does not refer to Them who created humankind; it refers to the humans who were created.

Them = Humankind

First God created the body of the man, and then He placed the spirit within the man.

Humus man = *Dirt man-meets-spirit* = Human

The integration of physical and spiritual generates a human; your body is *humus*, which is dirt, and *human* because you are a spirit. It was this creation that was given dominion over the earth. This means that the only creation that has the legal authority to operate on this earth is humankind.

This brings to the forefront the operation of a spirit without a body on earth, which is illegal. God will never violate such a law, and He followed after the precept's outline. For God to intervene on earth, there has to be a body made available for Him. For this reason, when Eve was in the garden having a conversation with the serpent and about to take the fruit, He did not intervene as He is Spirit. Had this intervention been done, the words spoken by the Creator would have been nullified and He could not be trusted ever again. Lucifer, the fallen, knew that in order to conduct business on earth, he would need a body; hence, he borrowed the body of the serpent and beguiled the woman. It was for this reason, when Adam and Eve had fallen, that God said He would come and save them, which could only be done with a body. "And I will put enmity between thee and the woman, and between thy seed and her seed; it shall bruise thy head, and thou shalt bruise his heel" (Genesis 3:15). This statement, when expanded over history, reveals to us that God was saying the same woman whom Satan used to cause the Fall of Humanity would be the same woman who would allow Him to enter into the world for the bruising of Satan's head. That was a promise given and a promise kept. Beforehand, it was prophesied in Isaiah 7:14 that a virgin would conceive and bear a son who would be called Immanuel.

The name Immanuel means "God with us"; it is "God inside humankind".

Im = In; Man = Humankind; El = Elohim

So God went to Mary, who was highly favoured, to borrow her womb to make a "legal" entry. "And Mary said, Behold the handmaid of the Lord; be it unto me according to thy word. And the angel departed from her" (Luke 1:38). The Word was spoken, and then the Word became flesh. The child's blood was never mixed with the mother's blood.

The child embedded in the womb by the Word of God was uncorrupted; for this reason, His blood would be able to cleanse. It so happens that Mary got saved by the blood she was carrying. Mary was to call the child Jesus. Mary's purpose was to incubate the body until it was time to release the child into the world. The child was born, but the Son was not; it was God who gave the Son to occupy the body. The Son was already in existence before the inception of time. Mary facilitated the body, the house, but God manifested the Spirit and the occupant. This makes Mary the mother of Jesus but not of Christ; Jesus is the body, but Christ is God. They both worked collaboratively because it was Jesus who made Christ "legal". It was a case of divinity clothed in humanity. It was for this reason that Jesus could pray on earth. God needs humans in order to step into earthly matters.

Prayer's Purpose and Significance

Prayer is the medium by which God receives requests from human beings to intervene in earthly affairs. This is necessary for His work to move forward; everything that has been done on this earth since dominion was given to humankind has been the result of human intercession allowing God's intervention. Humanity is utilized in the work of God as we are needed according to His Word; it's not because of the purity of humankind but because of the cleansing power of God. The Lord is always willing and ready to forgive because you are needed in His work.

Consultation Request

1. During the consideration of earth, a cleansing consultation was made with Noah; it was agreed and justified, and then it was so.

2. Before the destruction of Sodom and Gomorrah, Abraham was consulted and acted as the mediator for the people; however, based on the agreement, the two cities had to be destroyed.
3. God heard the cries of the people in Egypt, and He wanted to deliver them, but He went to Moses to request the activation of the process, and the people were delivered.

Prayer is a necessity for supernatural interference. Prayer is so vital that it gives humans access to the kingdom and access to authority we would not have been able to gain in the natural. There exists a mirroring relation and connection between heaven and earth through prayer.

The Body

Your body is so important that when it has expired, you too have expired and have no more authority on earth to do anything. The body is also important to God; hence, a restorative programme of healing is made available to prevent or reduce the occurrence of premature expiration. This programme can only be accessed by prayer. When the time of Jesus Christ had come to an end and He was crucified, Jesus died, but Christ lived perpetually. Expired on the cross was Jesus as displayed with the blood and water mixture gushing from His pierced side. Christ still existed even when Jesus's life was laid down; this was so because that portion of Jesus's work was done. The Spirit of Christ left and went to handle some business. During the resting of Jesus's body, Christ secured the keys to hell and death. When the work was over, the reuniting of Christ with Jesus produced the risen Jesus, "whom God raised again [and who] saw no corruption" (Acts 13:37).

To pray is to get yourself prepared to do God's will and not your own; it serves as the only way to release the power and authority that has been concealed within. Perspectives beyond mortal comprehension are activated with exponential and instantaneous responses. Prayer is enwrapped with the power to unlock the gates of heaven and close the gates of hell, shattering any intercepting barrier that keeps you from receiving your blessing. The manifestation of the power and authority will only come through practice; it nullifies distance, increasing proximity and intimacy. The impossible becomes possible, and control over the spiritual is gained.

Prayer Power

The time is now. Stop wondering when God is going to step in, and request His intervention. How else would He be authorized? Use the power you are given to regulate the outcomes. If you don't have initiative, then you lack a foundational principle. "Now unto him that is able to do exceeding abundantly above all that we ask or think, according to the power that worketh in us" (Ephesians 3:20).

The reason you should pray is that God answers prayer and He needs your request to activate that which is required. Requests cannot be answered until they have been submitted. As powerful as God is, He will not interfere unless requested. All things are possible. Once a matter is presented, though it can be done, it, like most things, only becomes possible through Christ, who is waiting to show you great and mighty things. Whatever good thing that you ask, it shall not be withheld from you. Your blessings will never be held hostage.

Though prayer is one of the most powerful keys to the kingdom, many people are hesitant to harness the celestial power to transmit their spirits' requests. Prayer will elevate from the earth, slipping through the atmosphere, moving from the terrestrial to the celestial atmosphere. The message is delivered directly to the intended Creator in the third heaven. This process is likened to taking air through time and space and back, which is delicately precise without interference or message interception or corruption. So powerful it is that before the thought is conceived, the answers have been delivered, even without the technical comprehension of movement through the troposphere and the stratosphere or the other interconnecting relays in finding the third heaven, which is the throne of God.

Comfort inducer, disease curer, addiction independency, restoration, healing, renewal, victory, unity, harmony, impossibility converter, giant defeater, sea divider, mountain mover, rains of fire, furnace quencher—these are some of the powers manifested through prayer. God is as close as your next prayer. He cannot and will not fail. If you need discernment to make critical decisions, if you need peace in your mind, or if you need things you did not build, vineyards you did not plant—whatever it is that is needed, just ask and you will receive. This is so because you have received the authority of His name, the power of His Word, and the sanctity of His blood.

Prayer Consideration

In approaching prayer, you must bring your concern to your Father, who is not of this earth. You must understand interdimensional communication while appreciating that your Father's name should be reverenced. Prayer is done in an effort to facilitate the kingdom's expression on earth, which should be a daily endeavour. In order to have the channel clear, you must be able to let go and forgive. You should ask God for wisdom in keeping upright, and you should conclude the process with worship.

1. Abiding outside the will of God will hinder the answering of your prayer.
2. To have your prayers answered, you must ask with the appropriate motive.
3. Self-serving prayers will not be answered in the way expected.
4. If you lack faith, which is needed to secure the work of the words, then ask that your faith be strengthened.
5. Only to those who desire to have a relationship with God will He reveal Himself.
6. Prayer should be done in Jesus's name; there is power through faith in His name.

7. The Holy Spirit is here to assist in the exercising of the power and authority enabled by way of prayer.

In order to address the Lord appropriately, we must use the right name for the intended purpose. When extolling His incredible power and might, we refer to God as Elohim, Yahweh. Derived from the Hebrew, it means I AM. Abba indicates Father. El Elyon means the God above all gods; El Roi, the God who sees; El Shaddai, the God Almighty. The provider God is Yahweh Yireh/Jehovah-Jireh. "The Lord is my banner" is Yahweh Nissi/Jehovah-Nissi. Jehovah Rapha is Healer, "the Lord who heals you". The God who sacrificed is Jehovah-M'Kaddesh. Our Master and Lord is Adonai, and Yahweh Shalom is "the Lord is peace". All these attributes exist in one God.

Daniel's Prayer

Prayer was never intended to be an experience of depression. Prayer was designed to be answered as it fosters the connection of the spiritual person to the Spirit of God, making manifest the will of God through humankind's purpose. For a more intimate relationship with God, including deliverance and revelation, one may practise fasting. Prayer and fasting are similar as they both allow for conscious intentional interaction with the Creator; however, fasting involves an intentional decision to abstain from pleasurable physical food in exchange for spiritual elevation.

As we read in Daniel 10:1, "A thing was revealed to Daniel in a vision." This thing was true, but the time for it had not yet come. So an interpretation of the matter was sought concerning the vision, during which time, three full weeks, Daniel, whose name was called Belteshazzar, ate no pleasant food as he was fasting. The answer to the prayer was not indicated at the same time when it was requested, even though all the protocols for prayer had been followed; it was soon revealed that there was a hindrance which had prevented the message from being relayed. It is encouraged that the intimacy of the relationship that is developed is maintained and seldom uttered in the physical, as the Receiver is the only one who can read the thoughts before they are formed. In breathing it in the physical, an occasion is given for the enemy to delay as then the plan and intent are known.

We read in Daniel 10:12–13, "Then said he unto me, Fear not, Daniel: for from the first day that thou didst set thine heart to understand, and to chasten thyself before thy God, thy words were heard, and I am come for thy words. But the prince of the kingdom of Persia withstood me one and twenty days: but, lo, Michael, one of the chief princes, came to help me; and I remained there with the kings of Persia." These verses reveal that the prayers were heard even though there was an undue delay. In the realm of the spirit, a war was occurring; this detainment slowed the process of delivery. Sometimes your blessings are on the way, and you may be wondering what is happening, why are things taking so long, and if the request has been forgotten. But you should be encouraged in knowing that all things work in the Creator's perfect timing: be strong and have courage while waiting patiently. In prayer, we have the ability to communicate with the Sovereign, who is immutable, infinite, self-sufficient, omnipotent, merciful, just, omniscient, omnipresent, and transcendent. Access the power that transcends the natural.

It should never be our goal to preserve and remember history as if it must be explored exclusively; if that is done, we will be stuck in the past. Instead, our focus should be on the creation of history. Breaking free from the past will position an individual to move into the future.

BAD COMPANY CORRUPTS GOOD CHARACTER

We read in 1 Corinthians 15:33, "Be not deceived: evil communications corrupt good manners." The character speaks to the facets that make up the consciousness that makes up the whole human. Character rests on similar lines of integrity, reliability, reproducibility, and accountability; it is the woven nature of the complex "fabric" which makes you the person you are. Think about it from the perspective of deoxyribonucleic acid (DNA). It does not matter from which part of the being DNA is derived; it does not make up the entirety of the person, even though it is a part. Character could be used synonymously with a principle because of its consistency. That is why the number one will remain as such, no matter where it is located, and the letter Z will be Z, no matter where it is transcribed, along with all the other characters.

It makes it manageable for us to understand that we are one person: each individual is one. Even though we have subdivisions of personality, there is still one entity within us displaying our character. We should not be different people when we go into celebrations, or when we go to work/school, or when we are in the house of the Lord; it should be remembered that you are one and the same person. The combination of all those varied aspects forms the character. An individual should endeavour to be one person, not righteous at church and unrighteous everywhere else, because the character is a reflection of the summation of all the parts.

A person who displays character does not live on feelings, trends, or that which is considered fashionable by the majority. Such a person's life is based on the principle of the Originator. These types of people are transparent, give full disclosure, are honest, and live based on integrity while evading biases and the desire to meddle in corruption. There are some positions which you must seek to avoid if you intend to maintain character because they will position you to sacrifice principles for popularity, not necessarily for that which is right or righteous. Once your character is void, it means that trust has been broken and you have been marred. We need to remember that we were created in the image of God, meaning that we were embodied with the character of God. The unchanging nature of our character was given at Creation which is a reflection of the Originator's image. It was not until the Fall of Humankind that the character of God was removed from humanity. We see this happening when the eyes of Adam and Eve opened and they realized that they were naked. Their nakedness was revealed because the glory of God had been removed since they'd become corrupted. At the corruption of humankind, worth, esteem, and understanding of self went for a nosedive; traction was lost; and the shame and consequence of the folly lingered. After being removed from the garden, humanity has been on a quest to find the image that God gave them. That is why appearance is more important than truth to humankind. That is why we have publicist management teams for damage control in the media and even personal image consultants.

We have gotten very comfortable in this world filled with lies and deception. This is because we have lost sight of who we are and, hence, we see a need to be someone else, causing us to create another person when all we need to be is one. When we speak of a person with character, we speak of someone who is unchanging with regard to his or her principles. If you realize that you are like a chameleon that changes to accommodate circumstances with your eyes peeled at 360 degrees, ready to stick your tongue out as if to catch prey, then you need to self-assess and engage in character development. Leaders must have character if people are to follow them; they must be people who are honourable, dependable, consistent, and in some regards predictable because the principle remains constant.

Character attracts loyalty so that there is a commitment to a value system without compromise. Joseph displayed character when he was in his master's house and when his master's wife made advances. The question that was asked is "How then can I do this great wickedness, and sin against God?" Joseph showed display of integrity similar unto none regularly practised in those times. In order for the character to be upheld and maintained, each individual needs to purpose the degree of sacrifice he or she will make for the cause of preserving integrity from within himself or herself.

In chapter 3 of Daniel, we meet three Hebrew boys in the providence of Babylon under the leadership of King Nebuchadnezzar who had an experience which tested their character. This king determined that it fitted his agenda to set up his image of gold to be worshipped at the sound of the music. He instructed that whosoever refused to fall down and worship this image should be cast into the midst of the fiery furnace. The sound rang through the air, and all knees bowed except those of Shadrach, Meshach, and Abednego. Another chance was given, but they still did not bow. This infuriated King Nebuchadnezzar; hence, he extended the punishment to those who were still standing: they were to be cast into the furnace heated seven times hotter. These three boys held their ground and were thrown into the fiery furnace. While those boys were in the furnace holding onto their character, something amazing happened that the king tried to explain: the appearance of a fourth person walking in the midst of the fire. The king acknowledged the presence of the Son of God as the fourth being in the fire with the Hebrews.

When your character is impeccable, the Creator can work through the vessel as a witness to proclaim His glory. The king commanded that those who were cast in the fire were to be removed and then examined by the prince, the governors, and the captains, and the king's counsellors. When these officials gathered together, they concluded the fire had no power over the body of the boys as their coats remained unchanged, nor was there any smell of fire passing over them. The king could not contain his amazement and truly realized the error of his ways. He declared blessings upon the God of those he was in the process of persecuting, executing, and attempting to exterminate. The name of the Maker was glorified because of the display of the character of these faithful boys. Even though they knew that they could have died, they still held firm to the principles of God. They knew with absolute certainty that they should have no other God before their God and should not even entertain the thought of worshipping any graven image. In those moments of existential crisis, the resilience displayed was made possible because the character was fortified in the principles of God.

These individuals valued the principles of God and in turn displayed that they valued themselves. They held the Lord in high regard, including His words and His outlined constitution, demonstrating that they understood their mandate and worth, which allowed them to maintain a standard of principled behaviour. If you value yourself, you will not short-change yourself; your intention will be to develop the best version of yourself, not to sabotage or cheat. If you value marriage, you will not commit adultery, because doing so would mean that you have no regard for the commitment made with your vows. Your values will protect you and others. The question you may want to ask yourself is, "Do I have standards?" Your standard defines your character, and if you violate your standards, you also violate your character.

This attribute of character is a self-imposed discipline, meaning you don't need anyone to keep you in line because you are already doing that. Your conscience and conviction are ultimate in monitoring your direction. You should never sell your principle for any price. If you do, at that moment, you destroy all that you have been entrusted with. Your character and integrity will protect your future. It is your duty to stand for that which is righteous; without standing, you expose yourself to being destroyed, embarrassed, and humiliated. Character intersects when your word, deed, and action become unified as one in integration. You can never confide in a person who says something, does something else, and promises something different from the two. With these people, you don't know who it is that you are speaking with when you do. It is as though they have a psychological disorder, a split personality (dissociative identity disorder); don't be associated with these types of people or become like them.

When you have character it means the following:

- You are willing to sacrifice friendship to protect your character .
- You are willing to leave a job if it compromises your character.
- You are will to exit a relationship which threatens your character .
- You are willing to refuse any money which will adulterate it.
- You will desist from going and doing certain things, which could eradicate your character.

You should never be so complacently addicted to the world as it is that you are willing to allow your subconscious mind to sever ties with reality, trapping yourself in a character "coma". If you should ever reach that state, you will need to be taken out with help, and it will be more like a hostage negotiation for your subconscious mind to be reunited with your body. Do not enjoy seeking after or facilitating those who encourage a dormant, hibernating character, since at all times control should be in your hands. A wave of dust like remorse will not be our cry as we maintain the tangible, intangible, tangible. Let's not be attracted to charisma; it is the character that is of value. When you become a person of integrity, you will soon realize that there is nothing that you may consider private. There is no private life; there should only be absolute transparency. If we want a life where we can hide selective things, then it means that we are not yet ready to embrace our character. A person with character simply needs to be present to be acknowledged; he or she doesn't need to say anything. That is the power of the character of God.

Your character can be referred to as a farming experience in which there is the preparation of land which is like the blank slate the child is born with. The "land" was predetermined by the combination of parents' input, the mother (wife) and the father (husband) dividing and multiplying through the natural process of life generation that was given as a gift from God. The experiences you go through and the company you are surrounded with will be the pollen and seed. The environment plays a crucial role in the developmental process of seed germination. The habits that you foster are then germinated and come up as shoots. Along with the good crop will be weeds, which are unfavourable attributes and traits. These should be eradicated by all means necessary to preserve the integrity of the crop. The crop will need watering with affirmation and constant focus from the beginning to the end. It needs the right amount of sunlight to light the way and the appropriate air quality of realism and positivity. Crops will need to reach maturity before their savour and flavour can be appreciated by the world, and then the seeds of the tree will be replanted to multiply this spirit of humanity combined with the Spirit of God.

In today's world, we see the propagation of a society which lacks a moral compass to hold itself accountable for its actions. It is one of the most difficult tasks to find someone who has character. Without character or integrity, no one desires to share their real self with anyone—hence the lack of meaningful relationship development. When considering those who are currently leading the world, we come to understand the dubious moral and ethical degradation that exists, causes us to cringe to the core. The media is filled with sordid stories about the ignoble action of the one who is expected to be setting examples and who claims to have societal development as a priority. These people include community role models, education leaders, workplace supervisors, sports personalities, political and religious leaders, and business executives. Unfortunately, there appears to be a general incongruity in our society between what we say we value and what we actually accept. This is true as in most instances we are only accessing the spirit of humankind and neglecting the Spirit of God.

No longer do we need to be surprised when it is uttered that the community role model is someone else during the day in comparison to the night, or that the education leader is miseducating society with fallacy and thereby imprisoning the thoughts of the young.

Other examples of such people could be:

- A workplace supervisor exercising sexual impropriety and victimization tactics upon subordinate staff
- Sports personalities found to be connected to illegal endeavours
- Political leaders buying votes and/or trying to sell a seat in government
- A business leader accused of and admitting to swindling funds from the poor and vulnerable with misappropriation methods
- Our religious leaders who withhold the truth from the membership while tolerating the errors of the members, to their demise.

It is not acceptable to do what you desire as long as you don't get caught. The real situation that exists in all the examples stated is a lack of character, morals, integrity, fortitude, and reputation of substance. These acts display precisely how humans have lost the image of themselves and are devolving into the unrecognizable.

Our character is determined by the subtotal of our choices. This means that we have the power to decide who we really are. We also have the opportunity to be one individual, the same person in public and in private. Though we may not have direct control of all situations, it is paramount for us to remember that we have a choice in how we handle situations. If we make poor choices involving such things as debauchery, depravity, deceit, greed, hypocrisy, abuse, adultery, avarice, extortion, exploitation, gluttony, fraud, treachery, lust, perversion, bloodshed, blackmail, bigotry, and bribery, or any other wrong conceivable, then we give up our character. It is for this reason that the Saviour came to take this cup of evil away from humanity and give us peace. The reverberation of the atrocity committed by the man in the garden has resulted in the calamity experienced today. Rebellion and rejection are displayed when the Creator's instructions are disregarded.

Pride often clouds judgement, which makes it necessary that we seek to maintain a spirit of humility in order to neutralize ego. While we maintain a firm footing on the promises of the Lord, we must execute the request of the instructions of Paul to be blameless and harmless in the midst of this crooked and perverse world.

Bad Company

It is imperative that we know that friendship with the world creates an enemy with the Creator and separates us further from His love. When we have studied the principles of God, we must assimilate them in order to find any usefulness in the knowledge that we have received. The virtues that should be on display are those things which are honest, sincere, just, lovely, pure, and of good report. Humanity should emulate the Creator as the human being and the Creator become one. One of the grandmothers of King David, Ruth was said to have been a woman of noble character and was considered a virtuous woman. Her state of nobility translates to mean strength and might. Ruth showed herself to have humility, faithfulness, industriousness, and godly character.

The foundation of one's character is seated in one's heart. It is only that which is in the person that will proceed from the person. It is therefore imperative to be responsible for safeguarding the heart and monitoring what goes in so you can filter what comes out. The only way you will do something is if you have fostered the thought and germinated the seed, and the opportunity for harvesting presents itself. Before evil is done, it has already been done. The reason for this is because the thought needs to have been cultivated. Jesus was right when he said that if a man looks upon a woman in lust, he has already committed adultery. The adultery will happen when the opportunity is presented, so the sin has already been committed.

Sin is manifested because of a failure to guard the heart. The heart needs to be trained to do that which is good instead of harbouring evil. This should not be in accordance with your eyes but with the eyes of the Lord. There was a display of keen leadership when an ageing leader filled with courage and tenacity encouraged the Israelites to complete the task at hand in which it was required for the nations around them to be removed from the land. Joshua 23 outlines that while the Israelites sojourned with these others in the land, they needed to be careful not to align with the unbelieving nations, associate with their customs, intermarry, or even be enticed to worship their false gods. These instructions were key, for if the Israelites were to maintain their nobility, they needed to refrain from a deviation of their own customs. In order to maintain purity, there needs to be a separation from that which is impure or conflicting with one's goal and direction.

Parental Instruction–Hannah

Hannah, a woman of faith, pleaded with the Lord for a child. With earnest prayer, praise, and worship, a covenant was made that upon the request being granted, she would return with the same unto the Lord. As it was recorded, the time elapsed and she conceived. The foetus developed, and then she gave birth to a male child, Samuel. When the child became of age, she gave him unto the Lord's service in accordance with the promise. This child was under the leadership of the priest Eli. Under the tutelage of the priest, the boy developed a connection with the service of God and a desire for the work thereof. In the revelatory experience of Samuel, the Word of the Lord was precious as there was no open vision. One night while Samuel rested, with the ageing of Eli and the dimming of his eyes, something phenomenal occurred: the Lord called Samuel. Thinking it was Eli, Samuel went up and went to enquire of Eli on the matter; however, Eli had no knowledge of making the call and so requested that the young man go back to bed. While Samuel was resting his head, the call was noted once again, and he responded in accordance. Eli gave him the same instruction of returning to bed. On the third occasion when Samuel went to Eli, Eli perceived the matter: that the Lord was calling the child. Knowing that

Samuel did not yet know the Lord and that the Word of the Lord had yet to be revealed unto him, Eli instructed him what to do if the call persisted. The Lord then called Samuel another time, and he did as was instructed. The Lord then gave him a message about that which was to come. Before we can answer the call of the Lord or be synchronized with His Spirit, we need to have a relationship with Him, which allows us to be able to hear and answer His call. Oftentimes it is our parents who position us in the direction of understanding what is required and expected of us in order to achieve the ideals that have been set so that we may become perfect. It is wise to have discretion in listening to our parents, but we must also remember the instruction of the Lord.

The only way we can do something that pleases the Lord is if we are doing that which is the will of the Father. While we have parents who are positioned to give us good advice, there are some who are not positioned to do such a task. As children or students, it is important that we assess and determine based on the principle of the Word and the integrity of the counsel we receive.

Our parents play a conspicuously subtle role in our nurturing and development. In the quest to provide the right environment, the parent can cause the child to become overwhelmed by the strains and pressures entrusted upon him. Though this may be evident, it is expected that parents/guardians have compassion on the child or children under their care. As a parent, you must show restraint in the undue provocation of the child or children under your care and place more effort in bringing them up with the fear of the Lord. This safely establishes the operating parameters for the parents. Exercise civility when aiding in the development of a child. It is important to note that the child/children under the parents' care should be fertilized with positive encouragement to facilitate the development of identity, self-acceptance, and esteem and to ignite the quest towards an actualization experience. Whatever is invested in a child from the root is what will be produced in the fruit. The values that elevate and cultivate the germination of pleasing fruits should be nurtured prior to infancy as untamed trees will only bring destruction, despair, and reproach. That which is invested in the child is what will be reflected by the child.

Unwise Parental Counsel–Esau and Jacob

In the story of Esau and Jacob, we see an incredible revelation of grave toxicity of ill-advised counsel, which led to deceit, betrayal, loss of trust, and destruction of a bond that should have been unbroken. Doing wrong will always be wrong, even when done for the right reasons. A woman named Rebekah had two children within her womb, whom the Lord had revealed to her were two nations, and the elder child was predestined to serve the younger. Despite that which was revealed unto the mother, she should have maintained a balance in love and affection between the two children; however, as they matured, both parents showed them different amounts of affection. The father, Isaac, loved Esau, while the mother, Rebekah, loved Jacob. Knowing this, the children walked in favour of the one who favoured them. It was good for them both as they reciprocated the support. The story continues with the birthright being sold by Esau in the field because of his appetite.

The two brothers shared time. It came to pass that Isaac, their father, was old and his eyes were dim. Unable to see, he called his son Esau, who was the elder twin, giving him instructions on what was required of him. In those days, it was the tradition for the eldest to be given the blessing of the father prior to his passing. During the conversation with Esau and Isaac, Rebekah, who favoured Jacob, overheard the instruction of Isaac requesting venison. Hearing this, Rebekah conceived a plan with Jacob as the executioner. In that plan, they created an illusion, exploiting the weaknesses of Isaac. The mother orchestrated the plan, giving instructions to Jacob to follow, which he did. It was as though Jacob was under a trance doing his mother's will. He went and fetched the venison and brought it to his as mother requested. Upon receiving that which was requested, Rebekah made the meal the father had requested of his other son. The two played the con, and Isaac was deceived. This deception was the blade that sliced the family into pieces for a season. After the blessing of Isaac was confirmed upon Esau, Esau returned home in anticipation of his blessing only to be hugely disappointed as it already had been given to his brother, Jacob. The moral here is that though we expect our parents to guide us, they may not be suitable for that "portfolio", especially if they have been corrupted. Hear your parents. Listen to God.

As sad as it may sound, it is possible to become defiled by those with whom we associate. Our character is not built in an instance; it takes time to be trained and cultivated. Those who desire to be noble must attain moral excellence through heeding the Word of the Creator.

Seven key character ingredients are as follows:

1. Honour
2. Diligence
3. Fruitfulness
4. Impenetrability
5. Vision
6. Communication—connection to the Vine
7. Humility

Honour

For any individual to function effectively in the way of his or her design, he or she must present the attribute of honour in his or her character. In order for this to manifest, the person needs to first be in a position to attain knowledge of the Originator and then be willing to be governed by the will of His instruction, after which there will be an emanation and reflection in how the person deals with fellow men and women. Hannah was seen giving praise and honour to God in her song, saying that her heart rejoiced in the Lord, and she declared there was none as holy as He! She was observed giving glory to the One who was capable of making the impossible possible, and for that she was duly rewarded, though she had to exercise great persistence. You are neither your mother nor your father. The conflicting practices of your relatives do not guarantee that you will experience the same things that they did. Just because your mother may have offered escorting services to survive does not mean that you will follow that same path. And it does not guarantee you will be derailed from the character "potentiator" from within. If your father was unknown or not the man you would have expected, it means that you need to make a little more effort in order to be someone who is desirable despite the fatalistic attraction towards that other path. Always remember that you are not your father. Each parent *does* have a responsibility to ensure that the appropriate skill set is communicated to the child or children; however, the choice is the child's to seek after that which is in accordance with the constitution of the Originator.

Your responsibility as a human being is to rise above the normative depravity of acceptable social mediocrity as you become the person you are intended to become: a propagator of the metamorphosis. The glory of God is the foundation of all light. When Moses was given the privilege to see the back side of the Lord, there was an instant transformation in his countenance. There was an overflowing glow that covered him. Before he could commune with the people, he had to veil himself. This should remind us of the honour that comes from the presence of God. A similar covering clothed Adam and Eve in the Garden of Eden while they communed with the Maker. It was this glory that left them upon the dishonour caused by their disobedience. The world is filled with sensual attractions; though short-lived in their alleged satisfaction, they have the capacity to impede development, making one unable to access the vast capabilities of the mind. The impediment of toxicity brought by dishonour is corrosive to the fibre and makes honourable development impossible.

Diligence

In order to please God, you need God. To develop and maintain the relationship with the Maker, you must seek after Him with urgent diligence. Being in contact with the wrong person can cause your life to slip away like butter in a hot pan on a warm day; it defies what should be normal. In an effort to adjust, you change your routine just to receive ease of mind. This state can be likened to a case in which you have a stalker trying to force access. You desire to be free from looking over your shoulder, breaking your neck in order to maintain an illusion of sanity and safety. It is a collusion of your neurons and imagination to manifest your worst fear; sometimes what you see is not what is actually there.

God is the only One who can solve all the problems that are created in the world by its occupants; however, there would naturally be a reduction in the problems created if humanity would be diligent in following the constitution and would learn from the examples set out as a guide.

Fruitfulness

When we have found our Father, we should be able to adapt His attributes as we shape ours to meet the standard of perfection required. As we are a reflection of His image, it is mandatory that when our understanding of self and value realization coincides, we are able to represent that which is expected. When a tree is planted for the purpose of bringing forth fruit, it will only produce the fruit which has been cultured within. By the bearing of the fruits, their origin can be determined. If there has been a cultivation of that which should be but it is not, then it means that there is a misrepresentation of the product; hence, it should be removed.

As people of character, we should portray what we profess and allow it to populate the area of planting. Those who refuse to produce fruits will be purged and cast away, and this fruitlessness will prevent matriculation to the higher call. Similar to this is the parable in which the one who was given five talents went out and produced another five. It is seen that all who increased were welcomed and accepted by the master; however, the one who returned only that which was given lost the talent because there was no level of multiplication or increase. That which was taken was given to the one who had ten talents, who displayed faithfulness in stewardship. The production of fruit is not limited to any one area of our lives. It involves all aspects: childhood accountability, chores, duties, the assigned task, studies, school, work, vacation, church attendance, tithing and offering, love and affection displayed to our fellow humans, and honour and respect of established institutions.

Impenetrability

Impenetrability speaks to the inability of two or more bodies to occupy the same space simultaneously, which gives an exclusive right to only one of them. In order for the character to be of an impenetrable nature, each individual must safeguard themselves against satanic and worldly influences. It is important to note that our fight is not against the physical realm but against the spiritual. We need to be equipped with the right tool in order to be overcomers and victors, taking the shield of faith to repel the fiery darts of the wicked. Even though we have the shield of faith, in order to be adequately prepared for what is ahead, we need the whole suit, the complete armour. This requirement indicates our loins be girded with truth; that we have the breastplate of righteousness; that we be prepared with the gospel of truth on our feet; that we wear the helmet of salvation; and that we clutch the sword of the Spirit, which is the Word of God (Ephesians 6:13–15, 17). Everything that is visible and physical is preceded by something invisible and spiritual; hence, in addressing the physical manifestation of all things, the invisible and spiritual cause must be investigated. If the spiritual route is not identified, an onlooker can be thrown off by the visible, physical fruit.

It is the Devil's desire to employ cunning devices to detract from your journey, discourage you, and create hindrances on your journey. This repugnant display of the Devil's influence is observed in the account of Ananias and Sapphira. They broke a covenant when they failed to return all that was collected for the sale of the land; that was the last time that either of the two lived. Infiltration has the possibility of destroying the whole.

Vision

It is essential *to know* the truth if you have the intention of being set free. The truth is the standard; once you know the standard, then you can distinguish what is right and wrong by way of deduction. That which is wrong, which is considered "wrongness", invites demonic engagement. This is critical as the enemy is a liar and a deceiver; that is why he does not want you to have a vision of the future God intended for you. As Proverbs 29:18 reads, "Where there is no vision, the people perish: but he that keepeth the law, happy is he." If you have the Spirit of God, you need to have a clear vision of what His plan is for you and for your life, especially as it relates to morality. In order for us to remain resilient, we are given a glimpse of the fruition in Revelation 1:6, in which our Lord has made us kings and priests unto God. An exercise of faith is needed if we are to embrace the reward of victory. Faith knows that God is telling the truth and acts as it is so even when it is not yet so, because it will be so simply because God said so.

Communication–Connection to the Vine

John 10:27 reads, "My sheep hear my voice, and I know them, and they follow me." If you are incapable of hearing (which you are not), you will not be in a position to realize or identify the Voice that needs you to be connected in order to complete your transformation.

There is a story about a diligent and dedicated family man who was struggling to find food for his family to sustain life. One day he went out to his farm to search for some food and consequently found what would change his life forever: a bubbling crude oil reservoir. After its extraction, the struggling family became mega billionaires. They never realized that they were always mega billionaires, having not known about the oil beforehand. Everything that they needed to live the life they desired, they had at their disposal; they just did not tap into it because they were only examining the surface. It is the same with us; thinking as this man limits us as to what we see. In order for transcendence to occur, we need to be connected with the Creator. Surprisingly, the family moved to the upper echelons of society but still lived as though they were scavengers. This should indicate to us that not everyone who has been enlightened is living up to their new position. The family was living in glory while acting as though they were in paucity. This is the elevation that occurs when one becomes united with the Spirit of God; the person is vertically propelled to celestial places. It is like an indictment where one is elevated by the enlightenment but remains complacent in former thinking. For this relationship to work, we need to stop existing in a self-limiting state and align our thinking to the standard of God. The mind needs realignment as everyone has been maligned by sin and circumstances.

None are worthy of trusting themselves. You cannot trust yourself! Don't do it. The sin we have inherited and the sin we have practised under overwhelming circumstances has confused our identity. We can only get deliverance when the branch is connected to the Vine. The undelivered person will create an undelivered practice. We need to remain steadfast at whatever level of development we are and study the things of God.

Humility

Elitism is an attitude of superiority which lifts itself or others up while demeaning people who are not considered worthy of recognition, acknowledgement, or equitable treatment. Elitism judges people based on false criteria that make some superior to others. Many individuals express elitism in varying forms without realizing that they have the picture twisted. Adolf Hitler is said to be someone who had the master race in mind. He then used his authority to mould this image of superiority into the minds of the German people. He believed he had the right to slaughter over six million Jews, not realizing that there has always been only one race, the human race.

There was a point in history where persons brought from various countries into slavery would not be considered totally human; hence, no discussion of equality was considered necessary. These people who practised and propagated these acts were mentally compromised as they were holding their own relatives captive.

It was custom for the Jews to consider the Samaritans as dogs because the Jews were the chosen people. Customs do not make such a situation correct. When Moses married an Ethiopian woman (a black woman), his people thought this was an interracial marriage. Miriam, his sister, and Aaron, his brother, went ballistic in condemnation. It could not have been a case of interracial marriage as all concerned were from the same race and the Lord had blessed the union. It is this type of behaviour which produces segregation and iniquity.

There is sometimes cultural elitism based on where you are raised. Education elitism speaks to the level to which you have been educated. Legalistic elitism indicates how many laws you have that need to be followed, and believing that because you have more laws, you are better off. The illusion of class elitism and financial elitism also exists, but amidst it all, God is concerned when people are made to feel like illegitimate beggars. These practices are in direct conflict with His Word. How can you say that you love the Lord and make an illegitimate distinction among His children? As we humble ourselves in the sight of the Lord, we are positioned for elevation. Humility speaks to the act of elevating our standards and reaching up to the level of the Maker. It is not looking down, as we have been culturally trained to do, but looking upon the perfect example while elevating our state of consciousness to be in harmonic synchrony.

Restoring Broken Character

Failure to deal with leadership effectively is greater than the failure of said leadership. When a leader fails, it is similar to closing the gate of trust. Trust is one of those things that you cannot pay for, play for, steal, or demand. It is a deposit in your account of integrity as you become known and your credibility increases. This is evident when your character is proved; however, if there is a policy violation, then all that would have been amassed becomes lost. Trust is one of the highest currencies of exchange that outweighs money.

Your talents and gifts have authority only in character. They become meaningless and are despised merchandise when used outside the parameters of character integrity (as seen above). Whenever we are gifted, that gift is not for us; it is for somebody else. What we have been empowered with is for those around us to benefit from while we serve as the conduit of that benefit.

Law has its foundation in ethics, from which culture and morality are derived. Whether written or unspoken, the law is of merit and significance, hence the reason for the conscience in keeping the individual on the right path. From the law comes the source of values as the law interprets values while establishing them.

It was so the integrity and value of humankind would be maintained that laws were established and given to Adam in the garden. We have access to these established laws of humanity from the Word of God. When we perform contrary to the law, we break it and require restoration. Character is then manifested when our values, principles, morals, and standards are aligned to overcome testing. This manifestation is generally apparent when we are under pressure by everyday trials.

When you say something and are able to prove it, that which you have stated is a display of the manifestation of character. Character is evident when self-sacrifice becomes more important than popular compromise. Your character will be tested most likely by appetite, fame, and power. Values play an integral part in character development as they supersede rules. Character lives beyond goals, sending a clear message that is identifiable and accepted while being believed. Character becomes woven into the culture of the group and then is shared by attracting similar values until it becomes the social norm.

If someone has the audacity to approach you to do something that is corrupt, illegal, questionable, or repugnant, it means that your values are not transparent and that you have a flawed character. You are already failing in your value system. There should be no comfort in enticement or in committing an error as people of light reflect only light while repelling the darkness. You can be fired from a job and still be going to work; check the story of Saul. Another was already appointed to Saul's position, and yet he was still going about business as usual. The Spirit of God had left him. Whatever is going to be done, you must be able to look at it after it is done and be comfortable knowing that it was well done and that what needs to have been done was done. If there is overwhelming doubt about the consequence of your action prior to it being done due to the negative complication outweighing the long term benefits, then you should not do it. Trust is an integral part of character: it is like glue. When there is a breach of trust, then everything that would have taken years, a lifetime, to build would be reduced to nothing. Trust that is violated by the self-imposed destruction of integrity and compromised morality will not be merely restored with forgiveness alone. The process of rebuilding will need to take place from the foundation.

Forgiveness should not be equated to the restoration of trust or confidence. It is the acknowledgement of a misstep and positioning one foot in front of the other on the quest to move forward in rebuilding that which was burnt down. It does not put the money that was wasted back in the account. We need to stop blaming people for not trusting us, especially when we possess no character and are truly deficient and void of truth. It takes a longer time to build trust than to destroy it and an even longer time to rebuild that which was destroyed. Having remorse or confessing or asking for mercy does not restore the total account of trust. As a child, it should be your duty to first maintain your commitment to your parents in accordance with the will of the Lord. This is one of your first opportunities to build character. There is a reward in upholding character. We must purpose in our hearts not to be defiled by the evil influence of this world or even to allow other people's desires to live within us. It is the parents'/guardians' responsibility to ensure that an example of good morality is displayed to the child/children. Parents should not position themselves to fail the child/children as failure will mar the intended prospect of child development, requiring remedial effort to rectify. Parents are expected to display honesty, integrity, and faithfulness in their obligation to the family and in other aspects of their lives. Only that which is upright and pure should be presented to the child to be consumed for equally beneficial output. As parents display their faithfulness and commitment to their responsibilities, having the child's best interests in mind without favour or prejudice makes the transfer more seamless. The child will then be equipped to reciprocate and expand based on the new information obtained. If the parents are ignorant or fail to display that which is required to foster character development, the child is prematurely ushered into the responsibility to lead the parent by example in the transformative change and constant growth in righteousness. This will occur until the parents/guardians have been realigned with an elevated thought process. The child is expected to maintain dignity, decorum, manners, integrity, and the principles of God as an example while the light is displayed.

If you have fallen in character and desire a restoration, you will need to follow a few steps. Knowing that restoration does not begin with the restorer, you need to get over yourself and stop asking people why they did not help you. What you should do is ask why you did not seek after help once realizing you needed it. People are not positioned to help someone unless there is a reaching out or an invitation.

The steps to restoration are as follows:

1. Acknowledge that you require help. No one will know what is in your mind unless you indicate it to them. One of the worst things that can be done is to give someone something that they are not yet ready to embrace. It is like detoxing a drug addict who has not yet accepted the need for cleansing. It means that the addict will go back to doing what they have been rescued from.

2. It is crucial to openly confess of your current state without making justifications for the infraction.

3. You should be accountable to an authority of integrity and reliability. This would be best, if this form of accountability is in effect prior to the need for character restoration which will serve also as insurance in reducing the likelihood of activating the need; however if the need should arise measures would have already been in place.

4. Completely submit to this authority, and show welcome obedience to the counsel and advice, as the one whose character has been compromised must never self-represent; all representation should be done by the authority of submission.

In order to get the best out of character development, we must ensure that the truth is known and practised. Without the application, the information will be useless. Let us seek to overcome the cycle as our character is maintained.

THIRD GEAR

The Virtue within You

Sustainability

Man of God/Son of God

THE VIRTUE WITHIN YOU

Virtue speaks to ideal behaviour by showing high morality in expression, referring to things which are right and righteous. Each individual has virtue within that needs to be minded and then refined to produce the glory that God desires. Virtue needs to be knitted in the essence of our being, producing pleasantly fragranced incense. It is expected that both men and women display virtue—and even the child who will become an adult. Proverbs 31:10–31 speaks to the virtuous woman, who has both physical and spiritual manners. In the physical/literal sense, this woman could represent the church; it is people and not the church who make the church (males/men and females/women), alluding to the fundamental roles and responsibilities that need to be fulfilled. The overview presents the indicated expectations of those connected to God. The spiritual meaning speaks to wisdom as the personification of the Hebrew feminine word for wisdom, which is *chokmah*.

Any individual desiring wisdom must first prepare himself to receive it; and if he does not prepare, then what he receives will be destroyed and be destructive. One should not look upon another until one has allowed refinement to take place within oneself, to the point of projecting through the person. The person of virtue must be one who is morally upright with the nobleness of character, soundness of mind, and dignity of righteousness. A virtuous individual has no price and cannot be bought. In exploration, there will be an intertwining of the spiritual and the literal. The book of Proverbs, primarily written by Solomon, son of David, outlines principles of high and holy endeavours that lead to godliness, which is necessary to govern our lives. Proverbs' intention is to demonstrate that only while we have living fellowship with God are we able to maintain purity of heart and conduct. The redemptive power of the Lord has a significant responsibility with regard to human thoughts, words, and deeds in ensuring that God's character is imparted.

Wisdom

Proverbs 9:10 reads, "The fear of the Lord is the beginning of wisdom: and the knowledge of the holy is understanding." Without wisdom, the knowledge that is gained and the understanding that is generated will be in error, if not even in confusion. Wisdom is a pure intellectual form that is only received under the direct instruction of the Lord. The wisdom of humankind is considered to be the quality of having experience, knowledge, and exceptional judgement. The wisdom of God is doing what He instructs, which is not being temporally minded; it looks far beyond the purview of humankind. No mortal himself or herself can ever access wisdom; when it has been grasped, it is identifiable. The acquaintance to the source of wisdom and righteousness is needed to express wisdom, which will restore us to His image. The acquired knowledge, learning, and skills we possess today fall far short of the dominion of the wise.

Everyone who desires what is good must go to the Giver of good gifts in order to get knowledge; it begins with the fear of the Lord. This is not knowledge as the world presents; it is unadulterated dissemination in an absolute state of purity. The acquisition of these virtues is interconnected and poetically calibrated. When wisdom walks into the heart, knowledge satisfies the soul and understanding keeps us on the path of righteousness, engaging in root cause analysis. In cause and effect, the spirit of discernment leads in the selection of the correct choice. This gift is absolutely free. As we read in Matthew 6:33, "But seek ye first the kingdom of God, and his righteousness; and all these things shall be added unto you." Wisdom is a principled thing which possesses extraordinary value. The thought to ponder is: how valuable is it to you? If the fullness of your life is within reach, then seek after wisdom and you shall find. If you lack it, all you need to do is ask the Giver of it. Access to this gift will become a life changer; things that you could have only imagined will become your reality in righteousness.

The Virtuous Woman

It is better to become a beacon of virtue so as to live virtuously; doing so will attract people of virtue. Becoming that which you seek after will develop you in preparation to receive it. Consistent diligence and care must be taken in the execution of virtuous duty. Who can find this woman of virtue, exuding virtuousness? How about becoming virtuous on the quest for wisdom? Each person should thoroughly purpose to live a life full of virtue.

The acquisition of wisdom is valued above rubies or precious stones. A godly person is becoming more difficult to distinguish given the normalization of evil. The desire to be godly is one that many have access to, but too few will actually access this desire. This is evident in the way humankind is destroying itself. Men and women who possess nobility in strength, beauty, character, and moral firmness are an endangered species. Many wish to find wisdom, but few do find it. When found, wisdom can never be taken away from you, except by the Creator.

Imagine a God-fearing, devoutly amiable partner who lives in perfect uprightness in righteousness. The husband and wife become one, walking the same path. In this case, there will be no lack as all that is needed is fulfilled. Psalm 23:1: "The Lord is my shepherd; I shall not want." So it is with the people of God; they should trust only in the Lord, who is the Bridegroom, knowing that all their needs will be supplied. The reason we can believe in wisdom is that it is derived from God, which is the equivalent of trusting in God. Inevitably, without the connection, there is no relationship and wisdom becomes absent.

Everyone desires confidence in preparation of the future. With wisdom, there is the anticipation of the inevitable hereafter; hence, a provision is secured for the family. Finances, among other resources in the present, and measures will be in place to mitigate undue liability. Depending on who you are and where you are during the selection of a spouse will determine the future you have, in comparison to the future that you may have had. It is wisdom that will guide you in the selection. Only the best must be given to the Lord, who deserves our total devotion, submission, worship, and praise. Wisdom reveals a life of deeds which is constantly and consistently in parallel with the cultivation of the best fruit from the husband with a desire for him to reach God's standard of perfection.

Wisdom seeks wool and flax to work with its hands. Clothing is not constructed haphazardly but with guided purpose, while exercising modesty in the selection of material and working to produce the garment desired. Most people today work only because of need or force; too many lack the willingness. Hence they find no joy, pleasure, or delight. The hands of wisdom are always eager to create and exercise radicalized thinking, accomplishing a task after understanding your gifts. This work is for the benefit of not only the immediate family but also the extended world. "Whatsoever thy hand findeth to do, do it with thy might; for there is no work, nor device, nor knowledge, nor wisdom, in the grave, whither thou goest" (Ecclesiastes 9:10).

Wisdom allows us to understand the responsibility placed upon a human to sustain life. In knowing this, it is imperative to ensure that food is available for the family. It speaks volumes that wisdom sees a need based on the wisdom of God endowed to it. This wisdom is shared with others. The wise woman engages in trading, meeting the needs of her family as they develop, while helping other families with their needs. It is wisdom which seeks to meet the needs of others.

Understanding that sleeping is essential and necessary in mortal rejuvenation, wisdom is not lazy or idle, seeking to exercise temperance in all things. While providing, sustaining, and delegating things which are foreign, the wise woman seeks help for better understanding to create greater efficiency, retention, and recovery. Worship is vital to the One generating the wisdom, so time is set aside for communion.

Unselfishly, the wise woman looks down in time to consider the possible desires of others, and she invests in the future for others' enjoyment. This is investing in one of the estates here on earth—real estate. This estate is not allowed to remain idle; it was planted with a vineyard, allowing it to produce. Wisdom displays a tenacity of strength, vim, vigour, and vitality which can only come from the Lord, as most are incapable of comprehending the dimension of trust in God. "Stand therefore, having your loins girt about with truth" (Ephesians 6:14). The girding process is to encircle like a belt. The wise woman must always rest assured in the truth of God. Her arms are strengthened as she works continuously and tirelessly.

She perceives that her merchandise is good, indicating that wisdom produces tangible fruit to be enjoyed, all of which comes from the Lord. The blessings of wisdom are on display for those who are permitted to partake of it. Our interaction with merchandise means that something is being contributed; it leads the mind to profit, gain, and surplus received from trade. Wisdom is presented as an all-rounded woman, curved in all the desired places while exceeding expectations. As Proverbs 3:13 reads, "Happy is the man that findeth wisdom, and the man that getteth understanding." With diligence and fortitude, with an unquenched and blazing fire, the wise woman works through the night.

Wisdom is skilled not only in survival but also in living and walking with God. This displays that not only did the wise woman seek out the material to have it sitting around but also that she was equipped to complete the task.

A parallel is seen in the humility expressed by wisdom, considering the needs of the poor, needy, and destitute, being able to recognize the spiritually impoverished. The heart of love is evident in this woman of wisdom, faithfully obeying the commands of God.

Wisdom is prepared for any occasion, even an unexpected occurrence of snow in a land where snow is seldom observed. This is the reason wool was acquired and prepared into garments. Even in the difficult times, dignity will be upheld, hence the colour of scarlet. It is the desire that all humanity might be clothed in the splendour of eternity after the sacrifice made to save our souls.

The wise woman is careful about her appearance and of things around. She is poised to know that she is a daughter of the King, so she represents herself in that manner; while maintaining etiquette of royalty in her industriousness, class, and elegant taste, she reveals herself more as she knows more about wisdom. She is adorned with exquisitely royal clothing likened unto the nobility of her godly character while avoiding the illusion of inclusion with the ungodly. She remains consistent in all areas. Wisdom is hard to hide when it is possessed; it will not be missed.

A remarkable analogy is seen in the relationship between the woman and her husband, in which the woman ensures that her husband is known within the gates of the community. Wisdom brings one to prominence as the gifts given are utilized for the glory of the Lord. Wisdom promotes purity. It facilitates sitting in counsel, allowing others to be edified, justified, and directed.

This woman finds it an absolute insult to consider the thought of relying on handouts. It empowers her more to deploy herself to create and use what has been given to her freely. The vision is made manifest as the future is anticipated. The product of the produce is without reproach, and that alone is given unto the merchant in exchange for trade. Wisdom dives into the inner resources of the soul to set the man free, asserting his manhood and causing him to liberate others while enjoying a meaningful life.

The presentation of wisdom is made with captivation, honour, and comfort. Its clothing is not available at any store as it was tailor-made from the Lord, peculiar and similar to none. The strength and honour of a wise woman are derived directly from the Source. She takes pride in knowing that she has the privileged position of ambassadorship. Having the virtue of wisdom will allow us to laugh in the time to come, clearly referencing that the future as preparation is already made and just peradventure the future is unknown. Wisdom knows who knows the future.

When wisdom speaks, all that can be observed is wisdom—no idle talk, no ill advice, no discrimination, no misleading statements, only truth and appropriate direction. If truth is not spoken, it is not wisdom.

The Law/Torah instructs the laws of kindness which are upon the tongue, meaning that the commandment is being upheld as indicated initially without modification or alterations. In Titus 2:3–5 we read, "The aged women likewise, that they be in behaviour as becometh holiness, not false accusers, not given to much wine, teachers of good things; That they may teach the young women to be sober, to love their husbands, to love their children, To be discreet, chaste, keepers at home, good, obedient to their own husbands, that the word of God be not blasphemed."

While the watchmen look for enemies and engagements that could overtake the city, the woman is alert, watching over her household to prevent pests from invading and thereby endangering and damaging the family. It is most important that deadly influence be isolated and destroyed before an opportunity arises to contaminate the home. It is very important to note that idleness and slothfulness are not in the diet of the wise woman as she values health and intends to maintain its solemnity.

There is no relegation in her family life as she is cherished by her husband and children. So too does she appreciate and care for them, blessing them with the same measure of blessing she has received. Wisdom excels knowledge and understanding; however, when there is an appropriate balance, the man will walk with God. Whosoever puts their trust in the Lord shall be safe. Let us trust in Him. External beauty is of value as wisdom looks beyond the physical. The evanescent nature of vain beauty is unreliable as an instrument for measurement as its fluctuation is unpredictably inconsistent. Imagine for a moment that there is a beautiful/handsome-looking individual who was once alive and is now dead; that beauty would come to naught as it becomes a beautiful feast for the decomposers.

What is given of wisdom if it is received unto itself? The deeds of kindness, purity, righteousness, and godliness are reflected as devotion is displayed to God in love for the wise woman's household, her contribution to society, meeting the needs of others and of herself in steadfastness. As people of faith, let us do the Lord's will.

The standard of a virtuous woman should be the goal of the well-thinking as that thought process secures your today in anticipation of the future. On this journey, seek not to confuse the voluptuous with the virtuous. There are two main classes of women who exist: a voluptuous woman of the flesh (curvaceous and sexually attractive, characterized by sensual pleasure) and a virtuous (godly/righteous) woman of the spirit. A virtuous woman is devoted to her family, delighted to work while demonstrating diligence, possessing integrity, displaying total dependence upon God, and caring for others and herself while maintaining a balance. And she is blessed of God. This type of individual is loyal, royal, domesticated, educated, rare, and precious, possessing inner beauty and living in love, knowing that she is well connected.

Most, if not all, are familiar with the voluptuous woman who is lewd and who finds pleasure in wrecking homes. It takes diligent effort to miss her as she possesses outer beauty that presents her as religious, bringing nothing short of destruction and damnation upon the family. Oftentimes these individuals desire not to engage their hands in constructive work but are more interested in killing their victims, who live by lust. It is integral to your survival that you stay away from the evil woman or become consumed with heresy. Though the flattery of her tongue will enthral, forsake not the guide from the covenant of your God. She has the capacity to turn her prey into harlots, taking them down the depths of the death chamber. In doing all this, she will never admit that she is wrong as she will convince herself that her wrong is justifiably right. Be not deceived by vain beauty that is allowed to engross thine heart, nor become a harlequin with the batting of her eyes. It would be more favourable to dwell on the housetop than in the clutches of her arms, as her loud and stubborn nature will be the end to anyone who seeks her demise. At your lowest, during the setting of the evening, you will be invited to take your fill of her love until the morning. The solace of her passion that is promised is filled with darkness. In the end, she seeks to terminate her victim's existence after subjecting his life to terror, destruction, displacement, atrocities, disease, untold suffering, despair, injury, and hate. In your best interests, stay away and don't be consumed by her or become her. Exercise the virtue of principle.

SUSTAINABILITY

Knowledge

Hebrews 5:12 reads, "For when for the time ye ought to be teachers, ye have need that one teach you again which be the first principles of the oracles of God; and are become such as have need of milk, and not of strong meat." The accepted definition of *knowledge* is "something that constitutes information and skills acquired through experience or education generally composing the amalgamation of the aspects of theoretical and practical awareness". One abundant commodity that exists is knowledge; people, countries, and nations go to war for its acquisition. It is exigent, so much so that specially trained intelligence agents are employed in ascertaining, extracting, and presenting uneasily obtained intelligence. Whether the information is accurate or not, it is presented as gospel, oftentimes used to control the narrative and behaviour and to manipulate those who have been fed the poisonous contaminants of deception offered in plain sight. People for generations have been destroyed due to a lack of knowledge and not necessarily because of the generational curses. Even so, knowledge becomes useless when nothing is done with that which is known.

The people of God on no account should be in a state of disarray in which they are lost due to lack of knowledge, especially when the information is available and evident. The reason many exist below their potential is that knowledge is averted and the wrong "child" is fed, causing death to humankind. A human being is a living soul, more spirit than clay or flesh. Without the manifestation of the spirit, the clay ceases to exist. The blessings of humankind are in the spiritual realm, which manifests the physical, which is more tangibly appreciated. Human beings need proficiency in knowledge to clutch doctrines and religious mysteries; people who receive matriculation in such things should be reproved and taught by the oracles of God. Apprehension towards diligent study weakens knowledge in things directly related to humankind's holistic development, disobliging the divine connection.

Not all knowledge is worth the process used in its generation. In navigating the bombardment of adulterated information complexities, it is imperative that truth is the guide if you want to avoid the ersatz information. Many people go to war to fight for a cause of which they had no clue; they eventually die, and it is then revealed to the family that the incitement was a waste. That is the power of misinformation. Reality and truth are God's declaration of character; everything of God eventually culminates absolutely. Throughout the ages, humankind has been given instructions for preservation after the information's administration; humanity will need to make the final move. Employing faculties of discernment will equip the person while improving intellect to the superlative excellence of divinity embracing the power and authority possessed to a position in the abounding of truth. With diligence applied, the pure infusion will eradicate any doubt or concern based on the presentation of truth. This knowledge received is noble in its submission, it is pleasant while contributing to the improvement of time, and tremendously useful in practice and application. It opens your capacity to grow, strengthening the overcoming powers held by the pillars of unchanging principles.

Human beings need not look puzzled at their own reflection, having incomplete knowledge of things now and of things to come, because all will be revealed and complete in its own time. Things will come to pass, and what was known can take another form, but love will remain. Knowledge is a useful tool which is needed as we have created many problems for ourselves; different areas of speciality exist in servicing these situations. In laying the foundation of the earth, wisdom was employed, but it was with knowledge that the deeps were divided. Proverbs 24:3–4 tells us, "Through wisdom is an house builded; and by understanding it is established: And by knowledge shall the chambers be filled with all precious and pleasant riches." It should be realized that wisdom, understanding, and knowledge are care partners, functioning most effectively in unison. Though wisdom foresees the building of the house, it is established to understand the knowledge of how to get it done, and then the house is finalized with exquisitely flamboyant decorations displaying its prominence.

Because knowledge is delicately relevant, it should be handled with love, for without it self-destruction will occur, taking along casualties of war. Without love, knowledge will be barren and even counterintuitive. Many with information will find themselves on a misguided projectile missile. Zeal should always be accompanied by knowledge. There is really no need to be destroyed for lack of knowledge. While on this journey in obtaining the ideal, we should be careful to avoid the fiery darts. It is time to put away childish behaviours. In the end, we must go with what we know so the world can receive the breath of life. The only way to live is to merge your faculties, placing them under the subjection of the Spirit. The best way to win is to lose; you win by losing the things which are weighing on your purpose fulfilment. Relieving self or being relieved of someone or something is referred to as losing. It can equate to a tangible or intangible loss. In contrast, winning is a continuous journey to becoming successful or victorious in the achievement of goals. How much are you willing to lose in order to gain?

Rich Young Ruler

Luke 18:18–23 gives the account of the rich young ruler. The Greek *archon* is translated as "ruler", referring to one possessing administrative authority, such as official or leader. The Greek *neaniskos* translates to "a relatively young man; youth; a man between twenty-four and forty years of age". The rich young ruler was also an individual of *plousios* (Greek), meaning "wealth". He had financial abundance while having earthly possessions that exceeded those of the average person. The young ruler made an enquiry into the process of inheriting eternal life. He called to Jesus as a good Teacher. The young ruler indicated that he knew all the commandments and said he had been keeping them since his youth. Though it seemed he was doing everything in accordance with the law, he appeared to be dissatisfied even while complying and noticed a lack; he wanted something more. In hearing his apparent plight, Jesus assessed the situation, told him precisely what was lacking, and provided a solution and direction. The young ruler rejected the idea of giving up all that he possessed as the solution to fill what he lacked and to satisfy his desire for eternal life. He kept all the legalistic commands on a ritualistic basis. It was demonstrated by Jesus that legalism and ceremonial practices are not sufficient to inherit eternal life. Eternity is not about temporal existence but about life after the life with the Great Commission for the saving of souls. When the ruler heard what needed to be done, he was waxed sorrowful because he was rich. Not all are ready to embrace the work mandated for them, which will determine their faith. You must be willing to lose vanity in exchange for eternity.

It should be absolutely clear that prosperity should not evade godly people. The degree to which an individual prospers is dependent on the location of the treasures that he or she has stored. This fact leads us to realize that our focus should not be on the earthly but instead on the heavenly wealth. It is the intention of the Lord that you prosper, and that is possible if you follow the indication and instruction of the Word. It is the wish that all people's soul will prosper; however, many will not choose this path. We should be sure not to allow people who are mortal to define us; we must fulfil the standard of perfection and be defined by it alone.

Three Hebrew Boys

In the account of the three Hebrew boys, we recall a statue was set up by the Babylonian king in his image, made of gold, that was to be worshipped. These Chaldeans—Shadrach, Meshach, and

Abednego—refused to oblige King Nebuchadnezzar because it was against their law. The Hebrews knew they could lose their lives by showing disobedience towards the king in their earthly existence, but transgression of God's law would have been an eternal loss. They chose not to fear the one who was able to destroy only the body but to fear the One who was able to destroy both body and soul. This allowed them to make the right choice in righteousness. They decided to obey their God, who saved them from the fire while giving the king a revelatory experience of His power. It should be the desire of our hearts to be willing to lose everything for the cause of righteousness, lest we become corrupted.

Daniel in the Lion's Den

It was also revealed that King Darius in Daniel 6 was placed in a complicated position when he was blindsided into passing a decree about worship. The proclamation, which was enforced by the king's order, stated that "whosoever shall ask a petition of any God or man for thirty days, save of thee, O king, he shall be cast into the den of lions". Daniel, being a faithful man of God and committed to His laws, worshipped according to the Hebrew customs at that time. He was accused of being noncompliant with the edict, and sanctions for the action's penalty were laid upon him. To the lion's den Daniel went. The king felt so uneasy that he could not sleep and petitioned for Daniel's safe return. When the morning light came, King Darius called into the den. Daniel, still alive, answered, saying that God had sent His angel to shut the lions' mouth. The Lord will watch over and care for all His children; let us remain faithful. Daniel prospered in the reign of Daris and also Cyrus the Persian.

It is time to move away from abusive relationships, inhumane treatment, lifestyle malpractice, conscious mental disability, lies, selfishness, destruction, rebellion, homicide, genocide, and suicide. Humans were created with a more extensive purpose than presently displayed; we need to accept responsibility and move in the restorative direction. If being around someone only causes you to reveal a side that is unbecoming, the best thing to do, if you fail to express control, is to remove yourself from that environment. When you consider the question of losing everything and evaluating what is left, and you find you have nothing, then you are mistaken. If you lose everything and you can still evaluate, it means that you have everything. You just need to claim it.

Honestly, none of us is in need of anything; once we go to the Source, from which all wealth flows, there is nothing we can do to increase the stature of the Giver. What is required is hallowed and sacred reverence and worship of the Most High. In the end, our reward will be greater than it ever was in the beginning. Is it of great significance if our souls should be sifted like wheat? What does all this knowledge profit us when not used?

MAN OF GOD/SON OF GOD

Understanding

Seize the opportunity in setting fire, examining and investigating a flame as the match is lit—when the stove has been ignited, when buildings or bushes burn. Many things are seen in the fire, such as dimension, colour, depth, burn pattern variation, and things which can affect its strength. All fires need oxygen, fuel, and heat to burn. If we look a bit closer, we can realize that all fires burn in an upwards direction. Fire defies the laws of gravity. The pull of gravity draws colder, denser air down to the base of the flame, displacing the hot air, which rises. This convection process feeds fresh oxygen to the fire, which burns until it runs out of fuel. The upwards flow of air is what gives a flame its teardrop shape and causes it to flicker. This is an illustration of understanding.

Wisdom and understanding can be found in one place: in God alone. These attributes are gifts from God, derived from the study of divine concepts and precepts. It should be accepted that hearing is not an assurance of understanding. Morality and character are developed with understanding.

There must be a realization and a need for understanding. Similar to with a new venture, one must seek and learn while refining skills and abilities. We read in Proverbs 4:5, 7, "Get wisdom, get understanding: forget it not; neither decline from the words of my mouth. ... Wisdom is the principal thing; therefore get wisdom: and with all thy getting get understanding." When understanding is acquired, we must not be tricked into giving it up or selling it out, betraying its integrity to please carnality. Understanding is associated with the personified woman of wisdom; they are walking partners, though they do not neglect their bond with knowledge. Proverbs 7:4: "Say unto wisdom, Thou art my sister; and call understanding thy kinswoman."

God is the most important thing for understanding, though the intellectual capacity that He possesses is beyond human comprehension as He is everything from which everything comes.

Lord help us!

A day is a gift; its utilization is dependent on the persons impacted. Adopting a set of beliefs to the exclusion of others can be considered a religious conversion. It means then that one has placed oneself in a position in which there is an abounding adherence to a particular affiliation. Many will have access to information, process, and source of application; however, few will utilize it. Peter was walking with the Lord and was still not truly converted even though he was given tremendous access regarding heavenly and earthly matters; these matters had not yet occurred until they were revealed.

God Wants You to Have a Bright Future

God doesn't want you to hold onto the past, being the same person when you were dissatisfied, but instead He wants you to move forward in your future, being catapulted by your present. Your human nature will compel you to focus on all your shortcomings and mistakes. But God's will is that you would forget your mess-ups and push forward to what He has in store for your future. Even if your life is a real mess right now, that doesn't really matter. What matters most is *now* and how you finish the race. It is not the intention that any be sifted as wheat; faithfulness must be exercised. As we read in Philippians 3:13, "Brethren, I count not myself to have apprehended: but this one thing I do, forgetting those things which are behind, and reaching forth unto those things which are before."

We are preempted to the blessings of the Lord, as stated in Psalm 1, when we walk in the counsel of God. The specific benefits of walking in the counsel of God are outlined; it is for you to consider if this is a path desirable to be taken.

You are considered, and there is a purpose in the life you live. We are interconnected; this interconnectivity refers to the state or quality of being connected. It is widely used in scientific disciplines such as biology, networking theory, and ecology. These elaborate systems interact with one another and cannot be analysed if considered alone. The Lord created the interconnectivity to allow us to be dependent upon Him. This representation of interconnectivity is flawed as God seeks after each individual independently, connecting them accordingly. Human beings are not trading cards or commodities, hence the reason for His concern for the soul. He understands when no one else seems to comprehend. It is His desire that you seek after Him as the experience of paradise awaits. Nothing will be kept from you as the relationship of love is immersive.

You Should Be on His Side

When you genuinely go to God for assistance and help, He will help you. The Father is a God of love and mercy and would much prefer to pour His grace on your life rather than get angry. God is patient, loving, caring, and compassionate; He wants the best for you and is daily trying to get your attention through creation, through people, and through circumstances. He desires you whole with thoughts of peace and not of evil. When God gives you instructions and commands for your life, it's not to hurt you but to help you prosper. Always ask yourself, "What does God want from me? What could be the possibilities for the future?" Does God want you to be in good health and have a sound mind? Yes. He also wants you to prosper in *all* things. That means your endeavours in life and your relationships, which include your finances and your career. God loves you.

You Will Enjoy the Results of the Journey

All experiences are uniquely genetically coded for you, and no one else will have the exact coding of your experiences. Some may come close, but not close enough. This demonstrates how much God knows you and understands your needs. He desires for you to reach a state where you can be perfect as you go through your *training exercise* for higher service. The situations you come upon aid you in understanding and appreciating the powers of God. In the state of destitution, there is overwhelming uncertainty, and you may even feel lost. In those moments, there is no need to go ballistic, and there is no need to break out into the deranged.

God's ways and thoughts are higher than ours. If we are God's people, it means that we need to edify ourselves. We should seek to be equipped so we know the signs and the direction we should take. Sometimes we find ourselves in a pickle because we do what we want but not what we must, expressing, "This feels like religion." We should not point fingers for the misguided concepts that we have and the misguided things we would have engaged in. In all we do, let us seek to express humility, knowing that we are God's disciples following His outline, humbling ourselves before the mighty hand of God that He may exalt us at the appropriate season. There is nothing wrong with being dependent on the Lord. It helps us grow as believers and become more like Christ. It helps with developing character *and* building our faith in the Lord.

God is saying, "Call, depend, and trust." Call on Him when you are in need, depend on Him when you need assistance, and trust in Him to render His will for His glory. Everything around may seem to be falling apart, the walls caving in and nothing seeming right with the appearance of no hope in sight. Let's remember that the Originator cannot be surprised. He will save you from your calamity. He will not abandon, forsake, or leave you. This is the time of God's favour.

Notes:

- **Knowledge** speaks to a fact, information, memory, and scholars.
- **Understanding** presents meaning, principles, reason, and teachers.

- **Wisdom** guides us as to what is to be done next. It entails application, action, and prophecy.
- All are gifts from God and should only be used in such accord.

Man of God/Son of God Mandate

In being considered or taking the title "man of God", one embraces a great responsibility. "Man of God" is a simple title, yet it is one enwrapped with profound riches, indicating a sacred privilege in which passivity is rejected when one understands the actionable nature which must be manifested in a person who is in possession of great diplomatic privilege. Dedication to God indicates that the man of God is determined to fight the good fight of faith and that he has his eyes fixed on eternal life. This focus will allow this individual to be drawn to righteousness and godliness while exuding character attributes of meekness, patience, godliness, faith, and love.

A formidable task was placed on Timothy in Ephesus as the commission placed upon him was to restore the church to the order of truth. The church had been turned away from God. False teaching, misunderstanding, and misinformation are dangerous to the truth; these need to be resisted for the glow of truth to prevail. Only knowledge, understanding, and wisdom can guide one on that path.

The man of God is a teacher of truth who has been dedicated and has accepted this dedication. This individual must be upright and perfect in his ways, thoroughly furnished for the good works that will be displayed. Some men of God include the likes of Moses. This man of God blessed the children of Israel before his death. Samuel was an honourable man, and as such, all he said came to past. Elijah was also considered in this category as he worked on the authority given to him by his Creator, and the people acknowledged him as a prophet. David was considered a man of God when he did according to the will of God. There are other individuals who exuded the character traits to indicate they were under the authority of God. An individual in this capacity should be perfect, upright, furnished with good works, and honourable and should worship God, exercising great discretion in humility when doing the Master's will.

Flee Sin

Sins are to be avoided at all times. The man of God must flee from sin in all its forms. The thought, planting, and cultivation should be avoided, lest the individual become consumed while allowing sin its reach to infiltrate and destroy others. The word *flee* is derived from the Greek word *pheugo*, meaning fugitive. It does not mean to stand firm or fight. We are told to stand firm against attacks of the Devil by putting on the armour of God; however, we should also submit ourselves to the will of God, resisting the Devil so he will flee us while we flee him. It is known that sin has the ability to trap and conquer. The Devil recognizes and plays on individualized vulnerabilities in an attempt to overcome us. In the exercising of prudence, we need to foresee evil and hide away from it. The simple-minded allow it to find a place within and are too soon punished by it.

Pursue God

In abiding in the will of God while pursuing Him, it is possible that before full matriculation is achieved, one may fall. The falling is a revelation of areas which need to be strengthened, which will be accomplished by getting up seven times. If one is consumed with evil, the only fall that one has the capacity to conceive is that of falling into mischief. On the quest to pursue God, one must maintain humility with eyes open in vigilance against pride. Imputed righteousness is received from God. He is the One who has saved us, and this is expected to be translated into godliness. The focus is on the inward qualities, in reverence of a sovereign God. Indeed we are His workmanship, a work of art created to bring the canvas to life when we walk with the light. Faithfulness speaks to dependability and trustworthiness in His plans and endeavours for our lives as we stay connected. John 15:5 tells us, "I am the vine, ye are the branches: He that abideth in me, and I in him, the same bringeth forth much fruit: for without me ye can do nothing." This connection will allow endurance in which the human being can bear up under pressure, striving through difficulties and trials while expressing the fruit which is epitomized by the fruit of the Spirit.

Fights for Faith and Eternity

We are in a battle of faith; it is a constant battle against the flesh. Faith is confidence in God, involving unwavering loyalty in the power, purpose, provision, and promise. Matthew 22:37–39 reads, "Jesus said unto him, Thou shalt love the Lord thy God with all thy heart, and with all thy soul, and with all thy mind. This is the first and great commandment. And the second is like unto it, Thou shalt love thy neighbour as thyself." Patience and meekness are prominent virtues completing the course. Patience allows the person to stick to the task without question, being kind and gentle with others, recognizing the development of self-control mixed with love. In setting our affections on things above, it brings home encouragement as we traverse this terrain of life, fighting the good fight for righteousness' sake. Let us offer prayer and supplication always in the spirit for the saints of the Lord so they all can be upheld by and for His glory.

FOURTH GEAR

Kingdom Concepts

Leadership–Service/Service–Leadership

Enjoy the Seasons

KINGDOM CONCEPTS

And saying, The time is fulfilled, and the kingdom of
God is at hand: repent ye, and believe the gospel.
—Mark 1:15

The Kingdom of God

The gospel mentioned here is that of the kingdom of God; anything else is a curse. To maintain its purity, the gospel was entrusted to the people of God whose hearts were tried by God. Those who had the foundational principles of God's kingdom were not self-appointed but divinely appointed to declare this message under the authority of the King. The gospel should not be diluted to suit humankind's appetite; it must be maintained in its purest form in order to evoke the change and transformation necessary for the transcendence of humankind. We should not be deceived or become ignorant of the illusions, misconceptions, and anomalies that were created to steer us away from the image of God. In this world today, people's eyes have been blinded by the gods of the world, which hinder the illumination of the glory of God. The beginning of the kingdom was with the gospel of Jesus Christ, but many are far removed from this gospel, spreading their own ideology.

The messenger is important, but care must be taken to ensure that the message from the messenger is received. Oftentimes, human beings can become so focused on the messenger that they neglect to receive the message and are no closer to accomplishing the work set out to be completed in the fullness of time. When Jesus had called His disciples and gave them power and authority, He sent them to preach the kingdom of God. This message was evident in the ministry of Jesus as it was the common theme in His parables and references.

Those who came after were also expected to teach this kingdom message, hence the reason for the appointing of apostles.

The gospel refers to the good news, and the kingdom refers to the government of God. The kingdom message equates to the good news of God's government, bringing joy, abundance, health, and peace for humanity, which it has lacked since the Fall. This kingdom will only be achieved at the end of the ages. Understanding this, the disciples enquired. Jesus then answered and told them to take heed to prevent the deception of people who would go in the name of Jesus with an alien spirit. They were informed that many would come in the name of Jesus, preaching of the good they have done, detracting from the message of the kingdom, and turning the focus primarily on the messenger, allowing the message to be lost. Not everyone who cries "Lord" shall enter into heaven. In spite of the deceptive vices, the gospel of the kingdom must be preached as a witness before the kingdom comes.

The kingdom of God is about salvation and His government. Jesus came to this earth as a baby and grew into a man; close to the end of His days on this planet, an account of the kingdom revelation was written. The identity of Jesus was verified when asked if He was the Son of God. Everyone who is of the truth heareth the voice of God. Luke 22:70 reads, "And he said unto them, Ye say that I am. Pilate asked if Jesus was a King," and in John 18:37 we find, "Jesus answered, Thou sayest that I am a king." It was for this reason that He was born to bear witness to the truth. If Jesus is a King, it indicates that He has a kingdom. Is this kingdom on earth? The answer is no, Jesus's kingdom is not of this world (John 18:36). Prior to the arrival of Jesus, there was a prophecy of the child who would have been the Saviour of the world, the One who would be called Wonderful, Counsellor, Mighty God, the Everlasting Father. When Christ's government is established, it will bring peace and justice on earth!

The Dream of Nebuchadnezzar

Most kings on this earth during the times of old were oblivious to the existence of other kingdoms that were not of humankind. In reminding humankind that there is a supreme Ruler, God allowed King Nebuchadnezzar the privilege to receive a dream that guided him to the realization of the coming of the new kingdom, which is supreme to all others that have been instituted by humankind. This image was separated into four distinct segments; at that time, it represented the future. Now this same image represents our past, present, and future.

Daniel 2:32, 38, reads, "This image's head was of fine gold, his breast and his arms of silver, his belly and his thighs of brass. ... Thou art this head of gold." This refers to Babylon's rule from 605 to 539 BC. The breast and arms of silver represent the Medes and Persians, the divided kingdom. Daniel 5:28 reads, "Thy kingdom is divided, and given to the Medes and Persians." This kingdom ruled from 539 to 331 BC. The belly and thighs of brass represent Greece's reign from 331 to 168 BC. In Daniel 8:20–21 we find, "The ram which thou sawest having two horns are the kings of Media and Persia. And the rough goat is the king of Grecia: and the great horn that is between his eyes is the first king. His legs of iron, his feet part of iron and part of clay." This is Rome, represented by legs of iron, during 168 BC–AD 476. "And the fourth kingdom shall be strong as iron: forasmuch as iron breaketh in pieces and subdueth all things: and as iron that breaketh all these, shall it break in pieces and bruise." The final segment, the feet and toes of iron and clay, represents a divided kingdom which will rule from AD 476 to the end of time.

> And whereas thou sawest the feet and toes, part of potters' clay, and part of iron, the kingdom shall be divided; but there shall be in it of the strength of the iron, forasmuch as thou sawest the iron mixed with miry clay. And as the toes of the feet were part of iron, and part of clay, so the kingdom shall be partly strong, and partly broken. Thou sawest till that a stone was cut out without hands, which smote the image upon his feet that were of iron and clay, and brake them to pieces.

When the end comes, all earthly kingdoms set up by humankind will be cast away as the eternal King comes to reign, presenting all that was promised to His faithful people. The message of the kingdom of God will have been preached to all the nations, kindreds, and tongues. In the end, a great multitude will cry with a loud voice, saying, "Salvation to our God while He is seated upon the throne."

Entering the Kingdom

In order to embrace the kingdom of God, one must be prepared to enter it. We read in 1 Corinthians 15:50–51, "Now this I say, brethren, that flesh and blood cannot inherit the kingdom of God; neither doth corruption inherit incorruption. Behold, I shew you a mystery; We shall not all sleep, but we shall all be changed." It basically goes on to conclude that if you are currently in a state of flesh and blood, you cannot enter the kingdom in such a state. It is only at the resurrection that humanity becomes qualified for entry into the kingdom. No church, country, continent, or empire is the kingdom of God; and in our corrupted state, we cannot enter. In speaking to Nicodemus about entering the kingdom, Jesus revealed that a new birth was necessary. This information indicates a qualifier to enter; there needs to be not a physical birth, because that has passed already, but a spiritual birth consecrated with submersion in water. Flesh is flesh and spirit is spirit; hence, a spiritual birth needs to take place before one may embrace the kingdom of God.

Is the Kingdom within Humans?

Luke 17:20–21 reads, "And when he was demanded of the Pharisees, when the kingdom of God should come, he answered them and said, The kingdom of God cometh not with observation: Neither shall they say, Lo here! or, lo there! for, behold, the kingdom of God is within you." Contrary to the misconception that was entertained to justify the Pharisees' holiness, the kingdom of God is not within any of us. There is no evidence to state that it will be set up within any person's heart. It could not be, as it has no dealing with the flesh or the corrupted. It would be similar to saying that the church is within you. Is that statement correct?

In speaking to the Pharisees, Jesus was referring to them, saying that the kingdom of God *is*, understanding that the kingdom has not yet come; speaking of it in the present would indicate that the kingdom that is not yet come could not have been the one He had mentioned. In the actual Greek translation of the passage, "within" refers to "among you" or "in the midst of you". So, Jesus is a representative from that kingdom who is in their presence. Humanity can be content knowing that the kingdom of God is not within us; it is impossible to be within. A day will come when death is swallowed up in victory. At that time the corruptible mortal form will be transformed to incorruptible immortality, a form where death has no sting.

Is the Kingdom of God Coming?

We read in 1 Thessalonians 5:2, "For yourselves know perfectly that the day of the Lord so cometh as a thief in the night." Though people believe they have the authority to bring peace, they cannot. Our feet should be directed to spread the gospel in preparation for the kingdom coming. The kingdom of God is coming back to receive those who are faithful to do its work.

Kingdom Basics

> But seek ye first the kingdom of God, and his righteousness;
> and all these things shall be added unto you.
> —Matthew 6:33

The kingdom of God existed on earth at the time of Creation. The government that was established on earth was the kingdom of heaven. The man was created in order to expand the kingdom of heaven here on earth. In essence, the man served as heaven's representative in the "colonization" process of earth. In order for the man to fulfil that role, heavenly principles needed to be executed on earth. In the creation of humankind, humans were created in the likeness of God. To initiate the creation, the word *us* was used, denoting a plurality of the union. After the man was created, humans were given dominion over all that was created. The thought process in the creation of humankind indicates that humans were finished before they had been created. What was needed for humankind to accomplish, contribute, and exercise was tabled prior to their existence. The mandate was established for humankind to have dominion over the earth. This is a reflection of the heavenly dominion over the universe. Earth was humankind's kingdom to be ruled and governed according to the heavenly kingdom, the statutes of the former modelling those of the latter.

The First Government

The first government that existed was *the kingdom of heaven.*

The first institution on earth was *the kingdom of heaven.*

The first government on earth was *the kingdom of God.*

The original mandate of God was the establishment of *the kingdom of heaven on earth.*

The first command of God to humankind was to govern earth for *the kingdom of heaven.*

Everything created has its place, purpose, and mission in the perfectness of its creation. The power and authority given to humankind was soon lost because human beings deviated from the statutes of heaven. It all went through the window when the woman was deceived by the serpent to eat of the fruit of knowledge of good and evil. This failure was the result of disobedience, causing humankind's exit from the kingdom. In protecting human beings from themselves and from consuming the fruit of the tree of life, God ushered humankind out of the garden and placed cherubim with flaming swords as a safeguard against their reentry.

When this cataclysmic separation occurred, humanity lost dominion; for this reason, the world has spiralled in the way we now experience it as the human being was disconnected from the kingdom of God and God's governance. Many ritualistic practices of sacrifice were used in seeking restoration; however, the governance that came after was unacceptable. Control turned into slavery, democracy turned into tyranny, order turned into chaos, management turned into failed stewardship, and leadership became repulsive as humanity was led to their destruction. The purpose of our creation was the administration of the earth. God purposed that for all of humankind, not just a few elite people. We were sent to earth to bring the kingdom, the governing authority of God on earth; the first assignment was to have dominion. The act of disobedience—the eating of the fruit—was treason against the kingdom of God.

Humanity lost a great deal. To this day, many have no idea of what they lost because of the Fall. It is for this reason that Jesus was sent, to remind us of the authority that we possess and can still access today. Many human beings behave in discordance with their commission, forgetting the bestowment of their Father. Humankind is from a royal lineage and is expected to act in that accord. This information is lost in the archives of the mind, hence the reason for behaviours that do not reflect the Father's glory. The same Father who has given us sonship just because has called humankind His child out of the darkness. The man was given the kingdom on earth, which he gave up. Today many seem to fill the void with religion, when in truth they seek after the kingdom which they lost when they gave up divine power. Diplomatic relationships with heaven were lost. No more did the Voice walk as intimately as it did in the garden when the man had his kingdom. Human beings have been consistently hiding from God after realizing their folly. It would serve a person more justice to himself or herself to go directly to God upon realizing this error.

Jesus Christ came as a representative to show how a person should operate, reminding us that we should not just live for water, food, clothing, shelter, and self-preservation. After these reminders, Jesus left, allowing the generations to linger in thought while directing their focus onto the kingdom. The desire for the perfect government is inherent in the human heart because we lost the government; this loss has placed us on a quest of seeking. The vision and mandate of God were to establish a heavenly colony of human beings on earth and to govern earth by His standards, conditions, parameters, principles, and values. There is an innate hunger and thirst that exists within us that can only be filled with righteousness, after which blessings will be realized. These were hidden in plain sight because the keys were not activated.

In living a meaningful and fulfilling life, one needs to discover, understand, and apply the kingdom on earth. It is the desire that growth in this kingdom be experienced and explored. If there is a yearning to be a peculiar treasure above all people, then there needs to be a relationship with the Source of all that is upon the earth. The Fall of Humankind was never the loss of heaven as heaven remains constant; it was actually the loss of the kingdom's government of heaven on earth. The spiritual, social, economic, and physical environment and cultural condition required a more superior government than is available on this earth. The only One who can restore the broken world is the Creator, but humankind will need to play an integral part in the process of restoration.

Keys of the Kingdom

In order to accept the kingdom, we must access its potential. For this reason, we are offered a guideline on how to tap into this wealth of knowledge. Luke 12:32 reads, "Fear not, little flock; for it is your Father's good pleasure to give you the kingdom." Jesus brought Himself as a manifestation of the kingdom when He came to earth, reacquainting us with the kingdom. Our Father, the King of heaven, gave us this kingdom when His Son was sent. We must turn away from our rebellion so we can access the rights and privileges that come with the kingdom, which is God's delight for His children. The kingdom of glory and the kingdom of this world cannot coexist simultaneously. The membership requirement is that we become a little flock, developing the characteristics God calls us to have.

Key #1–Knowledge Application

Kingdoms are unique in that the king *embodies* the government; the *will* of the king is the mandate of the government, and the word of the king is the source of *law*. The king personally owns everything in the kingdom, displaying *lordship*; the citizens of the kingdom are there at the king's pleasure, indicating the necessity of *worship*; and the king's reputation is determined by the welfare status of the citizen, demonstrating his *glory*. The thoughts of the King are of peace, purpose, and prosperity for all those under His authority. Everything in the kingdom belongs to the King, and this means that if you are a child of the King, you have access to everything that your Father has. He will never withhold any good gift from those He loves. You have an inheritance; it is time to claim it.

Key #2–Power and Authority

Matthew 16:19 reads, And I will give unto thee the keys of the kingdom of heaven: and whatsoever thou shalt bind on earth shall be bound in heaven: and whatsoever thou shalt loose on earth shall be loosed in heaven." We are given the keys of the kingdom and not the keys to the kingdom. These are keys that will unlock the power of the kingdom and make it work in our lives. We have been given the authority to command control over things in heaven and earth with certain limitations. Just saying that you have the kingdom of God does not give you the kingdom of God. It is made manifest in the execution of power. These powers can be seen when serpents and scorpions are overcome and when the enemy has no authority to hurt you.

Key #3–Prayer

In making your request known in prayer, you should utilize the name of Jesus to allow for the glorification of the Father through the Son. The one who has belief in the works that the Son did will be able to do more significant works for the glory of God. In asking in Jesus's name, we must ensure it is in accordance with His will so that the request can be justified. It was the Son of Man who made us pure and holy, giving us freedom when He paid the price (Himself) for our sin while meeting our needs. Thanks should be provided for all things unto God and the Father in the name of our Lord and Saviour Jesus Christ.

Key #4–Faith

Having the keys that God gave indicates that you have authority, access, ownership, control, power, and freedom. With this, you can actually speak things into being, just as God spoke and it was so. You may make a request that a mountain move, and it will respect the authority under which you stand and move to where it was instructed. It does not matter how small the faith is, but first you must believe. The greatest thing about the work of the kingdom is that it is manifested under the authority of faith through the Son of Man. The kingdom of heaven is like a mustard seed. Mustard is the greatest among herbs when grown, and it serves as lodging, but it is a grain in size that is the least of all seed. This seed becomes powerful when planted. With faith, little can become much and significantly increase because God is in all things. It is this attribute that is needed in serving and pleasing the Creator.

Key #5–Humility

Exaltation is a set-up for debasement, while humility is positioning oneself to be exalted. Humility is a virtue that is almost absent in modern society; in the world today, society is flooded with arrogance, pride, entitlement, discrimination, snobbery, egotism, narcissism, and hubris, among other vanities. This places society in a precarious situation, causing many to realize that humanity is a composition in which human beings exist and are treated with distinction. It is barbaric to self-promote or exalt oneself without the prerequisites; in knowing such, the ideal would be achieved knowing that only God is worthy of exaltation. It is better to have a humble spirit than to be found dividing spoils with those who are proud. In unlocking the kingdom, our minds' eyes will seek calibration concerning the spiritual as all things from the spiritual are made manifest in the physical. The world can only see the physical and lacks understanding of the existence of a far higher realm. To be the greatest, you must first become the least. A child's humility will allow greatness in the kingdom of heaven.

Key #6–Forgiveness

Forgiveness and pardon are necessary for moving forward. The parable is shared of a king who had a reckoning and brought unto him the servant who owed him ten thousand talents. The servant did not have what he needed to pay, so his lord commanded that he, his wife, and his children be sold until the debt was paid. The servant pleaded for mercy, and the debt was forgiven and he was set free. This same servant was also owed a much smaller portion (one hundred pence) by a fellow servant. He laid a hand on that servant, violently requesting payment. The fellow servant begged and asked for an extension of patience until he could honour the debt, but the first servant did not allow it and cast the man into prison until the debt could be paid.

When the lord heard this report from their fellow servants, he called the servant who had owed him and proclaimed that he was wicked because he had been forgiven of his debt but was unwilling to forgive another of his. The master asked, "Why did you not have compassion on your fellow servant, even as I had?" The master was upset and delivered this man to the tormentor until he was able to pay. This is what the heavenly Father will do if we are unable to forgive each other. We must forgive to receive forgiveness as we enjoy our prosperous lives.

Key #7–Follow Him and Never Look Back

Luke 9:62 reads, "And Jesus said unto him, No man, having put his hand to the plough, and looking back, is fit for the kingdom of God." In the account with the rich young ruler, there was only one thing left to be done as all other things had been accounted for—it was for the ruler to have a total separation from this world for the cause of the kingdom. He chose not to sell all his possessions and follow the Master.

This is like how Lot's wife, while leaving the riches of Sodom, turned, feasting on Sodom's destruction, and was made into a pillar of salt. So did the rich young ruler look back at his possessions and could go no further. The rich young ruler was so close yet so far. To this individual, it seemed unfavourable to do that which was required at the moment he made his decision. To human beings, it is impossible to accomplish things on a supernatural level; however, it is possible to overcome all things with God.

The paradoxical application of the kingdom comes with significant measures of treasure which should not be surrendered for temporal gratification when the eternal is at stake. People are easily moved to revert to what they are accustomed to, which is not the way of the kingdom. In living in the kingdom's principles, one must have a firm hold cemented in the Lord. Many are called, but only a few are chosen. Allow yourself to be chosen so you can start tapping into the kingdom's treasure house.

Key #8–Freedom

Matthew 8:25–27 reads, "And his disciples came to him, and awoke him, saying, Lord, save us: we perish. And he saith unto them, Why are ye fearful, O ye of little faith? Then he arose, and rebuked the winds and the sea; and there was a great calm. But the men marvelled, saying, What manner of man is this, that even the winds and the sea obey him?" Jesus was free. He knew that He had rights to exercise dominion over the world; hence, He spoke to the sea and it obeyed. It is this same liberty within Christ that makes us free, and as we receive this freedom, it should be our objective not to be entangled in the yoke of bondage and become entrapped again. Let us embrace the Lord, who is Spirit, as where His Spirit exists is liberty.

Key #9—Multiplication

There is a parable about the sower and the seed. In the account, the sower goes out to sow or scatter seeds, for which there existed multiple probabilities for landing. Some seeds fell by the wayside, becoming food for the fowls; some went on stony ground where there was not much earth, so they sprung up and were scorched by the sun; some fell among thorns and were choked while they sprung up. Then there were those which fell into good ground and brought forth exceptional fruit in abundance.

The seeds that fell by the wayside are those who heard the words of the kingdom and understood it not, so the wicked took it away. The seeds that fell on stony soil were those who received the words with joy, but because the words had no roots, they only lasted until the season of tribulation. The ones who received seeds among thorns were those who were tricked by the worldly snares and deceitfulness of riches, causing unfruitfulness. The seeds which fell on good ground were those who heard and understood the Word and made it manifest in their lives, bringing forth fruits in abundance.

The kingdom of God is a place of multiplication; there needs to be an increase, and the fruits are a quality witness. In the beginning when the man was created, the Creator stated, after giving humankind dominion, "Be fruitful and multiply." Each person was warned to abstain from fellowship with the unfruitful works of darkness. On the path to multiplication, care must be taken to exercise due diligence to safeguard the integrity of increase and to have no dealings with the world's deceitful practices while protecting that which is a blessing. The Creator of the created is insulted without an increase or evidence of fruit.

Key #10–Righteousness, Peace, Joy

Romans 14:17 reads, "For the kingdom of God is not meat and drink; but righteousness, and peace, and joy in the Holy Ghost." If it is your desire to access the kingdom's storehouse, then you need to drop some baggage in order to experience peace and joy. These keys are engraved in the laws of God, based on principles which have operated since the origin of time, generating the function necessary for you to be in accordance with the kingdom of God, which cannot be substituted. You are being charged not to be high-minded, trusting in riches. We should exercise prudence in trusting the living God. Utilizing these keys gives humanity access to God's storehouse and overflowing abundance. Prosperity in all things is a natural standard of kingdom living. We need to use the keys to open the doors. Remember, the blessings of the Lord make the holder rich without sorrow.

LEADERSHIP-SERVICE/
SERVICE-LEADERSHIP

It is more imperative and long-lasting to influence than it is to control. Control is momentary and demands constant supervision and micromanagement, whereas influence is perpetual and evident in the influencer's presence or absence. Influence is likened to yeast. When the dough realizes that it has been infiltrated, it is already evident by the transformation which has taken place. Upon the dough's awakening, it has already yeasted, similar to having been salted. It is obvious to note that during the process, there is seldom a sound during the operation. When salt is added to food, it sits there and extracts the flavour by creating the concentration gradient while working its way down into the food, quietly affecting the whole meal.

We are the light; if the light is absent, then darkness will overtake immediately. And when the light returns, the darkness will vanish. This is an expression and admonition of the process of influence. There is no need for light to fight the darkness; all light needs to do is to be present. The reason there is no need for light to fight darkness is that light is incomprehensible to darkness. In the same way, you would not light a candle and put it under a bushel. You would have more profit putting it on a candlestick to illuminate the house.

You should never give a permanent response to a temporary situation. This is your responsibility: to let your light shine as you uncover the dark and brighten the way for those who pass. You are only allowing yourself to be used as a springboard by the predestined. Those who you assume are your friends will turn into your enemies with this light, and those who were your enemies will occupy the inverted roles. The enemies will be waxed bitter with exasperation, but do not be in despair. The real reason is that people don't feel comfortable when you leave them in their nothingness. It is excruciatingly challenging and nearly unproductive to lead from behind. Though the righteous may be afflicted, the Lord will deliver them. Let's realize that sheep are not leaders; they follow the other sheep in front of them. When you have risen to the standing of a leader, you will need to design the course in unconventional ways which have not yet been done. It takes boldness, determination, and commitment to decide what is in the best interests of those you lead, realizing that you are accountable throughout your leadership journey.

Possessing the leadership spirit indicates that you are naturally created to lead; this spirit can only be awakened by the mentality that is owned. Some leaders are powerful but may still be in the bush of their uncultivated potential mental expression. Don't be afraid to come out and become the person that you are intended to be. Live your life based not on the opinions of others but on the purpose of the Originator. It is the Lord's desire that you be the head and not the tail. An exquisite attribute of a leader is that leaders are excellent followers, heeding the commandment of God.

If one examines the bird or the fish, one finds it is quite evident that neither needed to go to any school to learn how to fly or to swim. It is innate and wired within so that when it becomes time, flying or swimming can be expressed naturally. These creatures function from instinct. What makes us humans different is that we can choose to become what we were intended to become or we can choose otherwise. A seed, when planted in whatever soil, seeks to become the best of what is possible given its circumstances. It never murmurs or complains about the environment, the climate, or the seasons; it just allows itself to become. The tree does not limit itself to say, "I will only grow four feet in my lifetime." It grows as high as it possibly can, not looking at or comparing itself with other plants. The most significant limitation on a person is the person himself or herself, neglecting the untapped potential that is freely given. We should not be afraid to lead, because we were never given the spirit of fear. Instead we were given a spirit that is powerful and is unified with soundness of mind.

No one is truly ready for leadership without understanding kingdom governance. The reason we can lead is that we are royalty and have been given authority from our heavenly Father. Our Father is both King and Lord. As King, He has dominion/lordship/rulership, and as Lord, He has a domain. The dominion refers to the authority, and the domain refers to the territory. The kingdom principle teaches that the King is the owner of it all. There is genuinely no private property or ownership; there is only stewardship of a realm over which humanity has been privileged to rule. God is the King of all the earth, owning all the silver and gold. Let us give Him the glory.

Our King is Lord; He owns and has dominion over everything that can be possessed. Whatever is used and allowed access to is a privilege. We should understand that the King can give what He feels fitting to any person selected and in any proportion. The parable about the kingdom of heaven being referred to as a man travelling to a far country indicates that to one he gave five talents, to another he gave two, and to another he gave one. These were given according to the ability each servant possessed. The traveller left the servants, and while he was out on his journey, the one who had received five talents traded and made an increase of five more. The one with two also increased, gaining two more, but the one who had received only one went and dug in the earth and hid his lord's money. Time passed, and the lord returned. He took account of what had happened. He was pleased with the statements of the one who had five and increased to ten and with the one who had two and increased them to four. But as for the one who had one and failed to increase because of fear, the lord was displeased with him and said he was wicked and slothful. The servants who increased heard "Well done", as their works were good and they were faithful in what they had been stewards over. So too with stewardship: whatever is touched should be increased in value and not decreased. We have been commissioned since the beginning of time to multiply. This is a kingdom concept, one which says that whatever you don't use, you will eventually lose because it will be redistributed. Submission to the King means we are under the King's authority, and in obedience this is displayed. If you call on the Lord, be prepared to do what He says. The authority of God was transferred to humankind upon their creation. The first man was given his own territory, which was the earth, to rule. We are able to see when God created the earth, after which He handed it over to the man to have legitimate kingship. It is further stated that the man was to have dominion, meaning the man was to rule over that which was given and that the man had power and authority. This privilege was provided by the Creator.

Service

In the direction of leadership, the leader must become a servant in order to lead effectively. The service rendered should be not towards self but towards those who are being led. This can only be done under godly authority, as the natural person is selfish; hence Paul reminds us that we should die daily to self. Only then, when aligned with the mind of Christ, can we effectively manifest our leadership with the purity and integrity needed. The mind of Christ needs to be in the one who serves. If no one desires to serve, then it could be agreed that nothing will get done. It is those who render service who display their leadership by utilizing initiatives in filling needs and voids. This service will then create an elevation of living standards. No form of service to humanity is less than any other under the direction of godliness.

Jesus Christ was slain from the foundation of the earth; "who verily was foreordained before the foundation of the world, but was manifest in these last times for you" (1 Peter 1:20). Though He is God, He saw it as being justified to make Himself available to serve humanity, the same humanity that was created a little lower than the heavenly host. He became one of the created, taking the form of a servant in humility and obedience to the Father, even to the point of laying His life down. This is a display of selfless doing, because the choice existed when the Creator could have dissociated from the created, allowing everything to collapse. This selfless act of service must be displayed by leaders. The responsibility entrusted is not to conspire, victimize, manipulate, oppress, and desecrate; these are character attributes of evil and not of leadership. Leaders are entrusted to protect the poor. They should execute correct judgement with mercy and compassion and without bias or prejudice. Often these practices are mistakenly laid synonymously with leadership; however, it is not so. When an individual becomes willing to serve, he or she is almost ready to lead.

Chief Servant

The service rendered must be of the highest calibre, wrapped with love and kindness as the Lord is being honoured. The example laid down by Jesus Christ when He walked on earth is to be followed in an effort to modify your character. The more people who are serviced by your gifts, the greater your reach and leadership potential. It is about serving not to elevate self but to magnify God. Matthew 20:28 reads, "Even as the Son of man came not to be ministered unto, but to minister, and to give his life a ransom for many." *Ministered* is translated to *served*, and *minister* is translated *serve*. This humble expression of service was seen in the washing of the disciples' feet by the Master as He knew the Father's will and was leaving an example.

Leadership Spirit

Being under authority is a powerful place to be. The degree of power possessed is determined by the one whose authority the subject is under. The only authority that humankind needs to be under is God's; this authority is safe and provides freedom and mitigates against the world's cares. We should humble ourselves under the mighty hand of God so that He may exalt us in due season. For this reason, we must cast all our care upon Him as we remain sober and vigilant.

Being under any authority but the Creator's is chaos; submission is needed to enjoy the benefits of this authority. Similar to the birds submitting to the air to fly and the fish to the water to swim, so too humankind must submit to God, for it is in Him that we live, move, and have our being. In giving up your power, you need to step away from authority. This is what the Devil desires, but you must hold firm.

Spirit of Leadership

The spirit of leadership actually takes place in the mind, bringing with it the understanding of cause and effect, knowing that a decision has made an impact on the future. The principles of righteousness, justice, and peace are important. Effective leadership is a leadership that displays competence and compassion and is sensitive to that which is good and decent. In this reactive culture, problems are created and then acted upon. What should be done, more importantly, is to pray for the right people to be in authority and then to continue to pray while they are there. In fact, it would be ideal if we were to become the people of such authority, nurturing the virtues within us over time. Quality persons are needed in order to experience the execution of administration that is in keeping with what is right and righteous. The attitude of the leader should represent the future quality presented. This individual must possess a dream, a vision, a mission and be driven towards execution. It is this attitude that will be the architect of our future. The correct environment must be selected for optimal growth. Though a seed has a tree within, it will never grow if not planted. All leaders are accountable to the Lord and will be judged in accordance with the measure of His authority.

Humanity is a product of intelligent design which was transferred from the Creator, causing our innate desire to exercise intelligence in leadership for greatest efficiency. This spirit was entrenched in our origin. Our thoughts are the factors limiting our possible contributions. In getting the desired result, we need to expand our mental capacity through channels of unquestionable integrity. A charismatic person should mesh his or her charisma with character; the gifted leader should have conviction; those with power must display principles; those abounding in intelligence should exercise morality; visionaries need to display values; and spiritual leaders should reflect purity. The present calamities result from humankind's dysfunctional leadership, in alignment with which many are illegitimately operating. Leaders influence their environment as the leadership spirit is captured and cultivated. Authentic leadership is marked by the willing submission to authority and being inspired to extract the greatness that is within, making the ordinary extraordinary.

Those who are lacking the spirit of authentic leadership are unwilling, infecting those around them with sorrow and discord while infiltrating the mind with selective honesty and hostility, only giving to receive. They present pretentious values, in a moment willing to destroy, crushing enemies, competing, and committing to no one while keeping all in suspense. Leaders should not play on the vulnerabilities of emotion, needs, and fantasy only to achieve their personal desires, leaving the victims ravaged and in ruins. Investment should be made in the relationship between the leader and the followers, dignifying humanity. Those under the leadership, if not elevated, display poor leadership and a lacking spirit. Humanity should never be traded as a commodity, even though human resource is one of the most considerable resources. Perspective should not be reconciled, blurring the moral and ethical lines. A wicked ruler is likened unto a roaring lion.

Nehemiah

Nehemiah, though he was a servant to the Persian king Artaxerxes, was a valiant leader who used his connection of influence to benefit God's people. Hearing the distress of the Jews, he prayed earnestly for the people and went before the king. The king realized that Nehemiah had sorrow of the heart, as he was not sick, and hence allowed him to go on an expedition. In humility and respect, Nehemiah explained that the city of his fathers' graves was left desolate, and he wanted to rebuild. He also requested works and material, which were freely given, as the hand of God was upon him. So Nehemiah went and viewed the walls of Jerusalem and informed the people what the Lord had impressed upon his heart. The people were unified and ready to build, but the other nations surrounding Judah were not pleased. They constructed the city and sanctified it as each part was completed.

The walls were rebuilt because the enemies became uncomfortable, evident by their efforts to stop the ordained work progress. There were numerous attempts to intimidate and attack the people and stall the work, but the people's spirits were kindled with persistence. They worked to stop the breaches as they stood guard day and night with one hand dedicated to working and the other hand holding a weapon peradventure. Nehemiah dealt with the oppression of the people with rebuke while he dealt faithfully with his people. He avoided soiling his hands as controversy was averted. He received the captives who returned to Jerusalem, and he dedicated the wall that he had been instructed to build to the Lord.

Josiah

We read in 1 Timothy 4:12, "Let no man despise thy youth; but be thou an example of the believers, in word, in conversation, in charity, in spirit, in faith, in purity." Leadership is not hindered by age; it was when he was 8 years old that Josiah became king. He was not too young to understand what was right in the sight of the Lord. He walked in the way of his father, David. The more Josiah knew about righteousness, the more he acted upon the knowledge.

In the eighth year of his reign (at 16 years of age), Josiah searched for his father's God, and in the twelfth year of his reign (at age 20), he began to purge Judah and Jerusalem of the graven and molten images, breaking down pagan altars, until the eighteenth year of reign (when he was 26 years old), in which the land was purged. Throughout his reign, Josiah was faithful to God, the God of his father, the God of the universe; the purity of his leadership is mentioned in the book of Lamentations. When called to lead, you should answer, going assuredly with the support of the ultimate power in the universe. Remembering your Creator in the formative years as you despise the lustful pleasures of the world will serve as a guide for discernment.

The Prophet Jeremiah

Some leaders are predestined like the prophet Jeremiah, who was divinely created for a higher purpose than most men and women would embrace. The details in the tapestry of his mission were to venture into the uncomfortable in order to possess a sense of accountability and responsibility to the One who sent him. His Creator spoke to him, indicating that he was well thought out and was already known before he had been formed. Not only was he known before he was established, but also he was sanctified for the purpose for which he was created.

Jeremiah was seventeen when God called him to ministry and commissioned him to minister to the people of Judah. Upon seeing his destiny in front of him, Jeremiah was astonished and surprised. God told him that he was born to be a prophet. Though Jeremiah was a child, the Lord saw beyond the obvious and used the embedding within. The Lord will never send you until you are equipped, and fear has no place when walking with Him. Jeremiah fulfilled his purpose, something that many spend their lifetimes seeking after. Youth is malleable in the hand of the Lord, and He desires to perfect each individual, but only if they allow Him to.

Mary

Mary kept herself pure and circumspect so that her womb could be utilized as a nurturing vessel for Jesus. There is no role in leadership that is insignificant. All functions work for the same cause in fulfilling the heavenly mandate.

Queen Esther

She was born Hadassah, who became Esther, a Jewish queen of the Persian king Ahasuerus. Esther, before she became a figure of prominence, was a young virgin orphan girl who kept herself circumspect under Mordecai's instruction. She was willing to sacrifice her life for her people after she was made queen by going to the king without an official summons from him, saying that if she were to perish, then so it would be. It was the Lord who allowed the king to extend compassion and his golden sceptre.

The queen used her power and authority to bring justice and balance to the kingdom. We are reminded in the account that though evil should not be planned for others, those who devise evil may eventually receive their due. A countermeasure was used to protect the people of the queen without the impeachment of the king, which gave the Jews authority to defend themselves. Queen Esther went in to the king and made the request, and the king obliged. Our work should be a reflection of God's goodness, allowing all people to see it and know it, developing favour while following the ways of God. With the authority of his rulership, the king gave the decree, and it was done as requested.

The scribes were gathered, and the decree was written and sent to every province in their own language. When one is in service with honesty and good intent, trust will develop and eventually friendship. The king and the queen operated as a team in liberating God's people, allowing them to exercise their power in destroying their tormentors. Being connected to royalty induces a natural transfer. Mordecai received a reward and advancement and was promoted because of the excellent report and his contribution in preserving the integrity of the king's leadership, making him second to the king.

Ruth

Ruth's story is more about how she was opposed to leaving the side and counsel of Naomi. There was a famine in the land, during which

Ruth's young husband died, as well as his father and brother. The three wives were left alone and defenceless, having only each other. Both Moabitesses were extended the freedom to return home to their families. Orpah decided to do just that, but Ruth did not as she had been converted by Naomi's principles. Ruth shared the same loneliness, anxiety, and grief that Naomi had, and because of this, Ruth would not abandon her.

Loyalty was one of Ruth's distinguishing characteristics. Even though there was nothing to be gained, she still stayed to comfort and support Naomi. In listening to the good counsel of Naomi, her story of love, courage, and loyalty triumphed over adverse circumstances. Ruth met Boaz, got married, and had a son called Obed, the father of Jesse, who is the father of David. Trust was the reason the relationship worked; this trust brought protection as a voluntary submission to authority, which was established with accountability and perseverance until the goal was achieved. We read in Acts 10:34–35, "Then Peter opened his mouth, and said, Of a truth, I perceive that God is no respecter of persons: But in every nation he that feareth him, and worketh righteousness, is accepted with him." Both males and females have an equal opportunity to be leaders radiating the spirit of leadership.

ENJOY THE SEASONS

To every thing there is a season, and a time
to every purpose under the heaven.
—Ecclesiastes 3

A story is told of a youthful audacious voyager who set out on a journey distant from home, who covered all the paths that had been trodden until he encountered a strange place. This place excited his spirit. Even in his excitement, confusion loomed as he no longer knew his destination. At the intersection of an unknown ending, in limbo, the traveller stood. How long will this traveller remain in such a state? For a moment or a lifetime? It is necessary that each individual develop stability of mind with direct, purposeful focus.

This exact moment of your existence will never occur again. It does not matter if you are living in a loop despite having made choices; after it has passed, it becomes the past. You will never be the same as you were. With each ticking second that you age, you are moving closer to your future or are stuck in your past, maybe even becoming complacent in your present. Time's movement should never be equated with progress. It is not as growing older in number but remaining the same in maturity that is the mark of devolution. Life is filled with multiple phases, just as the year has seasons. It is unwise to become attached to a period, refusing to grow up, becoming an adult stuck with a child's intellect.

How productive were your last twenty-four hours, or the previous week, or let's say the last month or even year? Have you been living below your potential? We were placed in time to make an impact. God does not want us to only exist; He wants us to live. Phases that have passed are now in the past, and we should not hoard them whether they were underutilized or maximized. What we should do is look to the future today. Your past is dead except for the life you give it. We must not allow the past to define us, but allow it to aid in our refinement; the preceding prepares for the proceeding. In order to enjoy the seasons that life has to offer, we need to institute plans and set goals, actively enforced so that we accomplish them. Though projection may change, the purpose remains. Your purpose is more potent than any problems or challenges that may appear to overtake you. Rest on the surety that things work according to God's will, which is notably more evident for those who love Him. When you have been predestined, you will be called, and if you are called, you will be anointed and eventually appointed. This process is for the justification in anticipation of glorification as you are a child of the King. No matter what you have done, you will be placed on the path to your destiny, doing that which is in accordance with God's will. On this account, you can expect the best, prepare for the worst, and have an attitude that supersedes previous altitudes.

You are your past, present, and future. All that you need to survive and enjoy the beauty of life is already within you. In releasing your future, you must loosen the traps of confinement so as to allow the future you to emerge in the present as you walk with that future in hand. Just as Jeremiah was embedded with a plan, each individual has also been thought of and completed before creation. God has already chosen you, and only as a reminder, the thoughts that He has towards you are of peace, and His expected end for you is not one of inequity or ill intent. Your life has already been planned, so capitalize on the resources you have within. Your choice is the deciding factor: inferior or quality? You decide. God not only has your future plan but also has a way to get you there. You can move from small beginnings to enormous increase as all things are possible with God.

Time is a commodity of which we all have an equal measure according to the purpose intended for us. Time is never the problem; the situation lies in its utilization. Each human being gets the same twenty-four hours in each day. The difference exists in the turnover return. Since the origination of humankind, the Creator explicitly stated that human beings must be fruitful; this fruitfulness means to become productive and to produce. If you are given that authorization, you need to have provisions in place for it to be fulfilled. When you should be fruitful, multiplication is expected to take place; that which was produced should also produce. While production is taking place, there needs to be replenishing, indicating a distribution chain of efficient logistics. After the logistics are worked out, there needs to be domination—hence the word *subdue*. If whatever our hands find to do is approached in this regard, there will be an overwhelming abundance of fruits. The dominion that should be exercised is not over people but is that which the Lord created before the creation of humankind.

Die to Grow

First Corinthians 15:36 reads, "Thou fool, that which thou sowest is not quickened, except it die." The growing process requires death. There needs to be death. With the seed, before it grows it dies. Care must be taken to ensure that plans are in place to generate the required fruit, as preparation is needed for a meaningful return. You are where you are because you chose to be at that very point. You could generate more than you are, providing that you improve. Like converting the passive energy into kinetic energy to extract that which is within, the seed must be placed in the right environment, be isolated, die, germinate, be watered, be naturally fertilized, receive the appropriate sunlight, and be pruned while accepting the process of time.

The Keys to Bringing Forth Fruit

Environment

Proverbs 28:19 reads, "He that tilleth his land shall have plenty of bread: but he that followeth after vain persons shall have poverty enough." The environment should be one which is directed towards extracting the gift. When the "seed" is placed with like-minded individuals of equal or greater potential, it allows the prerequisites to manifest, determining that it should accept that these circumstances are the ideal course. If the soil is lacking the necessary nutritional requirements, the seed will fail to break free. The greatest gift that can be given is not giving your physical wealth but helping others to extract their own wealth.

The Four Types of Soil

1. **Ground.** This environment provides no usable nutrients that can be extracted to initiate growth. So in this case the seed will become food for another and will never get to grow. It will be a cycle where everyone is basically within the same scope.
2. **Rocky soil.** This environment provides minimal nutrients, causing the plant to grow quickly but to soon die because it has no roots. Without the foundation to improve upon, there is little progress and enthusiasm dies, along with the failing potential.
3. **Thorny soil.** The thorns grow up and crowd out the plants, eventually killing them. It is the toxic environment of negativity that strangles dreams and prospects and prevents the release of your authentic self.
4. **Good soil.** This produces, bringing forth crops thirty, sixty, or even a hundred times more than what was initially planted. This is made possible by the environment and the innate determination of the seed to grow. Some seeds may need soil transposition from where they are in order to become their best selves.

Isolation

Isolation is necessary for the individual to grow, as growth does not take place on a collective level but on an individual scale before the creation of a collective impact. This time is needed in the death phase preparation, the stage in which the transformation will become visible. This is the time when you are convinced and convicted that you can become that which the Originator intended for you, learning more as you draw closer to Him. The best way to make a decision is to do so out of respect for your Creator.

Dying (Self-Discipline)

As it relates to the season, for everything there is a time. The future can only be maximized if the seasons are invested appropriately in the right proportions. We have been made aware that those who are born in the mortal state will die; in the same way, the concept of gravity indicates that wisdom directs in planning the end at the beginning if there is an intent to enjoy the process. his stage takes self-discipline into account; those things which will weigh down and impede the progression will need dissociation. A clear mind must be maintained, indicating that no brain- or mind-altering agent should be used in the destabilization of health and well-being. All must be balanced as the being becomes one. Excel at what you do best. To those who are equally given much, it is expected as this is also the time to plant. In the end, the unwanted will be plucked and discarded. "For to me to live is Christ, and to die is gain" (Philippians 1:21).

Germination

After death is the resurrection; just as there was a resurrection after the crucifixion, so too will there be resurrection after the germination. Failure to metamorphize is equivalent to robbery and dishonesty. Do not rob yourself while robbing others. This is a transformation in which the being becomes what it is destined to become, what it did not yet know it was. In these moments, the growth takes place gradually as roots are sent down into the water reservoir, ensuring unquenched nourishing. Having power in your hands and not using it makes the power useless. We read in John 11:25, "Jesus said unto her, I am the resurrection, and the life: he that believeth in me, though he were dead, yet shall he live."

Watering the Seed

"But let judgment run down as waters, and righteousness as a mighty stream" (Amos 5:24). As the germination process takes place, water is needed from above and below. Without the water from above, misguided steps will occur, compromising crop integrity. The water that comes from above is life-giving. Vested interest and study are needed for understanding the transformation process. The waters that are from below will be the contacts who give guidance in accordance with the will of the predestination to allow distillation of the water above, which will allow the expected fruits to be produced. With this encouragement and motivation, the aim and purpose will not be lost as with withering leaves, but prosperity will be evident in action, thought, and deed, drawing all human beings to the Source of the living water like metal to a magnet.

Fertilizer

While recognizing that you are making progress, climbing the ladder, and elevating your thoughts, you should hunger to become the best within your area of expertise or speciality. In this quest, you revisit and refine information and evaluate the foundation. New information, trends, patterns, and changes are studied as you assess and create market needs and solutions. Education is not equal to the intellect, nor does it give you a seed; it only refines the seed. In the parable with the fig tree, the Master came upon it expecting fruit, but there was none. The Master instructed the keeper of the vineyard to cut it down as it cumbered the ground (using up soil), but the dresser asked for one more year to improve its state.

Sunshine (Networking)

"Let us therefore follow after the things which make for peace, and things wherewith one may edify another" (Romans 14:19). Though isolation was necessary for initial conviction, that phase has passed, and now it is time to seek after truly like-minded individuals by utilizing the network infrastructure. This will be the sunshine in order to gain exposure within and outside the circle created. Networking will naturally increase linkage and develop the scope. In controlling or impacting media, it is necessary to optimize communication channels. In a company of two, there is a greater reward for labour as one can help the other to achieve. And the two act as complements, reducing the weight of the work to be done.

Pruning

As a tree grows, it will need to be pruned. During this process, every branch that does not bear fruit is removed, and those which bear fruit are pruned, which stimulates them and allows them an opportunity to bear more fruit. When our reach has arrived at a satisfactory point, we always have the desire for more. In fulfilling this desire, we should uproot and burn the weeds that are part of our character. This involves cutting out bad or addictive behaviours, people, activities, circumstances, and distractions which hinder the progress of our destiny. Such hindrances could be attitude problems, negative people, people who are not yet allowed to experience our vision, entertainment distractions, circumstantial distractions, pharmaceutical or other illicit bondage, or experimentation, among all other hindrances that hinder our potential. If you are wise, you will walk with the wise, and if you dwell with stupidity, you will be destroyed by it.

Time (Accepting the Process)

Delayed/deferred gratification is always best. Even when you want to give up, you should still hold on. This is a process that a person often resists, the temptation of an immediate reward over preference for a later reward. With time, all things will be revealed and made manifest. Do not elope with your future; indeed, it will be worth it after all. And, yes, the value is enjoyment for you and all whom you wish to share it with. Allow yourself to be served by time. Instead of counting time, make the time count. After the fruit is produced, in time the fruit will be found, and people from afar will seek after it. Never have you seen a mango taking itself to the marketplace, but instead the marketplace finds the mango. Your fruits shall reveal who you are.

The Goal

In order to achieve anything in life, you need to make *goals* a priority. No one who has reached prominence got there accidentally. A child does not just go to sleep and wake up as a graduate of a higher-learning institution; neither does a person just stumble upon the land which is filled with a bounty that he or she accidentally owns. Perhaps the people going up the mountain miraculously reached its peak after stepping outside. Nothing just *happens*. Without goals, you will fail to have direction and purpose. It will also disqualify you from tapping into your leadership capability. You will never know when you have reached your destination, or where you are, or how much further you have to go. Do not live with ceilings; enjoy the open air as that is where plants thrive best.

A man went out to the sea and was standing on the shore for three days. A child, seeing the man, said, "Good day, sir. What are you doing here?"

The man replied, "I am waiting."

"Waiting for what?"

"My boat."

"Did you build it?"

"No."

"Has it left the harbour yet?"

"I don't know."

"Are you sure it is coming for you?"

"I don't know, I just have a feeling a boat is coming to change my life."

"Do you know where it is going?"

"No. I just know it is somewhere, not here."

The child's father called to him, "Let's go. You should not stick around people who know so little about their future direction."

The child said to the man, "Goodbye, sir. I hope you get your boat to *not here*."

The only proximity to success that some will ever get is in their futile destructive intention towards their goal accomplishment. Don't allow people to distract you or entice you away from the future. In setting goals, you must make them significant yet straightforward, consisting of both long-term and short-term components in order to assess progress while being unambiguously wrapped in the denominator of time. As enthusiastic as you may become, your goals should not be shared with everyone, as some may taint your judgement and create doubt in the possibility of your accomplishment, discouraging you from achieving the brainchild, while using your intellectual property and patenting your work as their own. Only your confidant circle should be considered. Reveal yourself with your development and goal achievement.

Law of Priority

Priority speaks to the degree of importance in an ordered sequence. The law is the governing principle designed to protect us. It's the blueprint to safeguard the enemy, who vehemently seeks to steal, kill, and destroy. When you are abiding in the law in accordance with the designated priority, success will allow you overwhelming authority and power. A single person's most critical duty is to become one with himself or herself as relationships are prioritized. The most important priority is God and His presence, as seeking Him will direct us on the path to achieving everything. Knowing God and growing in His presence is critical to maintaining a reflection of His glory. Love is of next importance: love your family, your neighbours, and yourself. As you embrace who you are and whose you are, it will be slowly revealed that you are a steward in a kingdom.

Creation Story

Adam and Eve were the human occupants in Eden. Before both, there were none. First came Adam and then eventually Eve. In preparation for humankind's creation on the sixth day, a systematic construct was displayed. Humankind, the prize jewel of Creation, was given everything needed before it was required. On the first day, the light was created so the man could enjoy the beauty of that which was to come. The waters were separated above the earth and under the earth on day two. On the third day, God created the dry ground, bodies of water, and plants in preparation for something much greater. Day four brought the separation of the sun, moon, stars, and planets. The air existed and the water existed, so on day five, birds were allowed to submit to the air and fishes to the water. On the sixth day, the animals submitted to the land as they were called into being. The "jewel" was formed from the dust of the earth in the image of the Creator; he became a living soul when His breath was given into his nostril. God created man. The seventh day was paramount because God rested. The creation of the world was complete, and as an example, God rested on the seventh day from all His work, not because He was weary but because He was pleased with the fruits of the manifested perfect goodness of His glory. After resting on that day, He blessed the seventh day and sanctified it. The beauty of creation was a foretaste of God's love for humankind.

The man, who was created from the dust, was allowed to commune with God and the angels. Adam was allowed to experience the presence of God in his mental fortification in holy education and intellectual awakening, completing the process of being connected to God; he was authorized to act autonomously and was given work. At this time, Adam lacked nothing after God had completed the creative process. Adam was allowed to engage in meaningful work in which he named the animals created. What he called them, those were their names. The Lord God put him to sleep a little while afterwards in preparation for a revelation. While Adam was sleeping, God took a rib from Adam's side and closed up his flesh. The extension of Adam was Eve. Eve was allowed to spend time in the presence of God, developing a relationship with Him. It should be noted that it was not Eve who woke Adam but God. Adam was awakened, and the rib, now flesh, was presented to him. Adam accepted that which was given and exclaimed that Eve was his bone and flesh. It was after the acceptance that the marriage ceremony occurred. As we read in Genesis 2:24–25, "Therefore shall a man leave his father and his mother, and shall cleave unto his wife: and they shall be one flesh. And they were both naked, the man and his wife, and were not ashamed."

God's priorities were to create, redeem, and restore humankind. From the action displayed in wisdom, we are seeing messages being sent by God to His people. We are seeing that both the male and the female must first have a relationship with the Creator; they must become one in themselves through the help of God. While becoming one includes self-acceptance and interdependence, they should explore their gifting and be productive.

Upon becoming complete, there is no need for another to complete you. Instead, another complements you. Even if you do not take unto yourself another, you are still whole. Prematurely, Eves seek to wake up Adams who have not been under God's direction, and Adams take Eves who are not theirs and not yet whole. This is what causes the complications in and the destruction of a relationship. If priorities are followed, all things will be revealed, and joy and laughter will be within all seasons.

Thought

A single human thought elevates or demotes. One big mistake people make is to concern themselves with what people think about them and not thinking about themselves. What people think about you is irrelevant in the changing seasons. If someone does not think highly of you, it should not matter how you progress; you should not be impeded, because you are not moving out of such a person's thoughts. Why should you *waste* your time *thinking about what someone thinks about you* when their thoughts have no direct bearing on *you*? If you are doing this, you are working on the wrong things. It is by no means your responsibility to be messed up, trying to be stewards over others' thoughts. *Get your head together*; don't let others get into your head. That is your private space.

A man had a portion of land which was passed to his son and future generations. This land, from the generation of this man, was used to rear animals. This property was transferred to another family, and it became a famous monument. It is the level of thought that determines overarching value. Goals can be set and achieved only at the level that you think. Though it was the same land, there were two families and two distinguishable results. What are you building on your "mind land"?

It depends on whose hands and minds are being activated. The same woman who someone said was nothing can be taken by someone else and allowed to become her best self yet. The same man who was unrefined can be transformed into a gentleman. If we look closely, we see that everything that exists came from a thought: a dress, an outfit, a suit, a house, a car, a chair, and electronics—absolutely everything! God has given us all that we need to survive and live; it is the intent that all people should use the natural aptitude they possess because the seasons of life should be enjoyed. The mind needs to be freed from our own imprisonment in order to embrace the road map to success. We need to impose a cease-and-desist injunction on the "hustler mentality" and become the CEO. Instead of becoming a flibbertigibbet, why not be the master communicator? Instead of branding nothing, why not start to become the brand and marketing manager? Exercise your analytical skills, assess the market, transform the negative connotations, and change your walk. You need to flip the switch so you can tap into the success reservoir. People with less potential than you have are doing more than you with forward thinking. The world is still looking for you. Have the courage to think beyond now. God asked Abraham what he could see when he was at a breakthrough point. He said that he could see the stars and see the sand. Then the Lord said that what he saw was exactly that which he would become. Don't limit God's potential for your life.

You are creative because you were made in the image of a Creator who is creative. He gave you tools to work with on your quest for creation. Everything you need, you already have. He gave us humans plants for medicine, and He gave animals and other life to study so we can understand Him better. He made gold, diamonds, and everything that is considered *raw material*. The more we learn, the more closely we move towards God. The raw material is for us to become creative and innovative, using our minds. You are one idea away from what you need to fulfil your purpose. Excavate and drill—the stream of knowledge is at hand.

Relationships

Relationships are a natural course engaged in over time; with the changing seasons, the engagement will shift and change gears. It is ideal to understand that not all relationships will move in the direction that you are moving; hence, some will need to be left behind, while some will only take you partway, and others will take you all the way. The quantity of relationships does not guarantee quality as humans are natural resources who can only operate within a given limit physically. All links have an effect, no matter what the level. It is a relational symbiosis which exists long-term or short-term. Every contact leaves its mark, but some are more difficult to decode. The same principles we live with will be displayed in the expression of obligatory or facultative (independently living) relationships.

Depending on your relationship selection, desirable or undesirable experiences can occur; appropriate relationships will be mind-blowing, lifting you to a state of success which may be strange waters. The wrong relationships have the potential to keep individuals tethered to mediocrity until the end of days.

In the distant future, will your life be better or worse based on your relationship indulgences? There should be no disconnection between who you are and what you have dedicated to the life given by God; you cannot choose the right and go left simultaneously—that is a disconnection. To say that there is a naturalistic relationship in which there is no effect would be to consider the existence nonexistent, as once the interaction has occurred, that is what has happened. We were designed to express the capabilities of interconnectivity. What is done affects us directly or indirectly. We will classify our interactions as competitive, amensalistic, parasitic, saprophytic, commensulistic, and mutualistic.

Competitive

This interaction is promoted as an accepted norm which is dangerous, destabilizing, destructive, and devious. Because competition is socially accepted as the way to achieve, one must battle throughout the day to win the "prize", wasting time with deceptive and obstructive tactics. The energies could have been better used collectively to conquer a problem with collaboration. This is usually the case when a male group sees some females and all of the males are pursuing one female, each trying to outdeliver the other. One eventually entices her, after which he is let go, only for another to take his place. Ultimately all parties involved are harmed, as you can imagine. This practice should never be facilitated or encouraged as your life is not a competitive binding experiment.

Amensalistic

In this relationship type, one's disadvantage is taken advantage of, ending in hurt with little effect on the perpetrator. This is too socially accepted in some forms and rejected in others. It is allowed when institutions have hidden fees and marked-up prices, contained in the fine print in legal jargon without explanation to the average consumer; when a vaccination is being given containing mercury, which causes mental impedance without the acceptance of liability or compensation; and in cases of genocide, among other redactions. The same practice is considered unacceptable when a woman is raped and allowed to suffer the shame, turmoil, and physical and emotional brokenness to the apparent perpetrator's violent satisfaction. Those placed in a dominant position to protect are the very same who destroy. What an ironic relationship. Only the narrative presented is consumed because the masses no longer see the need for critical thinking and action appropriation.

Parasitic

In this structure, there is a constant withdrawal and no meaningful deposit. The parasite benefits while compromising the host; if the parasite sticks around long enough, the host dies. The parasites vary in their methods of execution, all of which lead inevitably to the same end. The longer the parasite lingers, the more detrimental the danger.

Some people are like mosquitoes, micro predators; these types are subtle with their sting as they visit intermittently. They are there when they want something or when they know you have something. These people tend to be most evident on payday or days of celebration and special occasions with the expectation of receiving. A mosquito never gives you anything except a bite or diseases (dengue, chikungunya, Zika, malaria, etc.).

You may even have made way for the endoparasites which live inside, like the flatworm from the consumption of pig. It will suck you dry! The thing about its operation is that you cannot see it; however, if you don't seek professional help, you may die unless it dies before you do. It could be that person squeezing your heart, playing the lustful spirit. You are eating a great deal and still can't gain weight. People begin to become concerned, asking if you are well. When people start asking if you are well, it means that you are almost at your lowest point. Why did you eat that meat? Had you not, you would not have that parasite inside you. Leave it alone; it is unclean.

Then there are ectoparasites—these people are like ringworms, just eating at your flesh. If not stopped, the ringworm moves from the outside, mutates, and finds comfort on the inside until you are dead. Each individual needs space for cleansing; you don't need to be smothered alive. If things get too complicated, then you need to introduce another parasite, the cleaning symbiotic which will clean away the other parasite because it can eradicate it. It is always good to have people looking out for the parasites in your life, to clean them away before they get comfortable. These cleaners are normally mutually beneficial. In the arms of Jesus, you will be saved and safe.

Saprophytic

Some may wait until you are dead, so they can glean the insurance coverage payout and finally become able to take over your business or company and steal your patents, trademarks, and the like. They will enjoy what you produced and are willing to say, "Excuse me, this is my house. I have been living here for years." They are ready to live your life on your behalf.

Commensulisitic

The commensulistic relationship is one between two or more people. They practise imposing even when they are not invited; they desire to ride your coattails, saying to themselves that you are going somewhere anyway, so why not tag along? These people fail to say "good morning" or "hello", but as soon as you sit in your vehicle to drive, they are there. When the door to your home is open, they are there; they are very helpful in helping themselves to your food. In your bed, they are there and do not even say "goodnight".

Mutualistic

Though all these relationships exist, none are indeed God's intention for human interaction. The ideal relationship is mutualistic, in which there are equal and consistent deposits and investments among the parties involved. This relationship involves at least two individuals who benefit. It is similar to the relationship that hummingbirds and bees have—and let's not forget the trees. On the simplest level, two persons either can share their resources while supporting each other or can be independent of each other while still supporting each other. In the end, they are both interdependent.

It is this relationship that is seen between plants and animals, especially between herbivores who possess gut flora (bacterial colonization, pH, etc.) that aid in the breakdown and digestion of meals, providing both parties with the necessary nutrients while facilitating growth and development. Similar principles exist; however, both parties are always equal. Pollination is a mutualistic relationship between flowering plants and their animal pollinators; without animal pollination, harvesting yields would be low and eventually become nonexistent. Many plants that are pollinated via this method have highly specialized flowers modified to promote pollination by a specific pollinator that is correspondingly and instinctually adapted. It is the same with humans; only the specially selected can and should be allowed in the inner circle. That is why there should be a clear understanding of the reason why one certain person may not be suitable for everyone.

Engaging in multiple relations can actually make a relationship become parasitic as in such a case one cannot afford time for substantial investment, so all that is done is to withdraw. Identification of who each individual is, prior to engaging in a relationship, is critical to the relationship. It does not define you as incompatible with the person God established you as. A single, oneness mentality must be achieved.

All people must demonstrate a capacity, indicating that they are qualified to engage in a meaningful relationship. They should value themselves enough to note that they should not be a garbage can, collecting what has been refused. Instead, they should be like preservatives, keeping things fresh. The attributes of honesty, dignity, integrity, and confidentiality should be present at the beginning of a relationship, prior to consideration.

When Jesus responded to the cry of Lazarus's death, He went to his graveside. A large slab of stone lay before it. Jesus asked that the stone be removed, after which Lazarus was called out from his sleep, and he responded, walking out upon hearing his name being called by heaven's representative. Lazarus, who was dead, came forth bound in grave clothing. Jesus instructed that he be unwrapped, and so it was done. The deceased had risen. Let us look back at Jesus when Lazarus was in the tomb. Jesus did not go into the tomb; He stayed outside and called Lazarus to come out, reminding us that there are some circumstances that we don't want to get messed up in. Don't go near dead people unless you plan to raise them up.

The Process

During the process, sidetracking may take place, to the point of confusion. There will be challenges, but they must be overcome as you have already committed your way to the Lord, so He will act on your behalf. The fight that we must endure is not a physical one but a spiritual one. The reason battles are lost is because the wrong enemy is fought. When someone does something that conflicts with general morality and godly principles, it is not the person who has actually wronged you. The wrong experience is a manifestation of spiritual deviance/infestation. In attacking the problem, one should demonstrate love and forgiveness towards the person, knowing that it is a spiritual war. In fighting the wrong enemy, we accomplish little, if anything at all.

Conceptual fights are dangerous as it is the creative realm in which these fights are fought; the spirit world is the parent world, from which everything else emanates in the physical world. Visual impairment causes many to find comfort in safety, even when there is much peril around. In olden times, the church was fighting a holy war, whereas others were fighting for territories, possessions, and positions. But now, because we don't see these things often in the natural world, we embrace comfort. Every day, the angels are fighting for your preservation from the third that sided with Lucifer. The righteous can be safe using the name of the Lord as the fortified tower that it is. Circumstances may appear to shackle the mind and heart;

our morality is assassinated, our beliefs and integrity are skinned, and our emotions are mowed over, being placed in a death-hold with the past childhood brokenness crying out in desperation. Some will still be stuck at 40 years old acting like 10-year-olds, holding onto something that is unresolved—the daddy and/or mommy issues and all others which need a spiritual resolution. It is the enemy who steals, kills, and destroys, but the Lord has come so that we might have the abundance of life. The Lord will not allow you to be under satanic espionage.

In good times, we do not need to be thinking or focusing on that which can go wrong. In bad times, we wonder why we are in such a situation. We already know how we got there. If we did not want it, we should not so freely have embraced it. These actions are crippling. You are sleeping, but you are not getting any rest. You are tired when you get up; you are just walking around with a weight on your shoulders. That is not living. That is merely existing. While going through the process, your thought life is under attack, and the enemy wants you to give up. Remember that you are more than what you can see. All you need to do is to reach just a little farther. Cover your thoughts and your mind in the name of Jesus because to be saved is to be safe.

Similar to the way eagles manoeuvre in storms, they fly above the turbulence. So from their example, we have no reason to fly in the storms of our lives when we can fly above them. With Jesus, we can walk on things which people typically sink in, just as Peter was allowed to walk on water. Never lose focus on Him. God wants to bless you with a transfer into your "spirit account" so that it can manifest in the natural world. God does not manipulate people's bodies; He gives us a free choice. Accept the deposit He offers.

Joseph the Dreamer

Joseph, an upright son of Jacob, was 17 years old and dwelt in the land of Canaan. Jacob loved Joseph more than all his other children because Joseph was the son he had at old age. Hence a tunic of many colours was made for Joseph, causing his brothers to hate him and refuse to speak peaceably with him. He started to have dreams, and the preliminary interpretation of these dreams provoked his brothers to despise him more. This young lad was given a mandate, which he saw and shared. His dream caused him to be ridiculed. His brothers' hatred of him grew exponentially like a festering sore. In the dream, his brothers were binding sheaves in the field. Joseph's sheaf (bundles) rose and stood upright, and those of his brothers stood and bowed down to his. They asked if Joseph would have reign or dominion over them. Their feelings of hatred were kindled even more.

Just like it was revealed to Joseph about the things which were to come, God is also revealing things to you. You may not know how you will get there, but you will know once you arrive there. People around you may not understand. The same thing was asked: "Can anything good come out from Nazareth?" Jesus did! Do not let your current locality distract you from your internationality, thereby clouding the universality. Your family may not comprehend the possibilities, your friends may still try to decipher the cryptography, and others may have misguided beliefs. However, remember that God's sovereignty works outside the expected confines. He showed the end before anything was even considered viable, placing thoughts in your mind. The process is a systematic action that accomplishes a specific objective. Enjoy your process, as the process is what's vital in the production of quality.

Later, Joseph had another dream that confirmed the first through additional details for interpretation and was grander. He eventually shared his dream with his father. In this dream, the sun, the moon, and eleven stars made obeisance to him. Jacob, hearing this, rebuked him, asking if his father, mother, and eleven brothers should bow down to the earth before him. This was not according to their customs; hence his concern. Joseph's brothers envied him. With wisdom, Jacob kept the matter in mind. Not everyone will comprehend the vision for the life you were given. Break ceilings; enjoying open air should actually be your desire. Few will embrace the mandate, but your dreams should not die. If your dream dies, then, that is robbery.

People will appear to be doing evil to you, but they are setting you up to accomplish your mission. Count it joy when you are considered; if it had not been you, then who would you suggest? Being called into service is a privilege. The refinement process is natural. In attaining gold, a suitable rock with the proper chemical attributes must be selected, pressurized, heated, purified, cooled, polished, and finally presented. Joseph's process of refinement prepared him to become a man of God, seeing his dreams come true. It was Joseph's brothers who sold him into slavery after he went to check up on his brothers and their flocks. When they saw him from afar, they conspired to kill him. It was Reuben, the oldest brother, who heard and asked that Joseph not be destroyed but instead placed in a dry pit. The brothers stripped Joseph of his tunic of many colours. While eating their meal, the brothers saw a company of Ishmaelites heading to Egypt and thought to sell Joseph. They sold Joseph for twenty shekels of silver. Then they took his tunic and dipped it in goat's blood, creating the illusion that he had been killed by animals. They took the bloody tunic back to Jacob, who mourned for many days.

The lesson to be learned is that there will be times when you will be despised by those you love because of their failure to embrace the covenant upon your life even though it would be beneficial for them. It is always better to be alive during the process than dead. Almost dead but still alive, Joseph was sold by those who had the authority to protect him. In your own life, even though you may be correct, working with integrity and diligence, there will be some who seek to smother your reputation. Discern, ignore, and avoid them.

Greatness cannot be hidden even among the unrefined. People will quake at your presence when you walk with the authority of your Father because authentic leadership is recognized and utilized. Joseph was sent to the land of Egypt, where he displayed exemplary diligence while he worked under authority, finding grace in the sight of those he served. His promotion came at a time when many expected the worst; he was being trained for leadership. When you are being elevated, eyes will be upon you, and you will be desired in both godly and ungodly ways. You must hold God's principles. Do not allow your dreams to be diluted, to be compromised, to languish, to be dormant, or to be locked in a cave; remain resolute, no matter how far you decide to reach. Joseph was a walking blessing; all that he touched was blessed. Because your dreams cannot be stolen, the enemy will try to put your dreams to sleep with discouragement, distress, demotivation, and many negative and derailing acts. Just know that during these times you are positioned to catapult forward.

In time, the ungodly desires for Joseph erupted. In a moment of emotional weakness, maybe during the period of her ovulation, the queen, whose husband was away, desired comfort. She requested Joseph to work in a capacity in which he had no kingly authority, which he refused to do. The refusal of this advance was the result of the purposing in Joseph's heart not to do wickedly and not to sin against God. Because Joseph chose God and dishonoured humankind, Potiphar's wife lied about Joseph, only to have him placed in prison despite his being innocent. The Lord gave Joseph some time off so that they could get some "alone time" and strengthen his relationship with God in preparation for the gift He had in store for him. After Joseph's release from prison, God knew that things would be going at a fast pace; Joseph's time in prison was like a vacation, a training and networking phase. While he was there, he was a leader, managing the jail, ministering to and supporting his fellow occupants. Some time later, the cupbearer and the baker of the king of Egypt offended their master. The king of Egypt was angry with his two officials; the chief cupbearer and the chief baker were in custody at the same location as Joseph. Even though he was in a tough place, Joseph remained faithful while using his talents to interpret dreams that God gave him. Both the cupbearer and the baker had dreams which Joseph interpreted. As Joseph had interpreted, the chief butler was restored to his position, and the baker was hanged three days after the dream.

The pharaoh had a dream that none could interpret; it was then that the butler remembered Joseph, who had interpreted his and the baker's dreams in the past. Joseph was called and cleaned up to go before royalty. The dream was told to him, and he outlined the interpretation. The Spirit of the Lord was with Joseph, moving him from freedom to bondage, to service, to higher service, to prison, and then to the next-highest service, being second in line to the Egyptian throne. Joseph shows the triumph of faith; indeed, the dream came through as it was given. It was with the hands of the forgiving Joseph that he served his family, all who came around in his dream that existed to its fulfilment. It was the same dream which his father, Jacob, upon hearing, rebuked him, asking if Joseph's father, mother, and eleven brothers should bow down to the earth before him. The questions asked by his father were answered; his mother, brothers, and father did eventually submit to Joseph's leadership.

In Hindsight

Joseph needed to be at another place from where he started in order to help those who would need his help. His family had been instrumental in the process; his father treated him as royalty, reminding him of his origin. His brothers despised him; this was necessary for the logistics to be arranged that occurred when they sold him. Upon reaching Egypt, Joseph needed a "connecting flight" to be a little closer to where he should be. When he was there, he was sold again to Potiphar. Potiphar's wife falsely accused him, which inadvertently led him to have some alone time with God as networking took place while bringing joy to his associates and aiding in his refinement. Had he not gone to prison, he never would have met the baker and the butler of the pharaoh. If he had never interpreted their dreams, he would not have been given the opportunity to interpret Pharaoh's dream. All these steps were necessary for his transition to prime minister and administrator of service during the famine. Diligence, integrity, honesty, and purity were key attributes which allowed Joseph to serve his family and save their lives. The process was necessary for his refinement; all the happenings needed to occur in the exact way as they did. This unconventional manner highlights the anticipation of the Messiah, who brought hope to the dying world.

Conquer Goliaths

Ecclesiastes 3:5 reads, "A time to cast away stones, and a time to gather stones together; a time to embrace, and a time to refrain from embracing."

During the refinement process, you will have Goliaths that must be conquered because you are too gifted to be restricted. The battle is not yours; it is the Lord's. Humans tend to have the proclivity and propensity to approach situations from the wrong angles unless the mind is fortified in the way of the Lord. The wrong angles will encumber the yield potential. A substantial deposit and investment has been made by the Creator in our lives; the Goliaths are there to extract that which is in us as God is glorified. It is more about the work on the inside than the work on the outside; the crucibles are necessary. Paul had a thorn in his flesh which he desired to be removed; however, it was revealed that the grace of the Lord was sufficient to perfect and strengthen him, enabling the glorification of Him throughout the hurdles of infirmity.

God is looking within us, exactly knowing what has been deposited in us, and desires that it come forth from us. David was anointed as king, and after his anointment, he went back to caring for animals. The challenge with Goliath was strategically placed so that a depository revelation of that which was within David could be extracted. David was a child; the enemy was over nine feet tall. This was God's method of saying that no matter how much your giant overshadows you, the giant must be conquered so that you can move on to your destiny.

In approaching the situation, though it appears apparently insurmountable, the people of God should get excited since the bigger the giant, the better the reward. Walking in the anointing allows us to see, instead of the problem, the promises. When David arrived at the campsite, everyone was frantic, running for their lives, but the anointed saw God, who was the solution. Goliath was an uncircumcised Philistine who was never under God's covenant. It was already known that God was on the side of David and not on the side of the enemy. When there is unbelief, it is dangerous because it is then that the enemy infiltrates. Don't glance at the problem like Peter, who fell into the water. You need to look firmly at God. David ran towards Goliath because he believed in the promises of God and had confidence in the covenant He had created with Abraham. The anointing that came with David is that of a king, but Goliath was standing in his way. He was already anointed. This means that Goliath was what he needed to defeat in order to receive what God was bringing him into.

David came ready to step out in faith defending his Lord, but there were people discouraging him. They lacked the confidence to stand, and yet they feared when they saw him standing. Eliab, his brother, was angry when he saw David, who was there to take him food. The kindled anger against David was the result of the unfortunate, compromising situation which the soldiers had allowed themselves to be in; they were saddened that David had seen them so vulnerable. They had come to the realization that they were not willing to do that which was necessary and were angry because someone else was ready to step out in righteousness. Many people will not understand the power and authority that the Lord has commissioned upon you. Don't allow anyone to discourage you from the dream; just shake off the discouragement and move forward.

Walking by sight allows only the physical to be seen. The doors become open when there is a walk of faith. Saul expected the Lord to work in ways of the past, but there was a different plan. The old plan could not fit; David took off Saul's armour and stepped out with the whole armour of God. People who have never faced a Goliath will always have something negative to say; you should not allow everyone to speak into your life. Goliaths are conquered from your personal experiences and past encounters. Things happen gradually in stages; rest assured that the Lord will not give you more than is bearable. Young people and senior people have giants to conquer. Don't be discouraged While caring for his father's sheep, David was delivered from many situations such as a lion and a bear, so he knew that God could provide deliverance. If you are unwilling to move from one level to another, then you are not ready for progress; you need to be prepared on this level to move up to the next.

David entered the battle as a conqueror with a sling and stones, which were used to smite the Philistine. And when the Philistines saw their champion was dead, they fled. David reminds us of the Rock of Ages; this Goliath was conquered by the Lord. First you must believe. Enjoy your seasons and get ready for the next level as the best is still ahead.

Job's Experience

Ecclesiastes 3:6–7 reads, "A time to get, and a time to lose; a time to keep, and a time to cast away; A time to rend, and a time to sew; a time to keep silence, and a time to speak." There are three main types of people who manifest themselves frequently and noticeably in our lives: those whom we confide in, those who share a common interest, and those who are against a similar agenda. Those you can confide in are usually few; they support whatever cause is undertaken, expressing unconditional love. This minority will be with you until the end, through ascents, plateaus, fluctuations, and descents. They reflect the deep intimacy shared between David and Jonathan; they are willing to rescue you and to sacrifice themselves and support you even when everyone else is against you. Those confided in are needed to ensure that you remain on the path that God has positioned you on. Having one or two is a blessing as they are rare, these people who naturally value the individual.

The other groups that exist are not directly invested in you; however, their presence will be evident. As long as they remain in to the same things you are, they will labour with you. When their alliance with you is no longer suited to advance their agenda, they will leave you for another. Yes, these people will break your emotions. It is important that you not confuse these individuals with the elite group.

Then there are those who are against what you are against. They are not for you or for what you are for; they are only there because of the interests which you are against. These people operate in open shadows, causing people to come together to destroy and go against the same agenda. Care should be taken in identifying these individuals; you should maintain your distance from them. Immediately after the victory of the common enemy, they will move to another, grander project for self-promotion. At all times, you must remember that some persons are just like a scaffold that helps build the building; after the structure is finalized, they are no longer needed. They can be removed. Do not become too attached to this set of people. Remember that they were never for you or what you were for; they were only against what you were against. Only the confidants will stay; the others will eventually leave you. And for that you must be grateful. You can identify the people who are not with you; just enter a room and announce something good, great, or grand, and watch as certain people's countenances negatively change. When this happens, you know it is time to face the music.

The Lord is the only Authority who is above all authority existing in the universe. If your enemy wants to attack, he must obtain prior permission. The enemy cannot overtake you, as even to the will of your Father, the Devil must submit. In heaven there was a meeting, and Satan went to seek permission to test one of the Lord's anointed. Knowing what Satan was thinking, God presented a servant who could endure testing. Sometimes you are recommended for something great that you don't even know about. When you are going through your struggle, you must give thanks. The harder the process, the greater the reward. All that must be done is to remain faithful. God loves you so much that the parameters by which you can be attacked are defined when the hedge around you is lifted. The Devil was allowed to touch all that Job had except Job himself.

Job, a blameless and upright man who feared God and eschewed evil, had seven sons and three daughters. His substance made him the greatest of all men of the East. He possessed seven thousand sheep, three thousand camels, five hundred yokes of oxen, and five hundred she-asses, and he had an enormous household and he was righteous. His sons were having a feast, and their sisters were invited;

Job offered offerings in the morning according to their number, in the event that they sinned and cursed God in their hearts. In an instant, all Job's possessions and connections to them would be lost. Job lost his children, animals, and servants. Knowing this, he worshipped, acknowledging that it is the Lord who gives and the Lord who takes away. During his moments of agony, his wife, who was his confidant, spoke bitterly against his ultimate Confidant. His defence of God showed even more that God must be the first priority.

Job's wife, seeing him with sores and boils from his soles up to his head, asked him why he retained his integrity when he could just curse God and die. Realizing that her mind was compromised, he rebuked her, knowing she had never understood the situation. In all this, Job retained his integrity and refused to sin with his lips. It is best to maintain integrity, especially in challenging situations. All other confidants should come after God as they may speak foolishly outside of God's will.

Job had three friends—Eliphaz the Temanite, Bildad the Shuhite, and Zophar the Naamathite—who visited him, after making an appointment together to mourn with him and to comfort him. When they came, they were unable to identify him visually as he had physically changed. They sat with him on the ground seven days and seven nights, and none of them spoke a word, seeing that his grief was great. These friends were against what Job was against as none of them desired sickness to be upon themselves.

Eliphaz accused Job of folly, but this pitiless friend was reproached. Then he prayed for Job's relief. Bildad assumed that only the wicked were punished, suggesting repentance to Job, but still Job pleaded with God. Zophar urged Job to repent, like the others. Job indicated that he had direct wisdom from God and said that in everything he trusted God over his friends. These friends were for what Job was for as they wanted him to be healed so they could continue with their own lives. During the whole process, Job maintained his integrity and wisdom in God's remarkable works, defending the actions and justifying God's authority. Inevitably the suffering had to end, and the Lord revealed His omnipotence to Job. This situation allowed

God to be proven repeatedly, and Job's intimacy with God deepened with the challenges by his overcoming them.

Job was eventually restored to a more considerable measure than any person possessed. Losing what he had was not a punishment, so getting it back with an increase was not a reward. The Lord was only showing that He knew what was best for the universe at any stage, which mortal minds are not able to comprehend. Job received double for his trouble. He was restored to health, his life continued, his family was expanded, and he lived one hundred and forty years, seeing four generations. He lived full of days as his latter end was more blessed than the beginning.

The Mercy of God

The seasons that have been given should be enjoyed at all stages. It is better that Goliaths are challenged and conquered as we move to complete our mission. Would you find comfort in your Goliaths' repentance based on your influence? The book of Jonah, filled with literary pairing and symmetry, it is centred on the satirical narrative in which characters operate outside their expected nature.

Jonah was commissioned to preach against evil and injustice in Nineveh, Israel's enemy. Instead of going east, he went west, in the opposite direction, to Tarshish. While on his journey, in a boat, while he was asleep, a storm began; lots were cast to determine who was responsible for the term, and it fell upon Jonah. Jonah was allowed to explain himself. Imagine. Knowing that the Lord is God of the heavens and had made the seas, why would Jonah, trying to evade his Lord's mission, choose to be on a boat out at sea, which his Lord had created?! The consensus was that Jonah would be thrown into the water. The Lord provided a huge fish to "pick him up" and deliver him, through vomit, close to the place where his assignment was slated. When he arrived there, Jonah preached in Nineveh: "Yet forty days, and Nineveh shall be overthrown" (Jonah 3:4). And the people believed. Even the animals repented. Jonah was displeased exceedingly that the people repented and were saved; he was conflicted about the mercy that God showed, even to his peoples' enemy.

The compassion God shows to all people was unacceptable in his eyes. He disliked the idea that no matter how far gone you are, there is still a God who is willing to make Himself available to extend to you the lifeline; all you need to do is reach out and grasp it. Undoubtedly, the Lord falls the rain on both the just and the unjust, so why should He not make salvation available to both? Would you be comfortable if God showed mercy on your enemy? Indeed you should!

FIFTH GEAR

Health and Healing

Success Laws

Financial Abundance

HEALTH AND HEALING

Healing

John 10:10 tells us, "The thief cometh not, but for to steal, and to kill, and to destroy: I am come that they might have life, and that they might have it more abundantly."

The Contraction

In the world around us, people are increasingly being compromised through the advent of modern science with the focus on diagnosis and treatments advancing in exponential waves. Was it the intention that people should be sick, moving from one physician to another, one illness to another, trying to ingurgitate the next elixir with the intent of receiving its suggested curative properties and remedies of relief? Is medical science the hope for the dying world? Too many spend much of their lives suffering from the conditions of a cold or flu or even life-threatening illnesses and diseases. Many people have absolutely no idea why they are sick and, even worse, have no directions as to what to do about it. The system of governance in the physical realm has conditioned the minds of many into believing that they need expert medical advice when they are ill. The frequency of the population's ill health has caused overcrowded private practices, hospitals, and clinics; medical care is almost out of reach for many in relation to healthcare and efficiency. Many people will die prematurely thanks to the confusion as suffering abounds, lingers, and ushers out generations sequentially.

Throughout civilization, humankind has been plagued with diseases. Plagues have wiped some civilizations from the face of the earth. Medical scientists thought they had arrested the disease in question, treated it, and released the population from this humungous burden; however, their failure is documented in journals and other literature. It appears as though we are creating new diseases and mutating old strains, causing antibiotic resistance, virulent viral strains, and other abominable creations in genetic engineering. Casualties, debilitating illness, and death are among the widespread reports around the world. It appears as though there is no end in sight to restoring health ultimately. Indeed, someone is stealing, and destroying our health and our lives. This is not what the Creator intended. Is it that we have been refusing the invitation to abundance of life? The intention of the Creator is that our whole existence represent Him; this would indicate that our countenance should be a transfiguration of health. The infrastructure of our design is such that a display of robusticity should be evident.

After the creation of humankind in the Genesis account, God said that what He had created was good. This "good" means that it was as He intended, in a perfect state. We can conclude that no sickness or disease existed; it was after the Fall of Humankind that sickness was evidently expressed as the humans' eyes were opened. The expert on the matter of health is the Creator of the human; He is the One who has the authority to guarantee health and restoration, providing the outlined principles as followed. Ignorance is a state that people of wisdom must seek to circumvent with the truth. If we are to be in line with the expected, then our whole mental direction needs to be on the spiritual, putting the information together and in context. It is clear that all the support on the matter of health and healing will not be in one area but that, when ample time is given in the study, the whole can be appreciated. The revelatory experience is evident in the work of God as His grace, mercy, and forgiveness are displayed.

Healing was demonstrated in both the New Testament and the Old Testament. This shows how the degradation of society has increased exponentially since humankind's separation from the Creator. In the Old Testament, after the children of Israel left Egypt, they were instructed to follow the will of the Lord in order to claim the promise of healing. This indicated an established character attribute of God, Yahweh Rapha, which means "the God who heals".

The Wrong Physician

King Ahaziah, the son of King Ahab, was ill after falling down in Samaria. He then sent messengers to enquire of Baal Zebub, the god of Ekron, whether he would or would not recover from this disease. This request was an insult to God the Creator, who had given strict instruction about His jealousy in Exodus 20:5. Baal Zebub was said to be a god of medicine; this grieved God as the king had more confidence in something that was not real than in Him who had proved His greatness on multiple occasions. To put a rest to the matter, the Creator allowed the king to die.

If the Lord commits a promise to you, then it must be taken on the authority of God's character, which is unchanging. God had promised to fight for King Asa of Judah, who was initially a righteous king who trusted in God. His obedience was perfect, but his faith wavered when he joined an alliance with surrounding nations and paid monetary tributes to the king of Assyria. Another account brings our attention to King Asa during the thirty-ninth year of his reign, who had diseased feet. In the moments of progression, he sought not the Lord but the physicians. The records have him dead from his condition. The reason for his death was his choosing his physicians over God, and hence he deprived himself of the healing that was accessible to him from the original Healer. His lacking faith was what caused his needless demise.

Hezekiah trusted the Lord and pleaded for an extension of his life after the prophet Isaiah revealed the Lord's requirement for his soul. Upon hearing this, he turned his face to the wall and prayed to the Lord, weeping. The Word of the Lord came to the messenger Isaiah while in the middle court to inform Hezekiah that his prayers had been answered and that he would be healed and his life extended. Fifteen additional years were given, and the benefits that came with it. In this instance, his life was extended because the Life-Giver was consulted.

A Patient's Physician Contact

The New Testament's account of healing is evident with the advent of Jesus Christ, who preached the gospel of the kingdom of God. Jesus Christ was the *messenger* with the *message* of the kingdom of God. The gospel provided information and evidence of the existing healing power of God that was present in those days. The question of concern many may have asked on this matter varies: "Does healing still take place?" "Will I be healed?" "Can I heal others?" "Who has authority overhealing?" The medical society does not have the authoritative power to command healing. If that were the case, physicians, nurses, radiologists, midwives, medical technologists, pharmacists, and other allied health professionals would not die from the same diseases they aid in treating. The only authority on the gift of healing is the true church. When this power is executed, demons are cast out, myriads of miracles are observed, and lives are restored. It is important to note that faith needs to be exercised in order to become whole. Violation of laws has its consequences; physical violation can result in illness and death, whereas spiritual violation can result in eternal death.

Jesus Christ is the One who took our infirmities and bore our sickness. The reason that many have given up their privilege of healing is that they don't know from whom healing is derived; or those who know have chosen to reject the Source, leading to their own demise. The Lord cares for our intricate needs and desires; hence, He made provision for our restoration.

Faith Healing Amalgamation

People are eluded by the laws of God because they follow a counterfeit spirit; this is the spirit that works in the children of disobedience. This is the spirit of the Devil, which leads human beings into rebellion, causing them to believe that they can do what it is they desire to do without facing the consequences of their actions. This fallacy is corrupting the truth, forcing people to believe that medicine is the cure for all. Healing involves the forgiveness of sin. It came to pass that Jesus was teaching in the midst of the Pharisees and the doctors of the law, and the power of the Lord was present to heal them. There was a man of palsy whom they sought to bring in, but when they could not find a way by which to bring him, they went up on the housetop and lowered him through the tiling with his mattress into Jesus's midst. Upon seeing their faith, Jesus declared that their sins were forgiven. The forgiveness of sin brought healing. Those who were sick with devils had those devils cast out under this same authority. We see multiple displays of healing in the New Testament account—the healing of an official's son at Capernaum in Galilee, John 4:43–54; Jesus driving out an evil spirit from a man in Capernaum, Luke 4:31–36; the cleansing of a man with leprosy, Matthew 8:1–4; the woman with the issue of blood, who was healed when physicians could not help her, Mark 5:25–34; the healing of the blind men, Matthew 9:27–31; the healing of the deaf and the dumb man, Mark 7:31–37; and Jesus's healing of a servant's severed ear while He was being arrested, Luke 22:50–51. In being rewarded, one must exhibit faith with the diligent and earnest seeking of God, knowing for sure that without faith, it is impossible to please the Creator.

So now how do we go about getting our healing? Receiving healing is simple when you are looking in the right places:

1. Believe in the Lord.
2. Exercise your faith.
3. Go to the Source for restoration.
4. Seek forgiveness of your sin.
5. Embrace your healing.

Though it is not the desire of the Lord that our mortality become invaded by illnesses, provisions are in place should there be an occurrence; however, laws and principles are outlined to prevent reaching such a state of degradation.

In order to maximize our life satisfaction, we must uphold all the laws of God. It is possible that you can be healed and kept in health as humans were designed to prosper and be one and whole. The law of cause and effect is still one of the biggest challenges for humanity. We don't want to be unhealthy, yet our indulgences conflict with our utterances without our realizing that it is essential to note that the body is one, operating with a combination of multiple systems to create the functional machinery. When specific instructions are violated, consequences—which are unfavourable but justifiable by the cause—appear in the form of maladies. We desire to maintain weight, yet we eat more calories than we burn or even eat less than we need. This streamlines us towards a state of obesity or of being underweight, coupled with malnutrition. One situation leads to another when in a state of obesity. High blood pressure is induced, arteries may become clogged, diabetes develops, and renal failure results, among other underlying conditions. In trying to forget problems, one may engage in the consumption of alcohol, which induces cirrhosis of the liver, blackouts, and absorbance in the stomach that gives the appearance of pregnancy in men, followed by unnatural behaviours that are accompanied by regrets. Alcohol is like a gateway drug that may lead to smoking, which damages lung capacity, induces asthma, reduces blood circulation, causes poor mental functioning, stimulates addiction, and even leads to death. There are some who feel it fitting to eat anything that is available despite the adverse effects. This is a guarantee that all who keep the commandments and laws of God will be healed.

Food

In presenting our bodies as a sacrifice unto God, we must give care to what goes into, goes through, and is put upon the body. There are basic guidelines outlined from time's inception that can be used in our current environment to prevent the further degradation of humankind. Genesis 1:12 tells us, "And the earth brought forth grass, and herb yielding seed after his kind, and the tree yielding fruit, whose seed was in itself, after his kind: and God saw that it was good." This passage indicates that the food/herbs designed for human consumption should have seeds within, preferably in their original form as every green herb was given for meat, meaning that all we need to live was already made available before we knew we needed it.

During their journey in the wilderness, the Israelites were instructed through God's representative Moses about food that could be consumed. The instructions indicated that food that could be considered as being good for consumption included the following:

- *Land animals* with parted hoof and cloven-footed
- *Land animals* that cheweth the cud
- *Water animals* which have fins and scales
- *Air animals*—every flying, creeping thing that goeth upon all fours
- *Air animals* which have legs above their feet to leap—"the locust after his kind, and the bald locust after his kind, and the beetle after his kind, and the grasshopper after his kind".

Everything that does not fit in the class, as indicated, should be avoided. One thing we should not venture into consuming is blood or strangled meat. The life of the animal is in the blood, and so too are the diseases and death.

NEWSTART

This is a routine for people who make infractions of the physical and spiritual laws and then wonder why they are sick. They then, based on sudden enlightenment, rush to physicians, who are not in any position to help them; instead, what they receive is a drug. Or they have a polypharmacy experience, not realizing the items that are given merely hide their poor condition, increasing toxic build-up in the body and inducing other complications. These quick fixes do not go to the root of the situation; hence, a person will always be a repeat visitor to the physician and even, in some cases, a permanent resident until death. Most want to operate by breaking laws without experiencing the direct repercussions; for this, the children of Israel requested to be ruled by a king as they did not want God to speak directly to them and hold them directly accountable.

The medical society has its place in the world today; however, it should not be trusted more than God. If you lack absolute faith in God, you cannot be guaranteed healing. Certain conditions can be treated with medical intervention. The question is, why should you settle for treatment when you can be healed of all diseases, even the ones medical science has not discovered?

In maintaining health, each individual needs to regulate eight fundamental aspects in appropriate portions referred to as NEWSTART:

1. Nutrients
2. Exercise
3. Water
4. Sunlight
5. Temperance
6. Air
7. Rest
8. Trust in God

For the full benefit of this regimen, you will need to make a lifestyle change of consistent culturing of the basic principles outlined, which should be your goal to achieve. There is no real benefit in taking a haphazard approach to your health.

Trust in God

Trust in God is one of the fundamental pillars of health. Proverbs 3:5 reads, "Trust in the Lord with all thine heart; and lean not unto thine own understanding." We must first recognize that we were created by a Creator, who is the Originator and the Master Architect of the expanse and all that is possessed in it. With this evident appreciation, we can accept the fact that the manual of existence is in accordance with His Word.

Nutrition

Nutrition is a fundamental component of fostering, maintaining, and developing health. The body needs a daily perfect blend of vitamins, minerals, carbohydrates, amino acids, grains, nuts, fruits, vegetables, and oils to serve the body, and the body stores that which is needed from these things. All that is required, both the essential and nonessential nutrients, can be derived from the herbs and fruit of the land.

Exercise

Proverbs 24:5 reads, "A wise man is strong; yea, a man of knowledge increaseth strength." In order to build and maintain muscle coordination, it is vital to have measures in place to facilitate such growth. It is recommended that a minimum of thirty minutes of daily exercise be practised in order to have a comfortable start on the path of health. Exercise will increase the blood flow and aid in the expulsion of toxins while strengthening the muscles and sharpening the mind. Action is a law of life.

Water

Water is one of the most fundamental elements of the existence of any life form. The average adult human blood volume is approximately five litres; 55 per cent of the blood volume is plasma, which is 91.5 per cent water. The cells need water to survive. A 1 per cent drop in cellular hydration equates to a net 10 per cent loss of metabolic efficiency. Water is fundamental in waste management, aids in digestion, acts as a shock absorber in tissues, the spinal cord, and joints, and it regulates body temperature along with performing many other roles. The recommended daily intake is six to eight eight-ounce glasses, depending on your water output and state of hydration. Water is also essential to hygiene maintenance for the physical cleansing of the individual.

Sunlight

The sun was created to give light to the beauty of God's creation and to promote life by providing energy. In humans, sunlight is necessary for the activation of vitamin D, which is synthesized in the skin through a photosynthetic reaction triggered by ultraviolet radiation, which is required for a sturdy bone structure, to support the immune system, and in the providing of anticancer properties. It is essential for decreasing symptoms of asthma and strengthening teeth, among other uses. Sunlight is necessary to aid in the body's metabolism, its sleep–wake cycle, and its hormone balance.

Persons with inadequate exposure to sunlight are at an increased risk of vitamin D deficiency. Provitamin D is a steroid, and vitamin D is currently considered a hormone which is responsible for regulating transcription of over two hundred genes. It has pronounced effects on both dendritic cells and T-lymphocytes. In cases of chronic deficiency diseases, including but not limited to autoimmune diseases, cancers, hypertension, and heart disease are common. There are two forms of the vitamin, ergocalciferol (D2) and cholecalciferol (D3). The majority of the circulating vitamin D is in the 25-hydroxylated form of D2 and D3, called 25(OH)D. The plasma 25(OH)D concentration is an expression of both dietary and endogenous states. Sunlight is also necessary for drying room spaces while reducing the viability of germs, among numerous other benefits. As Ecclesiastes 11:7 tells us, "Truly the light is sweet, and a pleasant thing it is for the eyes to behold the sun."

Temperance

In exercising temperance, we must understand that there are things which we should do in moderation and other things from which we should totally abstain. Having temperance is knowing that good things should be enjoyed in their respective proportions of useful goodness. One should practise avoidance of sexual relationships outside of marriage and of defiling one's temple with impurities such as drugs and allowing the body to come addicted.

Air

The essential resource of air is necessary for the survival of the human being. In today's world, it is noted with the boom of industrialization that natural air is becoming a scarce commodity. An atmosphere that is free from pollution should be enjoyed for the full function of the lungs and the oxygenation of the blood in circulation to allow the body to absorb and utilize nutrients. Without air, humankind would not have existed, so a connection needs to be maintained for natural life. The man was only a form but became a living soul when God breathed into his nostril. Air is vital in the natural.

Rest

Psalm 127:2 reads, "It is vain for you to rise up early, to sit up late, to eat the bread of sorrows: for so he giveth his beloved sleep." The restoration and rejuvenation of damaged and impaired cells, muscles, tissues, organs, and systems requires rest. Rest is pivotal for growth, development, balance, mental clarity, and holistic reset. It is recommended that babies should rest for eleven to twelve hours, children for ten hours, teens for nine to ten hours, and adults for seven to eight hours daily. Humans are encouraged to engage in rest before 9 p.m., to ensure ample time for the body's recovery. It should be noted that the quality of rest is more valuable than the quantity of rest. Rest, though important, should not be abused, because when this is done poverty is the fruit.

Temperance should be exercised in all things. It is time to enjoy a new start and a new walk before it is eternally too late.

SUCCESS LAWS

Justice

The world that came into existence was perfect. The world, though asymmetric, is asymmetrically symmetric. Through the uncalibrated eyes, even though they still marvel at the world's axis rotation, the world is perceived as unbalanced, though delicately balanced and proportioned. The world is fair, as the Lord said that it was good; however, the problem is not in the creation but in unethical stewardship. Life is fair; it is the people in life who make it unfair. Female black widow spiders eat their mates, honey badgers are invasive and like picking fights, and a panda with twin cubs frequently abandons one in order to care for the other. In the animal kingdom, those things are acceptable; however, humans are not animals, which means such things are unacceptable. Those who practise these animalistic behaviours are considered barbaric, wrong, and unjust.

Justice is critical to humanity as human beings were set apart from all creatures that were called into existence because we were created with the hands of God in His image. This ideology illustrates that we are all created in His image, which means that all people deserve to be treated fairly, equally, and with dignity, no matter what the invisible lines of delineation created. After the Fall, humankind has been continually finding ways to redefine good and evil to their own advantage or someone else's disadvantage. Self-preservation is the direction that some people have led others to consider to be ideal, such as preying on, robbing, and stealing from the weak. This is the way of the wicked, which the Lord will turn upside down. More effort and care must be placed on executing judgement for the oppressed, giving food to those who are hungry, freeing those in captivity, and opening the eyes of the blind. The Lord is the One who raises those who are bowed down. And just remember, He loves the righteous, and He will preserve the strangers and offer relief to the fatherless and widows.

Self-preservation-related atrocities gradually take place in families, and then the cycle filters into the communities and societies, until the whole civilization finds it a pleasure to exploit. Then laws are established to secure the unethical practices. These are the practices from which Abraham was set aside in order to change the script and demonstrate justice as it is intended in righteousness. This righteousness shows the right relationships between people, treating people as beings made in the image of God with the dignity they deserve. "It is joy to the just to do judgment: but destruction shall be to the workers of iniquity" (Proverbs 21:15). Justice can refer to retributive justice, in which there is a causational deviation penalty; however, it is most often referred to as restorative justice, which means to seek out and help the vulnerable, the disadvantaged, and those who are not able to speak for themselves, among others. An advocation for the weak and a change in social structure to prevent injustice—for justice and righteousness to prevail in selfless existence—must be embraced.

The wicked are those who treat people as if they are outside the image of God. These are those who have the audacity to create inhumane environments and treat people as commodities and who are generally evil. Abraham's descendants, who were Israelites, went under Egyptian oppression and were eventually freed by Moses. Surprisingly, these are the same people who would have been redeemed and restored, but instead they went forward with the oppression cycle. Some purposely perpetrate injustice, some receive benefits or privileges from social injustice, and others are deceived into practising injustice in ignorance as a social norm. Wretchedly, throughout history, when the oppressed gain power, they often become oppressors themselves. The way they did not want to be treated is the same way they treat others. That is the reason Jesus was sent to display righteousness and justice, on behalf of the guilty, as an example. So justice needs to be sought for all; you must make other people's problems your problems. In understanding justice, you will be able to open doors while maintaining integrity and purity.

Opening Doors

Acts 12:1–16 gives an account of the doings of King Herod, who stretched forth his hands to harass people from the church. He had already killed James, John's brother, by the sword, which pleased the Jews, and then he took Peter. It was the time of unleavened bread, a religiously sacred period. During this time, Peter was apprehended and placed in prison, he was assigned four squads of soldiers to keep watch over him with the intention of bringing him before the rulers after the Passover. Peter was kept in prison while the church prayed ceaselessly to God on his behalf. Before the time that Herod would have brought him forth, that same night, while Peter was sleeping between two soldiers, he was bound with two chains and was guarded by a keeper at the door of the prison.

The angel of the Lord came upon him, shining a light in the dark prison, and awoke Peter by stroking him. Telling him to arise quickly, the angel caused the chains to fall off his hands that very instant. In preparation to leave, the angel told Peter to clothe himself and put on his sandals, which he did. He moved out of the prison, following the angel. At the time, Peter had thought he was in a vision. They passed the first and the second ward. They came upon an iron gate that led to the city, and it opened for them; they exited, passing through to the streets. And then the angel departed. Peter, now on the street, realized what had happened and said it was the Lord who had sent an angel to his rescue. He then went to the house of Mary, the mother of John, where some people had gathered to pray. A young girl named Rhoda heard the knocking at the door, so she went to investigate. Observing that the voice was that of Peter, in glee, she ran back to make the announcement of his return. Those who were praying did not believe her and thought she was mad, saying it must be an angel. Peter continued knocking. When they opened the door and saw him, they were astonished. Sometimes we pray for things out of formality, not realizing the power we have been given for the working of the Lord's will.

The magnanimity and merciful nature compelled the angel to hit Peter so he would wake up. Peter was in prison and in chains, comfortable to the degree that he was sleeping. One can imagine that he was confined to a small space with restrictive movement capabilities; on both sides, he was chained to soldiers. His life was restricted by the space he occupied, not only because he was bound by chains to people whose sole purpose was to keep him in that state but also because all of this was happening the night before he was to go to trial. In the cascade of events unfolding, Peter saw sleep as a fitting endeavour. The angel hit him for the reason that he had gotten oddly comfortable in an unfavourable circumstance. This circumstance was not anything that was even close to the will of God.

In order for some to get an understanding of their current state, they will need to experience hurt in order to find joy and be demoted in order to catapult their elevation. God does not want you to become comfortable in a dysfunctional situation; He is telling you that the place you are in is not your final destination: it is a piece of road on the journey. We should never allow the cement to harden where it was only to have been mixed. We see the process as Peter prepared to go through the door. The angel shined a light, which signalled Peter's revelation, and hit him, which portrayed his affliction. Then the angel told him to stand up, which was equivalent to his resurrection. So we need to stand up to the situation that may hover over us and try to define our limits.

When Peter obeyed the angel of the Lord and stood up, immediately his chains tumbled off his hands. He got up and started going through the door, and the third door that led to the street opened automatically, even before society had invented automatic technology. The process of his exit was realized when Peter had come to himself, knowing absolutely the Lord had sent an angel to deliver him from Herod and the corrupt Jewish leaders.

The Three Doors

This first door was the attack of Herod. This attack is symbolically about where we all have been positioned and are being divinely refined to go. When God raises up a deliverer for someone who is going to move into something exceptional, the enemy always raises an adversary. These adversaries are trying to prevent you from reaching where you need to be as they are intimidated by the reach God will have through you. So step through your doors. There is always a comparison with God and the adversary when you are moving through doors. Some of these opposing spirits can be seen below:

God	Adversary
Jesus	Herod
Daniel	Nebuchadnezzar
Moses	Pharaoh
You + God	Enemy + Adversary

The second door was the expectation of other people. The Gentiles received salvation through the work of Cornelius, and the Gentiles were endowed with the Holy Spirit. After Peter went to Cornelius's house, he was attacked by the traditional people/Jews, who refused to believe that salvation should be accessible to Gentiles. Attacks will come from people who don't see your vision or have your mission, but you must press on through that door lest you become imprisoned in those people's expectations. Never allow a stillbirth or abortion to take place, especially when God has something unprecedented prepared for your life.

The third door, which automatically opens, is the door towards your victory. You must remain tenacious and rest assured during your struggles in faithfulness. Knowing that you have been taken to it, you can go through it. For what God is getting ready to do in your life, you will need to let some people go so you can move forward. If you hold on to them, they will take you to your grave with doubt and negativity and small-minded thinking. You have the keys; use them.

Peter was knocking at the door, but Rhoda did not open it for him because she deferred to the people whom she had relationships with, delaying Peter's entry. She then went to the church members, who were praying for Peter but did not have the faith to believe that what they were praying for was a reality, even when it was right at the door.

We are shifting gears as we are leaving our past in the past and embracing our future. In bringing everything together, we must believe that our prayer will meet the desire. With this realized, all three doors will be open as we walk into victory.

Elijah at the Brook

We read in 1 Kings 17:3-4, "Get thee hence, and turn thee eastward, and hide thyself by the brook Cherith, that is before Jordan. And it shall be, that thou shalt drink of the brook; and I have commanded the ravens to feed thee there." Though this was a command from the Lord, it addresses a temporary situation that Elijah almost made permanent. He was there at the brook, eating and drinking, but God had a bigger plan for the prophet. God wanted to allow him a period to have introspection with meditation on the Lord without secular distractions. In obedience, Elijah went to the brook, and the Lord provided food through unconventional means. Then it was time for Elijah's next assignment, and the Lord allowed the brook to dry up.

With this occurrence, it was time for him to move forward. Elijah was then deployed to Zarephath, and he was informed that a widow would sustain him. The prophet obediently went, exercising faith in his Lord, and as was said, so was done. He blessed the widow for exercising faithfulness and kindness unto the servant of God. It is seen in the account that Elijah moved from being outside, waiting on ravens to feed him and drinking by a brook, to the inside of a dwelling, eating and drinking from a table. God will send you, too, to a place for a brief season where you will be sustained, but over time the brook of sustenance for you in that place will dry up. At the brook, Elijah only got what the birds could carry in their mouths. That is not what God wants for His children; He does not want us to become comfortable in a dysfunctional situation, living our lives on oddments. He is saying, "Young man [or young woman], you deserve more than just scraps." The Lord is able to provide abundantly, exceeding all that you can think, according to the power that works in us all for His glory.

When the brook dries up, it simply means that your assignment in that place has been completed and it's time to move to another place as God commands. Most people lack understanding of the will and working of the Lord. Despite having such doubt, exercising disobedience, and giving up your blessings, just rest assured that the Lord will always be there.

John the Baptist

Luke 1:41 reads, "And it came to pass, that, when Elisabeth heard the salutation of Mary, the babe leaped in her womb; and Elisabeth was filled with the Holy Ghost." Unconscious in the womb of his mother, Elisabeth, John the Baptist had a prenatal revelation of Jesus Christ. This same John doubted Jesus in his conscience while in jail, to the point that John called unto him two of His disciples and sent them to ask Jesus if he was the One or if he should look for another. This doubting of Jesus paralysed John's life with questions, and eventually John was beheaded. Whatever you do, do not allow the enemy inside your head unless you plan to lose it.

James's Beheading

The enemy is after your head; if the enemy can capture your mind, then he can make you cuckoo, mad, crazy, insane, psychotic, to the point where you will open up to the enemy's possession and mess everything else up. Your struggles are in your mind; the Devil makes you think he is doing things that he is not doing, making you a paranoid schizophrenic. The enemy tired to get in Jame's head; howere, they could not hence he was beheaded. Though th world may desire for you to comprpise, hold firm fearing not them who are only able to kill the body, but having true devotion to him who is able to destroy both body and soul.

In the wise providence of God, it was ordained that Jesus would be crucified on a hill known as Calvary/Golgotha, which translates to "the place of the skull". During the process of preparation, the centurions placed a crown of thorns on Jesus's head, before they pierced His hands, nailed His feet, or even pierced His side with a spear. The reason a crown was placed on His head was to show that the breaking and the breakthrough come from the mind, so the enemy aims to put the mind in captivity. Even when He was on the cross, He had His head "on straight", so He did not allow mortals to take His life, because He was straight when His life was laid down. When Jesus gave up His ghost, the biblical account declares the veil in the sanctuary was rent in two. The renting of the veil did not occur in a natural manner; it happened in an unexpectedly expected way. The separation in twain from top to bottom could not have been the work of a human; it had to have been done by a superior Spirit. It indicated that a new day had dawned and some traditions would be nullified in relation to sacrificing animals as the Lamb slain from the foundation of the earth was indeed slain.

Blessed

On the mountain, Jesus shared with His disciples words about some blessed things in which one finds comfort throughout the journey of life.

The Poor in Spirit

The poor in spirit represent those who are humble enough to understand themselves, knowing that of themselves, they are nothing without God. It is not the elevation of self-esteem but of sovereign acceptance. Being poor in spirit speaks to our state of powerlessness, knowing that if there is to be any life or joy or usefulness, it will have to be all of God and all of grace.

When Abraham was making an agreement with the Lord concerning Sodom and Gomorrah, he was exclaiming that only the Lord would give him such a privilege and it was not by his own merit. While Jacob was in exile, he wrestled with God in prayer, and as he did so, he realized he was not worthy of the least of all the mercies which had been shown to him. Moses was approached by God to bring the Israelites out of Egypt, but Moses asked the Lord for an identity check to ensure God knew who he was. Moses asked why he may have been gifted this privilege to go unto Pharaoh and bring the children of Israel out of Egypt. He thought to himself that he was not eloquent in speech. He was trying to disqualify himself after the Lord had personally qualified him. God was angry at the situation, not because of Moses's humble assessment of his own abilities, but because Moses overlooked God's ability. The Lord reminded Moses that His strength is perfect and only through Him can perfection and satisfaction be derived. People who trust in His power will receive the kingdom. That is a reflection of the poor in spirit.

Mourners

The blessings of comfort that are received by mourners are open to everyone, but they will not be accepted by all until applied as intended. People who fill their inadequacies, failures, unworthiness, and emptiness with successes, adequacy, worthiness, and the spirit-filling grace of God will be comforted after accepting and disclosing their grief to Him. Those who mourn shall be comforted.

The Meek

Meekness refers to the quiet, gentle, and submissive, to those who possess controlled strength and power. The meek are the people who wait on the Lord. We read in Psalm 37:11, "But the meek shall inherit the earth; and shall delight themselves in the abundance of peace." The meek should be still before the Lord and wait patiently on Him. Do not fret yourself over Him who prospers in His way. These individuals exhibit trust and total commitment to the ways of God without any fear of the wicked.

Moses displayed meekness when Miriam and Aaron spoke against him for marrying an Ethiopian woman. The Lord then rebuked both Miriam and Aaron and vindicated His servant. The meek have no real need for self-defence. It is done, the victory is won, and the servant of the Lord is justified and does not require revenge or have defensiveness. Meekness is reasonable. It cares about the truth and is wise. The meek are given the earth.

Those Who Hunger and Thirst After Righteousness

This hunger and thirsting is not for food or drink but for holiness. Holiness describes God as the creative force of the universe who makes all things beautiful; these abilities make God utterly unique. The sun is a consuming body of gas which destroys anything that comes in close contact with it; however, God's power is not of the same or similar composition. His immeasurable energy of purity produces such light and is also dangerous when one comes into close contact with it. God is more powerful than the sun, and for this reason we need to be purified by Him before going into His presence, or we will be destroyed.

The pursuits of humankind should be to do that which is right according to the Originator's outlined principles. In the book of Isaiah, Isaiah was having a dream in which he was in the presence of God and was totally terrified. Realizing his impure state and knowing his pending destruction in such an awesome presence, he accepted the cleansing of himself from a seraph who touched his lips with a hot coal, taking away his iniquity and purging his sins. The coal that the angel used to touch his lips removed the impurities from him, making him pure. This purifying process gives us a view of Jesus's first advent and what would happen. God's holiness did not destroy Isaiah but transformed him. In fulfilling the vision, Jesus touched people who were impure and made them pure, for those who had skin diseases, those who were dead, those who possessed all manner of infirmities, and even those with demons within. So His purity transferred to them and not the other way around. Purity, elevation, and righteousness must be our desire if we are to receive the filling of such.

Those who remain faithful can endure persecution as the world is ignorant about the blessings and rewards that have been promised. Through the grace of God, let us not fall into temptation, become corrupt and wicked, or give up the kingdom of heaven.

Those Who Have Mercy

Mercy comes from God. The Lord understands our state and makes provisions for our escape of that state so that we can be restored. God is more willing to use His power in restoration than in damnation and condemnation. As Psalm 145:9 reads, "The Lord is good to all: and his tender mercies are over all his works."

This same measure of forgiveness and compassion should be extended to all. That which is given will be received. In the parable of the Good Samaritan, a man had been attacked by thieves and was stripped of his clothing, beaten, and left half-dead. It so happened that a priest was walking that way and saw him but passed on the other side. A Levite did the same. But eventually, a passing Samaritan had compassion on the man. He bound his wounds and placed him on his transport, taking the man to an inn. He paid the initial cost of the care and agreed to any additional cost that he might incur. It is the extension of neighbourly mercy that allowed the one who had fallen by the wayside to be restored. This is the same approach that should be taken towards others. The merciful will see those in distress, responding with a heart of compassion, demonstrating practical effort to relieve the suffering of even an enemy. Mercy begets mercy.

The Pure in Heart

The heart is essential in order to see God, as only purity can embrace His presence. When solving problems, the centrality of God requires establishment; without it, only symptoms will be treated. The heart is very important because it can nullify the external. God sees far beyond that which humankind can comprehend, and this is significant. When Samuel sought after a king to anoint, it was not the one who looked the part who ultimately was chosen to play the part. God is more interested in the heart's state. David was the son who was selected, the one who was tending the sheep. This son had a clean heart and the right spirit.

The pure heart is one which has no connection with falsehood, deceit, or anything outside God's truth. If our hearts are corrupt, we cannot matriculate into His presence. In maintaining this purity, even our thought process will need redefinition. As dangerous as the mouth is, it will only speak the heart's will, and that will reveal the heart's concealed dimension. Our hearts need to be purified if we desire to see God truly.

Peacemakers

Peace is an attribute of the children of God. This becomes evident when we trust in Christ Jesus to fight our battles. In the past, it was customary to love your neighbours and hate your enemies; however, in this dispensation, it is indicated that enemies need to be loved also. This shows a society that is cultured but not converted. The enemy should be prayed for, that God's name is reverenced and that His kingdom and will are acknowledged in our lives. "If it be possible, as much as lieth in you, live peaceably with all men" (Romans 12:18).

If you or anything you are steward over damages something belonging to another, then there needs to be a restoration; whatever is missing should be taken and restored to wholeness. Reconciliation and healing broken relationships brings peace. Be not afraid or allow your heart to be troubled; Jesus came to restore peace and the fractured relationships between humans and their Creator, which He did after His death and resurrection.

Righteousness must not be compromised, even in order to make peace with your persecutors. Jesus clearly subordinates the role of peace to one of righteousness. Wisdom has it that purity will always take precedence over being peaceable, following in the order of purity, peaceableness, gentleness, mercy, and good fruits without hypocrisy or partiality. Purity must not be compromised in order to make peace.

Forgiveness

> And as ye would that men should do to you, do ye also to them likewise.
>
> —Luke 6:31

Forgiveness has been culturally touted as the process of intentionally and voluntarily relieving others and oneself from an offence that may come with negative emotions, vengeance, and reprisal eradication, in which there is restoration through the expression of Rakhmah. This process is synonymous with pardon, absolution, exoneration, purgation, and mercy. In receiving forgiveness, one must be reciprocal. Matthew 6:12 reads, "And forgive us our debts, as we forgive our debtors."

The degree of forgiveness can only be experienced by looking at the provisions made prior to humankind's creation and endowment of choice. Prior to humankind's sin, an arrangement was already in place for redemption and restoration, had that been humanity's choice. Knowing that this was possible, God still created the man and allowed him to choose. Humans find the process of forgiveness challenging because it cannot be done independently. Forgiveness is divine. With a constant connection with God, humanity can be elevated with the ability to forgive before it is needed; hence, if and when a trespass is committed, care should be taken to rectify the situation and make both parties whole.

Unforgiveness reduces the wholeness and completeness of an individual, fragmenting the person, compromising the impact and effect of the restoration. God's love is a fundamental requirement in exhibiting forgiveness. With the patience and kindness that love presents, it deals with wrongdoing in a civil manner without resentment, utilizing truth while enduring all things. It is known that everything will pass away but that love never ends; hence, love has the power to overcome even when it is absent. In the same display, the Son of God was sent to restore humanity by demonstrating the self-sacrificing principle. As beautiful as the admonitions are, too few will actually heed them and will then complain of their state. Though it is a supernatural venture, it is not by our own strength that we forgive. Things that are natural to the flesh are not so for the spiritual. In the natural, when we have been hurt, victimized, abused, or insulted, the approach is to plot revenge or simmer in bitterness. This is carnal; forgiveness is never overcome carnally, but spiritually. Providing that there is an unwillingness or inability to forgive, there is no use in asking God for such, because forgiveness should be based on a reciprocal action.

Putting on a show in hypocrisy is not forgiveness, and neither is living in denial. The factor that is challenging to understand for many is the concept of a "total memory wipe", though it may be possible that the majority does not experience such a thing. In remembering the incident, there will not be any negative bottled emotions, but instead purity and restored relations. If we make an attempt to counterfeit forgiveness, what we will produce is a bogus state, and this may confuse us into thinking that we have forgiven. Even though all the hurt is bottled inside, the emotional burden still exists, which will stymie our health. The intoxicating lure of a grandiose scheme of scorching retribution can become overwhelming. In these situations when anger overcomes us, let us not sin nor let the sun rest with wrath within us.

Forgiveness is absolutely possible. the reasonability that God exhibits indicates that nothing asked of humankind is unreasonable or impossible. Christ has forgiven, so forgiveness should be extended to our fellows as we personify kindness and tender-heartedness as we walk in the love of God. Forgiveness is not necessarily only for times when someone does you an offence, or when you have done an offence, but is also for times when someone is holding a grudge against you. If you are going to worship and you remember this, you should leave your gift at the alter and engage in reconciliation before proceeding with worship.

Philemon and Onesimus's Reconciliation

In the book of Philemon, Paul mentions the story of a Roman citizen from Colossae whom he met on a previous occasion who was a follower of Jesus Christ. Philemon owned slaves, one of whom was Onesimus. Onesimus and Philemon had a conflict, and afterwards Onesimus ran away and went to Paul for help. In the process, he became a follower of Jesus and a beloved assistant of Paul. So Paul penned a letter to Philemon asking him to embrace Onesimus as a brother in the Messiah and regard him no longer as a slave. Onesimus had to resolve the conflict with Philemon to reflect his conversion in the Messiah. In this situation, restoration was outside the socially acceptable norms. It involved taking in a slave and making him equal as one would with a family member.

Paul placed himself to pay the charge that may have been incurred during the transactional arrangement for completing the restoration. This act was similar to Jesus's sacrifice in our place. Paul stated that he had confidence in Philemon's obedience and that he would do more than that which was asked. That is forgiveness! For oneness, forgiveness is critical in order to enjoy success.

Faith

Hearing is simply the act of perceiving sound by the ears. If you are not hearing-impaired, hearing happens. Listening, however, is something that you consciously choose to do. Listening requires concentration so that your brain may process meaning from words and sentences. It is important that we listen. Forgiveness is coupled with exercising faith. Enoch showed the walk of faith, Noah showed perseverance of faith, Abraham showed obedience of faith, Isaac showed the power of faith, and Jacob showed the discipline of faith. "So then faith cometh by hearing, and hearing by the word of God" (Romans 10:17).

Elijah and the Widow at Zarephath

We read in 1 Kings 17:7-11, "And it so occurred that the Lord dried up the brook which he had sent Elijah and said unto him, go to Zarephath and a widow will sustain you. Hearing the command, he arose and did go to the city. Upon arriving at the gate of the city, the widow was there, gathering sticks. Elijah called and asked her for some water in a vessel to drink. While she was going, he also asked her to bring him something to eat." The Lord worked in such a way that Elijah did not know which woman he was going to meet; all he knew was where. The operation was quite precise; all the man of God needed to do was show up. This woman was in a predicament; she was at her "last". She was without a husband, and yet this was the woman the Lord saw fitting to sustain His messenger. When the Lord works, sometimes it conflicts with our expectations with things working out in an unexpected way.

The woman was on her way to fetch water when Elijah made a request for food. There was to have been the establishment of a mutualistic relationship as she was just preparing to have her last meal with her son and to wait on death, but her plans were about to change. In this situation, the prophet told her to have no fear and to do what was requested, and that was what she did. After he was fed, he asked that she make food for her son and herself. Remember that this woman was at her last and that she had sacrificed her life and her son's life so the prophet could be fed without holding back. She had accepted before she saw what the Lord had in store. She had to forgive herself for relying on her own sight; however, she exercised faith to go and prepare food from what was visually empty when she'd left. The prophet laid his blessings on this widow for her submission when she exercised faith. Her faith sustained the prophet, as God said would happen, as well as her family. All that was needed was the belief and submission to the will of God.

The Story of Cain and Abel

Both Cain and Abel came to worship before the Lord with their sacrifices; however, there was a difference between what they brought. Cain brought a sacrifice of the fruit of the ground, and Abel brought forth a blood sacrifice. As a result, the Lord Jehovah respected Abel and his offering, but He did not respect Cain or his offering. It was by faith that Abel offered a more excellent sacrifice than Cain. Cain presented his gift according to what he saw as desirable, while Abel gave what the Lord had required. It was for this reason that Cain's offering was rejected and why that which had been requested was accepted. Presumption should be avoided as it works in conflict with the Lord's will. It is an insult to offer the Lord something that is unacceptable while expecting acceptance. This should never be forgotten, because our lives are to live and then to live again. It was through the same exercise of faith that Sara received strength to conceive seed, delivering a child who fulfilled God's promise. With faith, whatever is requested and believed becomes possible.

Elisha and the Widow's Oil

In 2 Kings 4:1–7 we find the account of Elisha and the widow's oil, which shows employment of faith. This woman was in a peculiar situation; her husband, who was the provider, Elisha's servant, was dead. His being dead was not at all the end for her. This was a man who feared the Lord and was working in accordance with the Father's will.

In dying, he left debts behind. The creditors were coming to take the woman's two sons to be his slaves until the debt was cleared. If this woman were to give up her sons to the creditors, she would be left alone and could expect death to be knocking at her door prematurely. To her, this was not a viable option for consideration. It would have been better if the creditors came and took her stuff, but not her sons. In deep concern, she enquired what could be done to remedy the situation. Elisha asked her what she wanted to be done with what she had in the house. It is interesting the response to Elisha's question; the widow said she had nothing in the house but a jar of oil. Sometimes in a difficult situation, when we are between a rock and a hard place, it is challenging to see what it is that we have. All we tend to see is what we don't have. The Lord can use anything we have and do great things with it.

The widow said she had only a jar of oil, and that was enough for the prophet. She was already in debt, but she was instructed to go further in debt by borrowing vessels from her neighbours—empty containers, as many as she could secure. It is evident that the community impact was critical to her breakthrough; she needed to get them involved. So from them she borrowed empty vessels as many as were available. With God, we can access vast reservoirs without collateral; all we need to do is ask for help.

The widow was working with the man of God and was submitting to the instructions given. She got all the empty vessels possible, and into those vessels she poured the oil until full. After each vessel was full, she set it aside, doing this until there was not another vessel to be filled. When all the vessels were filled, the oil flow ceased. One's ability to access the immeasurable becomes measurable in direct proportion to emptiness. Once there is space for the blessing, it will be received. The prophet was not finished when the vessels were filled. One more instruction was given to the widow. She was told by the prophet that she should sell the oil and pay her debt, after which time she should live on the rest of the money earned.

The challenge that the prophet was called to solve was the widow's husband's debt. Sometimes we are shackled when we receive blessings as there is a tendency to keep it to ourselves, not realizing it was given to us to share. It was in sharing her blessing that the widow could acquire the resources needed to release the shackles from her sons' feet. The widow moved from not having enough to having plenty, and then she moved to having more than she needed—abundance. This was possible because she evaluated the situation and submitted to the process of restoration. This woman became a legitimate entrepreneur, affecting the community positively while presenting solutions to any problems they had. It was her faith that made this possible.

Faith, a powerful force, can transform the smallest to the largest and make the insignificant significant. It is the stabilizer for the unstable. This trust, assurance, and confidence in God is directly related to the relationship. It is through faith that we understand the world was framed by the Word of God; things which are seen came from things which did not appear. It was faith which caused the forgiveness of the debt.

FINANCIAL ABUNDANCE

He becometh poor that dealeth with a slack hand:
but the hand of the diligent maketh rich.
—Proverbs 10:4

A seven-year-old boy requested an advance of $20 from his father to buy a new toy; however, after the boy's request was received, the father (Dad's Abundance Inc.) denied the sum because of the boy's inefficiency in performing his chores and his inconsistent credit and repayment history. The CEO of the organization wrote him a letter of denial for the application, indicating that no further processing could be undertaken at that time but that a grievance procedure could be channelled through his mother if he felt that there had been a miscalculation in judgement. Never add price to the priceless as in doing so you will inadvertently initiate depreciation and misrepresentation.

Stewardship

Interestingly, in preparing the earth for humankind's inhabitance and dominion, God allowed everything to remain in place and also held back the rain because there was no human to manage what was prepared for them. Growth was quarantined momentarily until the arrival of humankind. Upon humankind's arrival, the cycles were started. We are given resources to manage. When these resources are mismanaged, then poverty, debt, bankruptcy, and demise overtake the people. Without management/stewardship, bills will not be paid, families will be destroyed, assets will be lost unnecessarily, and there will be an influx of liability acquisition, eventually spiralling life downwards. Stewardship requires living in, submitting, abiding in, and giving over the gifts of time, talent, temple, and treasure to the principles of the Creator.

Everyone each day possesses the same quantity of time. We all have different talents and different bodies. How these three gifts are used will determine the abundance in the treasury. The usage typifies stewardship, which is the timely, effective, efficient, and truthful use of property, possessions, or resources in accomplishing the delegated purpose with the intention of producing the expected added value. The mistake most people make is to think that they are their own, that whatever they have acquired is theirs or whatever they are placed in charge of belongs to them. If you are a steward, then what you touch must increase. Do not expect abundance if you are lazy. The laziness defect needs to be rectified as God will never give you more than you can competently exercise charge over. If you are lazy, you need to be worked on because you are mismanaging yourself. If you have an inability to manage, then things will be protected from you. That could be the reason you are still living the way you have been living since you first came to know yourself. You must be faithful over a few things before you may expect the increase. God wants you to enjoy the developmental stages in an effort to allow you to develop in order to accept a more favourable end than the beginning.

All individuals going in accordance with the manual will become economists, extracting the maximum from the minimum, producing excellent recovery without damaging or destroying anything in the process. It is an insult to ask for more when you have not yet explored the vastness you already possess. No one has the right to tell God they are broke because everything that you need you already have. Use it.

Stewardship of the Five Thousand

A depiction of stewardship was observed in Jesus's feeding the crowd in Luke 9. The people who were following Jesus became hungry; instead of scattering the people, Jesus offered them hospitality. He asked that they be arranged in companies of fifty. The request that they sit in groups of fifty was an effort at administration and organization to allow for resource management computation; the disciples stated they had only five loaves and two fishes. Jesus, in receiving what was presented, looked up and thank God for allowing an opportunity to utilize the resources in His hands. This is an expression of stewardship, and this example communicates the idea that even when we have all things in our hands, we still need a connection to derive from God's abundance. The food was blessed and divided. It was delegated to the disciples for redistribution after the multiplication. Miraculously exceptional service had been rendered; the people ate and were satisfied. The disciples were instructed to pick up every leftover, which they did, amounting to twelve baskets. This was necessary to remind us that nothing should go to waste because it is polite to leave a place better than you found it. This is an unquestionable display of stewardship. The waste culture will rob your inheritance.

Money should not run away from you. If it does, it means you are incapable of managing, and that is a reflection of your lack of stewardship. There is nothing wrong with money; it is the Lord's will that you increase as did Abraham, Isaac, Job, Solomon, David, and Joseph, among others, who were exemplary reflections of appropriated stewardship. It is true that when money is available, food can be secured, decay can be righted, and laughter and merrymaking can be enjoyed.

Distributions and Allocations

Tithing (10%) and Offering (Voluntary Contribution)

Adults have a tendency to be like children, chasing their shadows. This is because they focus on earthly things, looking down and not up. When we seek to assume the designed posture intended, we will find it easier to look ahead upon the kingdom principle. God does not need money, because everything created is His. We are entrusted with time, opportunities, abilities, and possessions to maximize and share the blessings. This process is about putting something aside. The opportunity offered in tithing and giving offerings is a privileged management training programme geared towards preparing humanity to handle portfolio diversification. Remember, all the increase belongs to God, who made everything. Requested is a tenth or 10 per cent in tithe and a free-will offering in accordance with our choosing. Still, all belongs to the Creator. Your faithfulness is under investigation in the act of tithing.

Tithing and offering are stewardship expressions of resource management. This account was observed and practised by Abraham, who offered tithes. We read in Genesis 14:20, "And blessed be the most high God, which hath delivered thine enemies into thy hand. And he gave him tithes of all." Jacob, after having the encounter with the angel, committed to tithing. This was a practice that God's children performed to ensure the continuation of God's work. Aaron and his sons, from the tribe of Levites, were called to minister in the priest's office. The Levites were set aside for this sacred duty and received no land inheritance, but they were supported by the tithes of the people. This contribution was a demonstration of obedience and love to God and not material possessions. In the process of tithing, love is shown to others whom you would not have been able to reach with the various outreach and in-reach ministries. Tithing refers to a portion of earnings equal to 10 per cent on the first increase. "And all the tithe of the land, whether of the seed of the land, or of the fruit of the tree, is the Lord's: it is holy unto the Lord" (Leviticus 27:30).

Tithing develops accountability. Each individual becomes responsible for the contribution that will be made when their eyes are opened to this requirement. It is an exercise of discipline to put apart from, develop control, and cultivate honesty—because no human individual is actually overseeing. Diligence is cultivated with the consistent employment of honesty, building character while faithfulness is being expressed. Letting go allows the hands to become open to receive the inflows.

Whereas the tithe is a specific amount in per cent, an offering is anything given beyond that but not in place of it. As we read in 2 Corinthians 9:7, "Every man according as he purposeth in his heart, so let him give; not grudgingly, or of necessity: for God loveth a cheerful giver."

Resource Management

Diligence with resources will reflect stewardship. Proverbs 13:22 tells us, "A good man leaveth an inheritance to his children's children: and the wealth of the sinner is laid up for the just." The Lord desires that his creation be prosperous, desiring His people to reflect the image they have been created in. If anyone is going to seek after accomplishing this, it is important to note that in being a good person, the individual should have an inheritance for the grandchildren who are not yet born. There is nothing wrong with wealth. There is something wrong with rapidly depreciating assets as they cannot be transferred as an inheritance; the transfer would be a liability. In the beginning, the man was given the land to have dominion. This was to direct our thoughts in such a way that we may grasp that real estate can be passed down from generation to generation while increasing in value; it is an asset. God gave Abraham, Isaac, Moses, Jacob, and other individuals land which was their real estate.

The wicked have the wealth because they are better managers—they execute the principles of God—while God's people only know and understand, but lack the wisdom to execute that which is known. It is for this reason that there is such great subjection and corruption with the clean and unclean. Diligence is needed to bring wealth. Diligent people, stewards, managers, take care of what they possess, allowing it to appreciate. Those who are lazy will always be in want and will always claim to have nothing, but those who embody diligence shall increase in substance.

All the money that ever existed and will ever exist on earth is still here. There is never a real crisis. Because of mismanagement and illegal counterfeit currency injections, economies collapse and the real money goes into hiding. In every crisis, one set of persons will always increase while another will continuously decrease. It comes down to your stewardship of resources and your portfolio diversification. In generating a revenue stream, we need to manage our ideas to produce water from the well.

Mismanagement

Most problems that plague humanity are surrounded by mismanagement, and taking the giant slice is the mismanagement of money. We read in Luke 22:31, "And the Lord said, Simon, Simon, behold, Satan hath desired to have you, that he may sift you as wheat." The enemy is trying to get your soul, and all measures conceivable are being utilized. He places his attacks on the family, human interaction, resources, conflict, and anything that can be used to distract attention from the big picture.

In Luke 16 we read the parable of the shrewd manager. There was a certain rich man who had a steward who was accused of wasting his goods. The steward was approached to give an account based on the accusation. This accusation would disqualify him from being a steward. The steward then said his lord had taken away his stewardship, and he was ashamed to beg, so he got innovative. He called on one of his lord's debtors and split the cost of that which was owed. This being brought to the lord's attention merited commendation of the unjust steward as he had acted wisely. This means that the job the steward was to have been doing was not done until after he was relieved of duty. Sometimes there needs to be a spring cleaning; the lord applauded this poor manager when he acted shrewdly as now he was demonstrating wisdom. It is never too late to start managing your resources.

Greed

The mismanagement of resources for personal benefit is greed. Greed will destroy a person as it is inside the human being. A person's life is more than what he or she will leave behind, as all human beings will leave all behind. Luke 12:15 reads, "And he said unto them, Take heed, and beware of covetousness: for a man's life consisteth not in the abundance of the things which he possesseth. Do not covet thy neighbour's, nor that which is they neighbours house, so stop cursing your neighbours for reaping blessing after following godly instructions and manage your resources with diligence while resisting greed and covetousness."

Gambling/Game Playing (0%)

You will only become who you allow yourself to be. Proverbs 13:11 tells us, "Wealth gotten by vanity shall be diminished: but he that gathereth by labour shall increase." In prudence, wealth should be amassed over time with consistent effort. It is unwise to think that ill gains will last. It is wiser to note that these gains will vanish like vapour as the epic state is outlined in Haggai 1:6: "Ye have sown much, and bring in little; ye eat, but ye have not enough; ye drink, but ye are not filled with drink; ye clothe you, but there is none warm; and he that earneth wages earneth wages to put it into a bag with holes."

Engaging in gambling or gaming is a sure way to delay or even halt your prosperity. Gambling is likened to a man giving away all he has, thinking a return is forthcoming. With gambling, the odds are always against and seldom in favour. When the debt cannot be serviced, it will eventually lead to death all around. These practices are addictive, and a person engaging in them needs help in order to overcome the addiction. Error in faith is evil, especially when money is love. This is a recipe to bring sorrow of spirit and of existence. This practice will ruin lives, directly and indirectly. Money has no place in the hand of someone who gambles. It is better to get wisdom than money as money does not actually exist.

Debt (0%)

This practice preys on individuals' inability to exercise self-control, purchasing that which they are not in a position to afford. Buying now, agonizing later, is far from the plan of God to enjoy financial abundance. Getting in debt will cause one to enter a revolving door.

So much can be wasted within moments which can take a lifetime to resolve. The bombardment by institutions practising usury (the lending of money with an interest charge for use) entices many to access capital, only in return to receive slavery. Proverbs 22:7 reads, "The rich ruleth over the poor, and the borrower is servant to the lender." When you are in such a predicament in which you love silver, you will soon realize that it will not satisfy you and that all the abundance will reveal itself as vanity. Would someone who desires life knowingly step into quicksand? Yet many find comfort in doing so. They cry about their bankrupt state, which they are in not because of a lack of knowledge but because of their inability to exercise control.

If a debit system rather than a credit system were used, the population would be forced to exercise more control or live on welfare programmes. The state prefers that everyone become someone else's problem, hence the reason no real control measures are put in place when moving from the quicksand experience. The state has a choice: to care either for the creditor or for you. Selected in your stead in many instances is the creditor. The best way to stay out of debt is to live first within and then below your means, exercising control. Stop comparing yourself with others and live in contentment.

Living within your means indicates that everything that enters exits, that income and expenditures are equal (income = expenditure = 0). In this state, it is hand to mouth, unhealthy and ungodly. Individuals in this predicament have not yet started experiencing the abundance of God. Living above your means indicates that you are spending more than you are generating (expense > income = (−)). This will lead you into debt. However, living below your means indicates that you are in an acceptable position to contribute to charities/religious organizations, pay taxes, pay yourself, cover recurrent expenditures, store away an opportunity fund, and invest as appropriate (income > expenditure (+)). Spending should be allocated as units and percentage in maintaining a balanced budget and reporting on the balance sheet.

Debt Calculation Formula

In order to plug the holes, one needs a budget so as to see where the money is going. Deuteronomy 30:19-20 reads, "I call heaven and earth to record this day against you, that I have set before you life and death, blessing and cursing: therefore choose life, that both thou and thy seed may live." If you are already in debt, this is what you will need to do to get out. Tithe 10 per cent, pay yourself 10 per cent, pay your creditors 20 per cent, and live on 60 per cent. The 10 per cent, when it has reached a substantial amount, can be invested in a system which protects the principal. You should engage in such a venture. It is copper to silver, silver to bronze, and bronze to gold. And if you continue, your gold will turn into platinum. There are treasures all around and oil to be desired in the dwelling of the wise, but those who are mentally decapitated will spend their money before it can be put to the most useful service.

Taxes (0%–60%)

Whatever the type of taxation that exists in a country, whether citizenship-based taxation, territorial tax system, income tax, or something else, it is advised that we pay the taxes. If you desire not to because the amount appears exorbitant, then exit the country, change your citizenship, buy an island, and live and do business elsewhere. With tax rates at this level, it is almost crazy to think people would have time to waste their resources. It is recorded that Jesus paid the imperial tax to Caesar. The Pharisees took counsel, trying to entangle Jesus, asking him if he thought it was lawful to give tribute to Caesar. Jesus, seeing their cruel intentions, made it simple and asked them to show Him the tribute money. When they brought unto him a penny, Jesus asked whose image was upon it, and they responded, "Caesar's." At that moment, they were given their answer: the things that are for Caesar should be given to Caesar, and the things which are for God should remain in their place.

The money was not created by you, which means it is not yours. You were only given stewardship over it so you can be motivated to work and be productive while driving the economy. Money does not really exist as it is an idea imposed on people to encourage corporation and desire. While in Capernaum, during the tribute money collection period, Peter asked His Master if He paid tribute. Indeed, Jesus expects the laws governing the land to be upheld, providing they are right and righteous.

Recurrent Expenditures (≤ 25%)

These are the expenses of independence, including food, housing, transportation, water, electricity, and any other necessary utility. If you are unwilling to work, you should also be unwilling to eat. According to 1 Timothy 5:8, "But if any provide not for his own, and specially for those of his own house, he hath denied the faith, and is worse than an infidel." This recurrent expenditure does not revolve around the stewardship of self but also around others under care. This expenditure should not exceed 25 per cent of wages. If needed, counsel with a specialist in the area of need should be sought in managing resources. Counsel should not be searched after if you are wishing to hear only what you desire to hear; it should be sought after if you desire to hear that which is the truth. Hearing flattery has the potential to bring you into ruin. Choose truth over flattery.

Opportunity Fund and Investment
(Split the Remaining Percentage Fifty-Fifty)

When the laws of God are followed, prosperity and success are guaranteed, though it is the case that riches do not hold trust. This means that you should never extend trust to your wealth. But in righteousness, secure your treasure where you desire your heart to be. The wise would choose the eternal over the temporal. Riches will be here in this moment and then be gone in the next. It is better to be connected to the source of riches than to riches, as the source will always have wealth. What you have acquired is measurable, but the source is immeasurable. "Wilt thou set thine eyes upon that which is not? for riches certainly make themselves wings; they fly away as an eagle toward heaven" (Proverbs 23:5). It comes down to creating, growing, and preserving.

In this preemptive preparation for the future, it is more about placing money in revenue-generating ventures which will allow growth and increase automatically, while still having access to an opportunity fund, which is actual liquid cash. In order to grow, you need to exercise gradual consistency and faithfulness. When this faithfulness is demonstrated, in time you will receive your own, to which others can apply their devotion as you did prior to your independence.

A wealthy man had sold all he had because he wanted to know just how wealthy he had become over the years. On his way to the bank, he was struck by a motor vehicle, and he died. The driver of the vehicle which made contact with this man also died. An advisory is now being given to all persons heading in that direction to change course as a pile-up has caused a bottleneck jam. It is not the lack of resources that keeps people in poverty but the lack of resourcefulness. Value-added relationships are critical, which equates to relational capital, which has a higher value than capital. It takes only one connection for things to turn, which is the power of the social currency. This is where passive income is critical. Immediately you are going to cease spending unnecessarily. Stop buying things you don't need or items for which there is a more reasonable alternative. When you receive an increase, you must pay yourself from the gross. How much is paid to yourself will determine where you want to be. To be broke, don't pay yourself. To be poor, break even. If you want an increase to become part of the middle class, pay yourself 5 per cent to 15 per cent. To become rich, 20 per cent is recommended. Anything above 25 per cent places you in a prestigiously exclusive category. Automate your payments to avoid late fees, maintain accurate records, and engage in market research. Money does not solve problems when misused.

Financial literacy is what's important. It is your responsibility not only to have money but also to ensure money does not have you. Invest in assets and not liabilities. Something that it is costing you more than it is generating is not an asset; it is a liability.

In preparing for your grandchildren, you need a system that is automatic. You must be willing to change your thinking. Count the cost of all actions, use a guide, and manage your resources with diligent stewardship. Earning is necessary, but more important is spending. This is what causes the grave problem for the struggling individual in poverty. The poor will be on this earth always. "The poor" does not mean those who are lacking. It more means those who are nonproductive in resource utilization. If people make themselves of value, they will extract the natural resource and present it as a precious commodity. The process for wealth creation involves fruitfulness (production), multiplication (reproduction), replenishment (distribution), and subduement (control); at the end, abundance will be actualized. Genesis 1:28 reads, "And God blessed them, and God said unto them, Be fruitful, and multiply, and replenish the earth, and subdue it: and have dominion."

It is the blessing of the Lord which has the capacity to make rich anyone who desires it and who is willing to follow His principles. These riches presented will in no way carry the baggage or burden of sorrow with them when accessed at the appropriate time. It is vital to engage in employment while preparing for deployment. Upon doing just this, the increase from service should be secured while keeping back a tenth (10 per cent). This percentage should be invested in an income-generating enterprise which guarantees the principal while increasing in interest. At the appropriate time, real estate should be sought after; this investment type often appreciates with age. Expenditures should be controlled, and debt should be avoided. If incurred, debts should be cleared in the shortest possible time, but not at the expense of paying yourself. With an increase, many will seek to share in that which you have patiently acquired. Do not become an emotional victim, because if one is unfaithful in little, he or she will fail to be faithful in much. If your help is desired, give it without allowing the other person's burden to become yours. Indiscretions are costly and have the ability to destroy quickly all that has been long laboured in acquiring. The emotional obligation will not help anyone but will serve a more useful purpose in destroying both of you. There is no such thing as "good luck"; life is to be enjoyed with blessings entrusted by the Creator. Follow these wise counsels, and you will enjoy financial abundance. "And whatsoever ye do, do it heartily, as to the Lord, and not unto men" (Colossians 3:23).

SIXTH GEAR

Esteem and Worth

Seductive Manipulation

Love Principle

ESTEEM AND WORTH

We read in Philippians 2:3–4, "Let nothing be done through strife or vainglory; but in lowliness of mind let each esteem other better than themselves. Look not every man on his own things, but every man also on the things of others." The concept of esteem is confused with humanity's perception, which is in direct conflict with God's standard. When a person speaks about esteem, it usually refers to the promotion of self and interest, in which image, love, and life revolve around the idolatry of the person. In reference to the standard, it is evident that self has no place as it is totally devoted to God. Love is shared with others. Humility expressed as the Originator is the standard. Self-esteem refers to the values and measure by which you hold yourself accountable, and deviation from this creates discomfort and depression and may even lead to suicide. It reflects the cumulative worth of your life base on the human standard. When we look at esteem from a human's perspective, we see a value system which includes appearance, brilliance, wealth, and talent; however, according to God's standard, value is focused on character, attitude, benevolence, faithfulness, and so on. The Lord in no way sees as humanity sees. The Lord looks at the heart, while humans are stuck in the fixation on externality, which is transitional and vanity.

Slavery Mentality

The mind of humanity is so entrapped in the past, hence the present state of self-imposed oppression. In the past, generations were challenged by their circumstances which were passed down in a seamless fashion, which caused the free to remain within the confines of the past. The minds of many have not yet worked out the difference between liberation and enslavement as both expressions are indistinguishable because of the potency of mental scarring. When a nation is defeated psychologically, it can be considered the end of that nation unless a maverick rises to restore it. For nations which have facilitated this psychological defeat, hundreds of years later their minds are still trapped, not only because of circumstances but also because of the strategic miseducation of the people by the oppressor. The cycle continues. The people have been oppressed so long that they find more comfort in the predictability of the oppression than in the idea of taking charge of their future, stepping outside the lines of the past. The plethora of socioeconomic issues that arise are of such significance that they give rise to the problems caused by a lingering identity crisis. The thought that a specific set of persons are not fully human has torn society's fabric and has left the current generation with the lingering smell of an infected sore. With this mentality, the illusion of low self-esteem and immorality is created. It still lingers as the thoughts are shared and cultivated even though the reality does not exist, thus creating a reality inside a reality that is absolutely imaginary. The same mindset existed with the children of Israel when freed from Egypt. They never really wanted to leave, having become comfortable with oppression, although they claimed they were waiting on the promised rescue. Change must be allowed to overtake our lives as we make the choice as to which state we desire to thrive in. It is time for a mental liberation. Let us seek to change the narrative, moving away from the victim mentality and towards the victor reality.

You cannot hold time; in this life, you need to invest time with the rule of seventy-two (compound interest). The best investment that you will ever make is the investment in yourself. When you realize that no one else can see you for what you can become, you will steer towards becoming that which is your purpose. No one else can hear your conscience but you. Within yourself, you need to focus on your ability in an effort to minimize any disabilities. You will need to push yourself in order to get where only God can take you, doing all with all you have got until you become no more. In light of this revelation, you are encouraged to understand yourself and the uniqueness that you naturally possess. You need to stop thinking small and begin to think unlimitedly as you determine the level of your success by the limits of your mind. You need to be relentless, resilient, and resourceful, knowing that you are going to be the best. Do not be defined by your past defeats or pain. Be prepared for your opportunity. When it comes, you will be ready. Envision yourself in the future, in the present, so you can propel from your past into your future, which will be your present. You should just keep moving as you will always have something achievable in front of you.

Esteem

Esteem existed and is evident in the third chapter of Genesis, where there is a transition of consciousness. Prior to their eyes being opened, both Adam and Eve were God-conscious, but after the dark enlightenment, they became self-conscious to the degree that they realized they were naked and sought to cover themselves. Their actual state had not changed in its physical nature; it was a divergence in the processing of the information which caused the alarm. Prior to that occurrence, Adam was incidentally and peripherally aware of himself as he exclaimed upon the presentation of Eve, "This is bone of my bone and flesh of my flesh." This awareness did not detract from his focus on God. It is important to remember that it is all about you being royalty. As such, you are expected to behave in that manner.

The mind is the control centre of our being, giving us the capacity to think and make logical and sequential decisions. Though we possess this magnificent capacity, nothing will change until our mindset has been modified to suit the transformation. The sooner it is realized that the volume of information is negligible, we can change in relation to the application of information which is more meaningful in the transformative process. In effecting this transformation, we need to exercise humility, though the desire to use earthly resources will tempt the sensual appetite to validate its worth in misappropriated pride. James 4:6 reads, "But he giveth more grace. Wherefore he saith,

God resisteth the proud, but giveth grace unto the humble." Humans' attempt to validate their worth based on the standard of humankind is an error, which is the reason multiple people have lost their way while seeking to exist as someone else. Because of the ill alignment with the standard, many have fallen into great depression and even have become casualties of attempted suicide or suicide. In humility, self and selfish desires are laid aside, especially when our existence is parallel with the reality, knowing that apart from the Lord, we are nothing.

Attitude

Your attitude determines your grasp after you reach. The mentality you possess determines the fulfilment of the promises of God in your life. You are the limiting factor in what the Lord desires to be done in and through you. Even if it is yours, if you don't believe it, there is no guarantee you will receive it; just maybe someone else will receive it on your behalf. A table is prepared for you, but you must also be prepared for the table. Physical relocation coupled with intellectual motivation can still cause you to end with spiritual paralysis, meaning that the starting attitude is equal to the outcome even though a change has taken place. Whatever you do, it is imperative that you never allow anyone to break your spirit. Keep on keeping on; maintain your standard to enjoy your altitude. When your spirit is broken, you will be shackled to oppression. Authorize your attitude to chart your course, because it is God who works in you according to His pleasure.

Confidence

Confidence is essential if we are to take charge and command of our outcome. Confidence is the belief that you can do a thing; however, without God, you can actually do nothing. Proverbs 26:1 tells us, "As snow in summer, and as rain in harvest, so honour is not seemly for a fool." A fool is one who conflicts with the ways of God and believes in the strength of his or her mortality, neglecting the immortality of God. Self is a carnal expression of deprived spiritual empowerment. When working on the world system, individuals must be subjected to the world's economy standard in which unhealthy and ungodly acts are performed, which creates a lot of friction if one is suspected or found out. The great thing is that when we have confidence in God, He can lift us up and promote us with our character and integrity in check. The world has a false economy adapted from God's economy; it has maligned the concept of the original kingdom economy. This economy is not understood by the world as it is discerned spiritually and not naturally received. Pride is at the base of people's deceiving themselves to believe themselves to be something that they are not, but we are warned that pride goes before a fall. Such are the consequences of having confidence in self and selfishness. The world's standard truly desires that you fail in all aspects of your life in order to gain an understanding of a none existent reality. It is a distraction to prevent you from focusing on what matters, which you could lose if you do not realize it soon. With strong faith, confidence will be on display. We are asked to come boldly, meaning without fear, worry, or concern.

Comparison

Deception is apparent when an individual thinks himself to be something when he is nothing. Deceiving someone else is something, but fooling yourself is deadly. It is not advised that you compare yourself with other people or compete with others as this will present inadequacies and create jealousy, hatred, segregation, and despair, nothing but negative emotions and energy, which is detrimental to existence. It is preposterous to consider comparing your weakness with another's strength; the results are already known. To avoid comparison and competition, the best alternative is to collaborate, in which the advantage of the parties can be maximized to accomplish goals and objectives rapidly. It does not matter how you feel, as you are in representation. God wants you to *be* safe and not just to feel safe. Safety is a part of the package for royalty; it is a part of your inheritance when you know the Creator. You already have it, but if you don't know that you have it, how will you seek to use it? Your heritage condemns any tongue that may rise against you. No weapon has power over you as you, not the created thing, are designed to prosper. People who are still in the world's economy fight with the natural, thinking it will bring a resolution. This fight usually is carried down for generations. The people of God exercise authority over the spiritual, which is the source of manifestation of the physical. Humankind is more spiritual than physical, but the world has it twisted; hence there are people who solve the same problems, treating the symptoms since the recording of sin. It is similar to the treatment of a headache; the medical team prescribes some analgesics to numb the nerve so that you will no longer feel the effect. The fact remains that though you are not feeling the impact, you still have a headache, but now you just don't know. As the pain intensifies, you get an increasingly stronger dosage until you die. Only now, at the autopsy, does the medical team realize that the headache was caused by a brain aneurysm. This occurs because of people's inability to understand the source and the appropriate restorative option to be employed. The Devil does not mind you hurting as long as the eyes of your conscience remain closed.

Insecurities

Insecurities exist when we forget who we are, whose we are, where we are from, and where we are going. There is no need to feel less than secure as there has been no one similar and there will be no replica after as you were purposefully genetically engineered to be distinguishable from all humanity. Work is set aside for you. There is a need for you to contribute. Only you are positioned to make that contribution. You will need to reach out and allow the Holy Spirit to lead you in righteousness. Your security should not be derived from that which can be perceived with the eyes after feasting in the mirror, or from those with whom you have associated, the tangibles you have amassed, your address, your transportation selection, or your educational fortitude. Your security should not come from any of these things, because if such were the case that these things provide security, then when they are stripped away, you would believe yourself to be vulnerable. Your worth and value are based on who you are in God. This means that if your circumstance should change, the Lord will love you the same, and you will retain your value. Let's not have an identity crisis; that needs to be a thing of the past.

I Want My Sex Back

After experiencing the agony in thought, conflicted in ignorance with how beautiful they had been created, D could only remember the doctor asking that backwards counting be initiated. As the count began, 10, 9, 8, 7..., he realized the reality while under heavy sedation. In that white room, the last thing his senses recalled were sounds of the machines beeping, fluid filling the lines drip by drip, the smell of chlorine in the air, the sight of white as the lights were the object of focus, and his body slowly disconnecting. Suddenly at the count of seven there was the absence of photons. When he opened his eyes next, things would never again be as they were. Life itself would change into the facade the surgeons were creating. But was it the moment when the process was to be completed and satisfaction finally reached?

The first question that D asked was, "Did it work?" Questions flooded his mind: *Are we finally on the other side of the genetically illusive fence? Was the impossible made possible by the mortal surgeon's hands?* Or have we been deluded into conceiving such a thought, challenging our mental fortitude? In change, we have created an apparent shift that remains the same. It seems as though it is true what we often hear: "The more things change, the more they remain the same." Or have we convinced ourselves that things have really changed?

Initially it was thought that only if the hormone therapy was able to work, that would be fine. Prior to D's receiving hormone therapy, conflicts erupted as the fantasy outweighed the gravity of reality. Next, the idea of getting his voice to the desired pitch was the target— which was done. This should have made D happy, but there was the lingering sense of incompleteness. Thoughts of chest adjustment came into play. *This surely will make me look as the originals are purported to be.* Surprisingly, it was not enough. It then came time for the final act. Gender reassignment would mortify that which should not have been.

It was a great hope that when the final sex realignment took place, D would experience completeness, but it was different from all the other gradual and drastic modifications which did not bring the joy as expected or anything close to that which was desired. It was instrumental in bringing D to the revelation that things would be more complicated compared to those which were done previously. It was realized that naivety allowed the flourishing ill-equipment in truth digestion. There was no resolution to the plaguing identity dysfunction. What was created was ascetically pleasing; however, never had the surgeons explained that it would be just that, painful to use and virtually useless for the purpose intended, thereby creating more dysfunction than functionality. With the failure to reach the expected pinnacle, more evident was the gender dysphoria at its brimming peak. With no release, such a person is morphed into becoming a social pariah while being driven to despair.

The free spirit was marching to its diabolical drum, only to be burdened with baggage that cannot be packed or checked. Cosmetic is what it is as it is not really what is possessed, as it was truly never meant to have been how the mind perceived, but as it was in the initiation. Is it too late for a detransitioning? With a gasp for air like the drowning soul, D's eyes were opened only for him to realize he had not undertaken the procedure with jubilation. His thoughts were cancelled out as the gender reassignment surgeries were all the product of the union of a nightmare and a daymare. For you, it may not be a dream but an aspect of your reality; the good news is that it is never too late. Liberate and emancipate your mind. This humbling reminder indicates that there are some experiences that you don't need to have as the consequences involve a death sentence.

The Engagement

If you engage in a relationship from the wrong perspective, you will go through three main phases: lust, rust, and dust. For this reason, it is essential that you follow the process so as to minimize any regret. It is not every experience you should have for yourself, especially when you can learn from the experiences and inefficiencies of others. The big S, sex, is a single person's fantasy and sometimes the untrained married person's nightmare.

SEDUCTIVE MANIPULATION

Jezebel, Attire of Disgrace

One day King Ahab, as we read in 1 Kings 21, was visiting his summer palace in Jezreel. While looking out from his garden in admiration of its beauty and wonders, his eyes were filled as he continued engaging in mental computation of his possessions. While he was in the process, a thought of how to increase his territory filled his soul. Suddenly he noticed something over the wall of his garden. It was a beautiful vineyard with vines heavy with fruits. Based on the quality of fruit produced, the king determined the land was good. Immediately he had a growing desire within him for the vineyard, as this was what he thought he needed to enlarge the territory. Excited by the discovery, he felt the grapevines could be removed, and then whatever his heart desired could be planted. The king went to see the owner, Naboth, requesting to purchase the vineyard at any price. To the king's surprise, Naboth said that the land was not for sale as it had been in his family for generations. It was God who had given the property to his family as an inheritance, so he thought that care must be given to guarding it. The law at that time indicated that the heritage was for whomever it was given to; not even the king could capture the land. The king was angry as he was denied the estate, so now his large possessions meant nothing in comparison to the small portion of land that he had been denied.

Upon returning to his courts in Samaria, he thought about his disappointment. The more his thinking increased, the more miserable he became, to the point of depriving himself of communication. He refused to speak to anyone as he lost his appetite, creating alarm among his servants. The queen was informed. Queen Jezebel was a powerful, vindictive, malicious, wicked, cruel, immoral, and selfish woman. Israel was under the rulership of King Ahab, but Queen

Jezebel ruled the king. Hearing the concern, Queen Jezebel when to attend to the matter immediately after confirmation, laughing as she soothed the king. Queen Jezebel wrote a letter to the rulers of Jezreel, the city where Naboth lived, signing the message with the king's name and stamping it with his seal. The rulers of the city were forced to obey the writings of the king, and they did just as the letter instructed. So they brought Naboth before the people, and two wicked men were found who swore that Naboth had spoken against God and the king. The concluding instruction was that as a consequence, Naboth would be stoned to death. While on trial, Naboth indicated that the allegations were false, but the judgement was already sealed before the hearing. The people believed the story of the false witnesses, and that which was to have been done to the guilty was done to innocent Naboth.

After the orchestrated plan was completed and the news was reported that Naboth was dead, Queen Jezebel instructed the king to go and possess the land that he wanted as now there was nothing in his way. At this point, there was no need for the property to be paid for as he could receive it for free. With glee and excitement in the cunning devices of the queen, King Ahab was comforted to have his heart satisfied.

Ahab had forgotten God, but God had not forgotten Ahab. Elijah, the great prophet of God, was instructed to meet the king in the vineyard. The journey concluded with Elijah's indicating that because of the wickedness, the existence of King Ahab would be wiped from the face of the earth, including the queen and his sons. In that day, it was evident to King Ahab the price that had to be paid for engaging with seducing spirits. King Ahab's alignment with Jezebel was an alignment of Israel to hedonism. Jezebel was a Phoenician princess and a pagan. She persuaded her husband to build an altar in Samaria dedicated to the false god Baal, thereby displeasing God. This is a typical example of bad company corrupting good character. Baal was the most popular of the Canaanites' gods, indicating that the people who knew better wanted to be in style and move with the flow. These idols were oftentimes made in the shape of a bull, representing strength, fertility, lust, sexual pleasure, and power. This is what is needed to entice the appetite of men walking in darkness!

Seduction

Seduction has been used since the beginning of time as we know it. The first known seduction which occurred was seen in the Garden of Eden when the temptation to eat from the tree of knowledge of good and evil was introduced by Satan. This spirit has not left the human being and will continue to plague humanity because humankind became corrupted and now lives in corruption, with most people finding pleasure in damaging others. It is crucial for each individual to understand this lingering spirit as it is oftentimes used to manipulate actions, especially with unstable-minded individuals who have not yet cemented within their hearts that they must not sin against God. Seduction is an enticing appeal which plays on desires of fantasy, which are harmful. It is a subtle form of deception, presenting the party being deceived with the idea that he or she has situational control to do his or her will, when in actuality he or she is doing what someone else desires.

Manipulation

Manipulation is similar to being a puppet on a string, doing the will of the unseen hand. This practice is an art and takes time to develop, playing on emotional vulnerabilities with the employment of physiological social engineering, fascinating the unsuspecting mark and taking him or her out of character—while revealing the stranger within by the sleight of mind. This is the same effect observed by Satan; the propensity to engage in deviant behaviours without the connection to natural inhibition is the effect of manipulation. The paradigmatic shift suggests that we need to be vaccinated against such behaviours. "Thou wilt keep him in perfect peace, whose mind is stayed on thee: because he trusteth in thee" (Isaiah 26:3).

When an operator creates a fantasy and sells it, you begin to desire something that was initially imaginary until you allowed your imagination to manifest it in the physical. This is highly sexual and sensual in nature as it transports the unsuspecting person to perceive pleasure. It is like placing a frog into a pan of cold water on a stovetop; the frog will sit in the pan of water even as the temperature is increased. It will not move and will stay there unto death. If the water were hot, the frog would have realized it instantaneously. It is the gentle introduction that is detrimental, giving no time to recognize the end until the lights go out as the distraction covers the obvious. This approach utilizes vain appearance and decoration to entrap. It may be obvious the motive when observing disloyalty, dishonesty, and amoral behaviour; however, desires are so stimulated that it appears unthinkable to let go. The feeling of abandonment seems to be better than not to be pursued at all. This overwhelms the repressed side and breeds the need for freedom from virtue, giving the other party a chance to be the reformer or the illusion in rehabilitation. Naturally, some people will be entrapped by the broken spirit, thinking they can be fixed, as that is one factor needed to gain mind control.

The majority of people will go about things in an unprescribed fashion and as a result will encounter the shattering glass moments, which otherwise would have worn them down with time. This disappointment and conflict between the reality and the dream creates for them a burden which they wish not to carry, though it is of their own doing. With this reality in mind, and in desperation, one reveals in most instances much desired detail. This information is used to present what is lacking, filling the voids of disappointment, offering a second chance and an opportunity for restoration. Once this spark of fantasy is established, a projection will be observed, and this is the opportunity given by the unsuspecting. The aesthetic of this interaction is beautifully tabled in favour of the facade of perfection, causing the captivation and long-lasting seduction, appealing to detail vanity. This combination is time-consuming, exercising patience, mixing sensuality and spirituality, and transforming the whole charade into a memorable experience filled with the undertone of ambiguity.

Transformation

Some people naturally seek to escape the confines of the expected norm by increasing or decreasing their gender roles to those that are more tolerable, playing on masculinity and femininity. The male tends to decrease in masculinity, thus increasing in the softer, more feminine side, causing those of the opposite gender to be comfortable while reducing the intimidation of those who are masculine. Females might seek after a more commanding masculine persona in order to blend with the masculine group. These persons tend to entice as their classification is difficult as they fashion their own image, creating alluring enthusiasm. They then use that power to exploit, creating the fantasy of childhood behaviour to encourage ease and a reduction in vigilance before the venomous sting is employed, as it often is. These types may be subtle, may blend in, or may even stand out as stars, bringing escape to those who interact with them.

There are seducers who manipulate with teasing and enticement, generally with that which is provocative. They titillate desire and trap people emotionally. While they are emotionally detached, they make use of their inherent understanding of emotional imbalance by way of selective withdrawal, keeping the victim unbalanced, unstable, and always wondering. This is a game which causes the enslavement of desire. Such people bait others with promising rewards, giving hope for satisfaction and bliss, both of which are elusive. The relational intertwine causes the continuation of interest. These individuals may be considered narcissistic.

Many individuals like those who are charming. These individuals seduce by hinting at sex, creating sexual tension; however, they will go no further. The tension created is used as the rope to lure the victim. It is like placing someone in a trance, reducing one's analytical reasoning ability by appealing to self-esteem, ego, and vanity while periodically applying a light touch to keep the attention during the exploration of desires. This is done by making the unsuspecting person the centre of attention as the revelation of who they are becomes evident. It operates on the principle of employing flattery individualized to account for the person's insecurities.

The charismatic is compelling on a large scale, in which droves of people are hypnotized simultaneously as the presence of the charismatic excites. Success in this area comes from the quality of being self-assured, confident, and contented and possessing a sense of purpose. Possessing what most people lack creates this following. People lose self in the cause because of the promise of an adventure. This natural display plays to the desire for something to believe in, creating mystical mystery.

The Process of Seduction and Manipulation

Seduction and manipulation are carried out strategically in systematic stages. Always the process is initiated with selfish desires. The seduced is the one who loses the most, losing time, stability, energy, power, and even self. Before any seduction is done, it begins with a thought, and this thought leads the seducer to accomplish the challenge which has been set. To the seducer, this is all a game to be played repeatedly with as many people who are willing to be enticed. Understanding that everyone lives in their own world, the seducer seeks to take the unsuspecting person outside that world, penetrating his or her mind with thoughts originating from the seducer. The victims are lured and then captured in an evil net, similar to a bird being caught in a snare.

Scouting

In the beginning of the process, there is a scouting period in which the prey is selected who meets the predetermined criteria and is able to produce or give access to that which is needed. The attention of this individual needs to be captured. After the selection comes the idea to be marketed. During these formative stages, interest is stirred in the prey towards the seducer. The approaches may vary based on resistance. It can start with friendship development or theatrics, creating a mystical atmosphere or creating covetousness as an attractive idea. Once the prey acknowledges the seducer, intimacy develops with an appeal to desire. A void is identified, and the individual will create an opportunity for it to be filled. The one who is being seduced will be lured with the impregnation of his or her mind through fantasies and ideas, for which inclination exists to be fulfilled. This was the tactic Haman used in his vendetta against a Jewish man named Mordecai, tricking the Persian king Ahasuerus into issuing a decree calling for the elimination of the Jewish people. Further in the story, it is seen where Haman himself is deceived, expecting honour at a banquet, only for his plot to destroy the Jews to be revealed.

False Security

In the process of creating a sense of security and developing trust, attachment, and dependency, the seducer shifts control in favour of his or her agenda. He or she sends mixed signals to keep the interest of the prey, causing the prey to desire the seducer. Such desirability is created by the seducer's putting on a persona of monopolization, creating an illusion. In order for this to work, a need must be manufactured. It should be noted that a person who is whole with a grounded mind and focus cannot be easily seduced, as such a person has actualized contentment. Jael, the wife of Heber, as shown in Judges 4, lured the Canaanite general Sisera into a false sense of security, and when he least expected it, she drove a tent peg into his temple.

The Injection

The seducer injects himself or herself with that which is needed to solve the problem, overcome the challenge, or expand the limits with the insinuation and constant suggestion to become one with the spirit of the other. When this is achieved, then comes the temptation, which preys on the victim's weaknesses. This is the same play Satan used on Eve. "For God doth know that in the day ye eat thereof, then your eyes shall be opened, and ye shall be as gods, knowing good and evil" (Genesis 3:5). Now that the temptation is presented, the prey will be led astray by the seducer against his or her better judgement by way of the use of words, paying attention to details and then subtly omitting those details, creating questions and doubts in mind. For the best effect, the prey is penetrated in isolation. When doubt sets in, the trust that was developed is then relied upon as a safety net, with the prey not realizing that the seducer has a different agenda, one that will result in destruction.

The spiritual veneer created causes the individual to find more comfort in thinking the move will elevate the mind to a higher dimension, luring the prey to consider transgression. Manipulation is then in effect in which the seducer mixes pleasure and pain, attaching and detaching, maintaining both closeness and distance in equal measure while closing in on desire. All the seeds have been planted for the final execution of causing the prey to give in to that which the inhibition otherwise would prevent. Seducers tend to place their victims between a rock and a hard place; the seduced, already confused and disoriented, is now much more likely to comply.

Execution

In Genesis 27, Jacob and Rebekah (Jacob's mother) conspired to trick Jacob's father, Isaac, into giving his blessing to Jacob instead of to his twin brother, Esau. This caused a separation of the brothers for a while. Jacob fled with his brother's blessing and went to stay with his uncle Laban. While there, Jacob was overtaken with affectionate emotions towards Rachel. His uncle agreed to his serving for seven years in exchange for his daughter Rachel in marriage, but after the seven years passed, Laban got crafty and gave his daughter Leah instead, who was older to marry. In order to receive Rachel, Jacob would have to serve another seven years.

Having the will controlled is the final move in getting what was intended from the very first moment. Seduction and manipulation are acts of deception and are evil. You should avoid engaging in such acts. The aftereffect upon the prey's realizing what has happened when the trance is over is damaging as the seducer moves on to another. The reality is more disappointing than the fantasy created. "But evil men and seducers shall wax worse and worse, deceiving, and being deceived" (2 Timothy 3:13).

The mind must be clear at all times in order to discern the evil snares of the Devil. The family is expected to be a safe place and a safe space, but it is not always as expected. Too often unfitting behaviours are practised and members engage in the carnal seduction of each other without counting the destructive cost, only concerned with self-gratification at others' immediate and extended expense. While in the land of Zoar, Lot's daughters induced intoxication upon their father and lay with him, the older one night and the younger the night after. Both were impregnated, and eventually each bore a son. The firstborn son was Moab (of the Moabites), and the younger son was Benammi (of the Ammonites). This great evil caused war between the two both tribes. One indiscretion produced generations of war.

The Playground

Seduction and manipulation are from Satan, and they are evident in schools, work institutions, social interactions, advertisements, and almost everywhere your eyes can be focused. In order to overcome seduction and manipulation, a follower of the Creator should study the things of God, rightly dividing the Word of Truth. Humans are enticed into seduction because of carnality, thinking on things in the temporal without subjecting them to the law of God, thereby creating enmity against God. Confusion is necessary for the wrath of the Devil to be unleashed. It is the same manipulations which have been used for generations. The introduction of sin into the world placed a divide between God and humankind.

This same seducing spirit has been passed down from generation to generation. Humanity should never underestimate the competence of Satan to deceive. Let us no longer allow our souls to become consumed with things of a fantasy, but let us consider the reality within the reality. "And the great dragon was cast out, that old serpent, called the Devil, and Satan, which deceiveth the whole world: he was cast out into the earth, and his angels were cast out with him" (Revelation 12:9).

LOVE PRINCIPLE

The feeling that you feel when you have the need for healing, which compounds the feeling, is nothing but the feverish excitement preceding a bowel movement. This should not be misdiagnosed as anything other than what it is. Three often misused words are *lust*, *infatuation*, and *love*; and though all serve their purpose, a distinction needs to be established.

Infatuation

Infatuation is considered as an intense but short-lived passion for something/someone. It is a state in which one, being smitten, is carried away by extravagant passion, developing strong romantic or platonic feelings. This is typically experienced in dating. Infatuation is sometimes referred to as *puppy love*. Intellectual infatuations do exist as infatuation can be extended to activities, ideas, mindsets, and objects. The fleeting nature of this feeling does not qualify for love as it exists on no foundation, principle, or moral. *Infatuation* comes from the French word *fatuus*, meaning "fool/foolishness; making foolish to affect with folly to weaken the intellectual power of, or to deprive of sound judgement", as defined by *Webster's Dictionary*. This is a counterfeited virtue of God made prominent by the work of Satan; this forgery in its primitive state is indistinguishable. In an effort to reduce the deviation from the original template, one must take time in the process of testing. On this quest, the mind must be in a stable state or else an illusion will be created that is only a figment of the imagination, causing great delusion. It causes one to fail to see that which is before one as one floats on the clouds of misconstrued emotions. If you ever think that you are suddenly in love and you have an overriding sense of better judgement, it could indicate infatuation.

Feeling thrilled but not happy, longing to trust yet overwhelmed by suspicion, one becomes, in the absence of the infatuated object, compromised with misery, jealousy, and a sense of incompleteness.

Imbalanced hormones and surges of dopamine rush through the dopaminergic projections, causing an inflated sensation of mellowness, initiating a cascade of subsequent reactions in which norepinephrine flows through the brain, stimulating adrenaline production, which increases the rate of blood circulation, breathing, and carbohydrate metabolism while preparing the muscles for exertion. Already laced in the consumed products is phenylethylamine (PEA), an organic compound, a natural monoamine alkaloid and trace amine which acts as a central nervous system stimulant in the human. This in combination with the others causes bliss. This powerful compound is coupled with oxytocin, which acts as a neurotransmitter and is premier in sexual arousal. Oxytocin signals the inevitable feelings of emotional attachment and induces the desire to cuddle, which can override logic if allowed to be expressed in the untrained neophyte's relationship. Similar to the effects of drug usage in which there will be no other time like the first, the corruption of the pure creates an exotic ecstatic compromise which can be fatal. Over time there will be a natural development of tolerance to the chemical effects, making it more challenging to reach the pinnacle. Attempts to reach such a place by many are futile with only the knockout effect to remind them of the attempt. The rain stops and the flood ceases, the sun comes out, and all the water is returned from whence it came. The drying of the hormones can give the disillusionment that the relationship has ended, along with the affection and the infatuation. The actual question is, can something end that never started?

Infatuation can be identified after the expression of the symptoms, in which one exhibits a complete reliance on emotion and has tunnel vision for the object of infatuation while developing an inability to perceive anything outside the narrowed vantage point. The feeling occurs instantaneously, even at first glance, as the system lacks the durability and robustness to stand the challenges and test of time. Fluctuating interest causes emotional destabilization and manic attacks. The infatuation destination is reached when the object becomes the only existing item in the universe, with both parties clutching and wrapped around the bodies of each other, similar to the relational orbiting of the earth around the sun. When there is the revelation, even the blind eyes will see and appreciate that which is seen.

Obsession

Obsession could be considered a half-shoot of infatuation. It is based on weak emotional development and mental immaturity and involves an interest in irrationality and addiction. To be obsessed is to have one's thoughts continually preoccupied with the object of desire, with the untamed intrusion of this object in mind in spite of the lack of mutual reciprocation. It is next to worshipping (a person, thing, place, etc.), being fixated—the expression of obsessive-compulsive disorder towards the object, which is a trap as in idée fixe. Affections and attachments are strictly based on fantasies of perfection or on your wishes exclusively, no matter the concerns for the other party. The severity of obsession may increase to the degree that one neglects necessary functions needed for sustenance, including eating, sleeping, working, exercising, and attending to one's hygiene.

Stalkers

Infatuation is dangerous as it leads to obsession. Eventual it may lead to stalking, which, if not arrested, may cause death to self and others. The stalker is a person or group who engages in the process of stalking. Stalking is unwanted repeated surveillance by an individual (the stalker) or group (governmental or nongovernmental agency), resulting in harassment, intimidation, and entrapment without permission. These techniques have been repeatedly used to compromise individuals on the quest towards dehumanization. The stalker typically calls on the phone and hangs up, tracks the victim's patterns of movement, and follows the individual around to gather intelligence. After pattern recognition is developed, alongside continuous monitoring, different interventions and intrusions are made, creating discomfort and unease. The imposition of the stalker and his or her integration into the life of the victim may develop and eventually become fatal. This behaviour is long-lasting and creates emotional, mental, and even physical scarring of the individuals involved, to the point of a person choosing to live in hiding in order to remain anonymous to the stalker, be it an individual, a governmental agency, and/or a nongovernmental agency.

Samson's Infatuation

Samson was a legendary Israelite warrior belonging to the judges. An angel of the Lord appeared to Manoah and his wife, who were trying to conceive, informing them of Samson's conception. He was to be a Nazirite, meaning he could not drink alcohol or eat unclean food, and no razor was to touch his head. The child's prenatal plan was given prior to his arrival; this brought great joy and hope for the family and the people. The people considered him a glimmer of hope against the Philistine oppression. Like any child, Samson explored, but he soon realized he was not like any other. He was endowed with the Spirit of God in the form of strength. In his youth, while surveying the land, he laid his eyes upon a woman in Timnath, of the daughters of the Philistines, who was visually satisfying. At that moment, he demanded of his parents that they get her for him to be his wife. This was not the custom, but his eyes were blinded.

Samson's expression reveals the effects of infatuation as he appeared to be experiencing "love at first sight". He did not realize the grave incompatibilities that existed between his people and the woman's people. The Israelites were under oppression from the Philistines, who worshipped gods and whose ways were in conflict with the purity required of the Israelites. The possible destruction in forming a union with this woman was evident, but Samson's emotions took charge of the situation, to the point that he commanded his parents to get the woman, who failed to actualize the standards of God. This was a woman who was not known by Samson's people. Nor was any time allotted for courting and introducing her to family and friends. Importantly, there is no indication that counsel was sought from God prior to Samson's moving on with the decision. In a display of misguided youthful exuberance, he compromised the whole process and did it backwards. Had it been a pure expression, the Lord would have been consulted and His instructions heeded. Making the decision and then expecting God to fall in line would not have emerged.

Samson, who was strong-minded, decided that this relationship was in his best interests, against the counsel of his parents. He went down to seek after the woman again, but a lion attacked. The Spirit of the Lord came upon Samson and allowed him to conquer the beast. On his return journey, the same lion's carcass had a swarm of bees and honey around it. Knowing the vow he had taken, Samson was not to touch the dead or anything pertaining to it, yet he took the honey and ate of it. He also took this honey to his parents for consumption, who had no idea of its origins, and they ate it.

The Philistine woman who pleased Samson was to marry him. A marriage celebration in those days lasted seven days. A riddle was given to her people about the occasion of the lion and honey that none could solve. So members of the philistine community threatened the family of the woman so as to extract information about the matter Samson had revealed to her, which eventually was disseminated among her people. The reward for solving the riddle was thirty changes of garment, so it was time for the matter to be expounded. Samson declared his disgruntlement with how the mystery had been solved as they'd solved it with the use of extortive vices. In honouring the reward for answering, he slew thirty men and took their spoils to give as the reward. Again it is observed that Samson touched the carcasses of the dead in order to get the garments. Samson was angry about the situation, and he ventured to the woman's father's house, only to find out that his wife had been given to his companion who was a friend.

In time Samson nearly realized the deception. It was at the time of the wheat harvest that Samson visited his wife with a kid, believing that he could go to her chambers, but her father did not suffer him to go in. Her father presented another of his daughters to Samson because the one he wanted had already been given to another. In a release of his anguish, Samson used foxes tied together to burn down the family's vineyards and olive trees. After this manner, the wife whom Samson should have had and her family were killed by their own people.

Sometimes disappointments are presented before us, not to dishonour us but to secure our future. If these people were so vile as to kill their own, it shows the corruption that would have entered into the Israelites' camp, which not only could have destroyed Samson but also could have taken his people's heart away from God. A little while afterwards, Samson settled with his people. He served them as a judge for twenty years. There is always safety with those who are like-minded and connected to the principles of God.

Lust

Many have been deceived by an error which fertilizes the thought that love is an accident. There is no evidence to support the claim of accidental love. Any accident resembling love is actually lust. No one falls into love; it just does not happen. However, individuals can fall into *lust*, believing they are in love. The hostility of humanity towards the principles outlined by the Originator is the reason for much demise. Proverbs 6:25 reads, "Lust not after her beauty in thine heart; neither let her take thee with her eyelids." If there is such a strong caution being given to us to stay away from these situations, then the probability of an unfavourable outcome is compelling. Lust can be characterized as a psychological force that causes an intense wanting within someone, an effort to fill the emotional reservoir. These cravings can be mundane or unorthodox, ranging from a distinct desire for a specific food or particular item to a more common longing for money, power, sexuality, and sex in conventional and unconventional forms. We must abstain from coveting our neighbour's house, husband, or wife. The eyes of a person should not become red with covetousness or green with greed.

The operation of lust is effected in the expression of self-interest to the detriment of both involved parties. If the only reason you speak with someone is for sexual gratification, then all between you is rooted in lust. These types of objectifying relationships are unhealthy; they inevitably lead to loss, distrust, and misery. The personality and character of the individual should be of the highest priority in lasting relationships. Prudence should be exercised when engaging in a relationship with strangers, and controls should be put into place to monitor relationships with friends and acquaintances as lust can be conjured in the heart and expressed in a moment. Entertaining the manifestation of lustful passion will end in its victim's being filled with shame, regret, and remorse. Lust is exclusively motivated by selfish interest and the intent to fulfil one's own wants and desires at any cost. Society has not seen it fit to address the root cause of the problem but feels more comfortable to capitalize economically, placing a Band-Aid over the festering wound. Instead of encouraging total abstinence and expression of self-control, society finds it more lucrative to encourage the young, adolescents and adults alike, to engage in the practice of feeding their lustful desire as the corporations will provide the condoms to prevent pregnancy and diseases allegedly. They have marketed these things very well, in line with a greater hidden agenda in which they encourage abortion and make facilities available when the medication fails to work as intended. These corporations have many research facilities to study humans like animals without the subjects' realizing they have been caught in the trap of a science experiment. Today more diseases exist than have been recorded in previous times. Society will not reveal the grave effects of ill deeds, because if that were done, then whole industries would collapse, meaning that more people would become financially free and more interdependent, instead of being exclusively dependent on the oppressor.

We read in 1 John 2:16, "For all that is in the world, the lust of the flesh, and the lust of the eyes, and the pride of life, is not of the Father, but is of the world." The passage prior describes how humanity has been robbed of their inheritance simply because they have a desire for that which they do not need. It is unwise to become a co-labourer with the carnal, with the eyes being the open windows to the world, which desires those things which are in the physical. It is often forgotten that humankind is more spirit than flesh. Having the spirit of pride is the cause of blindness among many, preventing them from seeing that all human beings are equal on all levels and should not be discriminated against based on status, wealth, religion, locality, or any other measure. In deviation, individuals live outside of the structured parameters of the Father and Creator of the world. Because of the natural inclination towards self, selfishness, and pride, capitalism is allowed to prosper and flourish. Though many are bombarded by the temptation of lust, people should be encouraged to shun the very appearance of this evil. Relationships based on lust end in sexual gratification, which conflicts with the principle of God as sex should only occur within the confines of marriage. This type of exploitation and exploration damages the relationship and creates unnecessary baggage, which is routinely taken into subsequent relationships and typically requires spiritual intervention is one is to experience freedom. The flesh and the spirit operate on two different frequencies; however, if we walk in the spirit, we will not fulfil the lust of the flesh.

Many individuals place themselves in compromising positions and seek after relationships with individuals who are in the clutches of the Devil, believing they can create any form of change in such individuals. That is a deception. We are not able to change people; it is only the Holy Spirit that has such a capacity. We need to be reminded that what we do today is a contribution to the future because our lives are the subtotal of our choices. This indicates that it is imperative that we choose appropriately in the present in order to enjoy a desirable future. The young and ageing population go on dates of varying types, such as in rum bars, at strip clubs, at other clubs, at parties, at carnivals, and at astrological gatherings, and engage in speed dates online, which dating eventually goes offline. These endeavours indicate a direction for which the end is known. Why are these the only places that stimulate interest and participation? Could it be a reflection of who we are but one that we have not yet realized? If you are engaged in a relationship with someone in any of these areas that conflict with the Spirit of God, it would be unreasonable to expect you to make a radical transformation upon request. You should keep to a strict path while on this journey to secure your lineage, sanity, and peace.

Amnon's Lust

The type of sordid relationship revealed between Amnon and Tamar is undesirable on all levels. Their relationship depicts the lurking dangers involved with lustful thought, which waits on an opportunity for expression. Amnon had sexual desires for his sister Tamar. We know this because of the expression of his vexed sick state for Tamar, because she was a virgin. This strikes a chord. As a dagger in his eyes, she was perceived by him to be fair, indicating his attraction to her physical countenance. Surprisingly what he did had already been done before it was done; in his heart, he had taken her virginity and violated her purity, leaving her to disgrace. What was lacking was the opportunity, which was finally created by an alleged friend called Jonadab. Bad company corrupts character or reveals that which need not be seen. Amnon's lustful relationship with his sister was overwhelming. In an effort to execute his plans in the physical, he schemed the mode of attack for the undertaking.

The plan was to pretend to be sick and then request his sister to bring food. The food that she brought was not the food that he had the intention to consume; instead his passion was set on having her as the meal. "So said, so done." Tamar, who was being lured, went in to her brother as the king had instructed and made food before him to be eaten. After the meal preparation was completed, the food was laid down to be eaten, but Amnon refused to eat. Instead, he sent out all the men before him. When Tamar had brought the food, Amnon asked that she lie with him; however, she refused and explained that to do so would conflict with the practices of Israel as it was folly and would bring shame. Upon explaining the situation, she offered a solution, namely that he could ask his father for her, having confidence that the request would not have been refused.

Though Tamar had given Amnon a way of escape, he refused that path. He abused his strength over her and deflowered his sister whom he claimed to loved. After Amnon defiled Tamar, he hated her exceedingly to the point he put her out and shut the door upon her. It was not because of anything that she did; it was the conviction of his sin that was destroying him. He was consumed with iniquity, and he robbed his sister whom he was to have protected, just because of a selfish desire and the enabling of a bad friend's advice. He left his sister weeping and placed her out as a stranger. The cost of lust is nothing less than destruction. In the end, two years later Absalom, the brother of Tamar, gave the order for the death of Amnon. Amnon lost his life because of his failure to follow protocol, exhibit good manners, and observe proper etiquette. His indiscretion caused the defilement and exile of another individual. It should be noted that being raped is not the fault of the one assaulted under any circumstance. Adultery, avariciousness, covetousness, fraud, exploitation, fornication, gluttony, lasciviousness, lewdness, pride, rape, and uncleanness are all lustful expressions. Though an exhilarating thrill is experienced when one is infatuated, care must be taken to ensure that decisions are not made based on a short-term effect with a long-term repercussion. Let us make all things honest in the sight of all people.

Commitment, Emotion/Intimacy, and the Passion-Based Classification of Relationships

Low Commitment and Low Intimacy with High Passion

This is typical of bloated infatuation, almost an obsession. It is to be trapped in the thought of the person more than in the person or object of infatuation. The intoxicating nature of that which is overwhelming causes a longing for something that, or someone whom, has not necessarily been experienced prior. It may be manifested with physical arousal, producing a fluctuation of high and low sensations. If the object or subject is perceived to reciprocate, it is appreciated; however, if not, a continuation in the fantasy of passion will satisfy.

Low Commitment and High Intimacy with Low Passion

This is experienced in the initial stages of a friendship relationship. There is an emotional connection with the person and the interaction, causing the release of dopamine, giving rise to closeness, warmth, and caring interaction. Confidence is developed over time, and because of the lack of commitment, the relationship can fade into the background without notice.

High Commitment and Low Intimacy with Low Passion

In Eastern culture, this marks the beginning of a marriage relationship, or the plateau of the relationship in Western culture. Passion and intimacy can develop at the appropriate time given the changing dynamics. In this relationship, there is a commitment to the cause based on the predetermined arrangement of the relationship's framework and its future for the greater good.

High Commitment and High Intimacy with Low Passion

This type of relationship is experienced with a best friend and is typically long-lasting. The two people have a genuine affection towards each other, bringing warmth, closeness, and confidence. The relationship is not fuelled by a passion for devouring in a carnal manner. Commitment to the relationship is well established, and it is expected that each party may assuredly count on the other.

Low Commitment and High Intimacy with High Passion

This is often confused with romance, leading to a "one-off" sexual experience or multiple on-call experiences without the desire for commitment, as there is no need to provide it. It is similar to getting milk from a cow that is not yours, so there is really no incentive or desire to commit to the care, development, nurturing, and maintenance. These types of relationships are classified as lustful.

High Commitment and High Intimacy with High Passion

This is the ideal relationship for a marriage union, one that is balanced with regards to commitment, intimacy, and passion. Love is being displayed based on the combined effect. The engagement will allow the marriage to last as long as it was designed to exist—until death. The stick-to-itiveness enables the relationship to continue as it is nurtured and protected from harm, and as damages are fixed and constant restorative work is done. In this experience, each partner considers the needs of the other and places them above their own, making the necessary sacrifice for the relationship's growth and development, which is embodied by loyalty.

Love

Seeing and understanding all the challenges and deceptive counterfeits that exist, we may become hastened in assuming paralysis, but I submit to you that the only thing you need is the truth. All the other "love-like" relationships are irrelevant when you have the truth about love and its purity. In such a relationship, we are now mentally emancipated and liberated, reconnecting the nerve endings which have caused convulsions and paralysis as we become energized with courage. There is no need to study the counterfeit as it can take varying forms, looking as though it is the original; if we know which one is the original, we are in a position to identify the deceptions that exist. The question is not if we can identify. It should be, will I choose to fall into the open trench even though it is known that it will take me six feet under?

Even the precocious have only developed a transient understanding of love, which gradually dissipates with the external influences of society when the foundation is not adequately excavated and developed in the appropriate areas. Very few have any idea or concept of the gravitational magnitude of this most overused and misunderstood word. The government does not understand it, politicians fail to grasp it, entrepreneurs neglect to exercise it, celebrities are evaded by it, clergies seldom teach it, the law fails in its execution and adjudication, and society is in a drowning confusion because they know not of it. Those who have been allowed to experience it are likened unto slaves who were in bondage and are now free and will die before returning to slavery. Had love been evident in society, there would have been no need for either bond or free, separation, discrimination, inequalities, corruption, injustice, genocide, homicides, or suicides, among other debilitating vices. The simple solution to the world's problem is in four letters which make up one word (LOVE), and that one word roots back to three letters which equate to one word (GOD). Love is a principle that has its foundation in God. It cannot be expressed by someone who is not connected spiritually with the Originator. If a person becomes convinced that he or she has expressed love as an unsaved individual, such a person is gravely mistaken. "Love-likeness" does not qualify as love; it is counterfeit. It aids to create a net of safety that does not exist.

In an effort to amplify the principle, we will journey to the beginning. We read in John 1:1–4, "In the beginning was the Word, and the Word was with God, and the Word was God. The same was in the beginning with God. All things were made by him; and without him was not any thing made that was made. In him was life; and the life was the light of men."

Our understanding and appreciation of existence leads us in the vastness of nothingness, becoming something through aseity. The self-existing nature of God reveals the information that we need to accept. Our Originator is an eternal, self-sustaining, and self-existing God who was, is, and is yet to come. He has unlimited capabilities of existence; it is impossible for Him to run out of energy as He is energy, and it is improbable for Him to go out of existence because He is existence. He neither ages nor dies as He is so constant that He changes not. Our Father is independent and does not need any part of His creation for existence; uniqueness is His natural attribute, which no one can match or measure. In trying to size God, it is like comparing a grain of sand to the vastness of all universes, or hydrogen and oxygen to water in all the world of worlds. God, in His wisdom, was mindful to have reminded Job of the infinite distance and imbalance between God and humankind when God was explaining how the foundations of the world came into being.

Though we are incomparable to the Creator, we know we have a Creator who regards us highly. In His speaking of His sons and daughters from the ends of the earth, we see humanity is created for the pleasure and glory of God. He chose us to be the recipient of power, peace, joy, grace, and eventually eternal life. The Word was in the beginning, and the Word was with God, and the Word was God. This idea directs our minds to the idea that all existence came from God and His power. This display of authority and command of existence is profound as the Master Architect demonstrated delicate precision.

What is about to be revealed in the coming moments will shock most people in the world today. The ideology you have been previously served by persons suffering the same symptoms they warn against is made up of error and lies. Human beings have been designed with the capacity to love; however, they are not able to manifest love until they are connected to the Creator. Humankind, being evil, has an inclination in the conscious state to present a gift which is good to humankind, but there is a heavenly Father who is holy and wants to present an even greater gift, the gift of the Holy Spirit. Giving gifts is not necessarily equal to love. It may appear as such, but it's not the case. Evil people do offer a gift out of need, want, or abundance with underlying motives and intentions. Love-likeness is a display of affection and attributes similar to those expressed by people connected to the Source of love without any foundation, understanding, or attachment. This expression of love is basically a mirror of the expected norms of people connected to the Creator.

We read in 1 John 4:8, "He that loveth not knoweth not God; for God is love." The message that should be transcendent and resonant is the principle the world has missed in its quest to solve its problems. Ungodly men and women cannot express love. Love can only be manifested and expressed from a converted heart, and any other expression is love-likeness. Sad to say, many in relationships today, both married and unmarried, have not yet experienced love or its surrounding dimension; it is for this reason that the world has such increased rates of divorce, deceit, neglect, rape, violence, and so on. The proclivity to sin will ruin lives. Meaninglessly, lives are being lobotomized, and persons are being institutionalized because of the destructive concepts of damnation fed to them. It is unfair, unjust, and unmerited for any more people to needlessly experience such a fate, either in this generation or the one coming up. You cannot possess something if you are not associated with the Originator who manifests it. God is love. If you have an inability to love, it means that you do not know God. The reverse is true: if you don't know God, you cannot love.

In having a relationship, you need to understand the other party's principles, standards, and values so that you may determine your compatibility. It is for this reason that we synchronize with our friends in relationships, operating within the predetermined parameters. Two can only walk together if they agree. It is urgent that we agree with the leadings and principles of God if we wish to experience the benefits of love. Love is everlasting, unchanging, and pure, similar to the attributes of God. It is for us to find comfort in His promises and His will. In order to display our faithfulness, we must uphold and maintain the commandments to love God and love humankind (Exodus 20). Love is so principled that it does not need to carry feelings; it is love in spite of, not love-likeness, which operates because of. Now that we have grasped the concepts and understood the root, it is now time to enjoy the fruit. The expression of this principle is in whole and not in part. It encompasses the dimension of the body, mind, and spirit while revealing its beauty as time progresses, dancing the delicate balance of dignity and integrity. Love is given freely as life itself, not because of any owing, but just in case there comes that time. Heed the good Word.

Love is necessary for the law to be executed; without it there is riotous living wherein things fall apart, the house is in shambles, and the society is decadent. Many today would rather receive than give, and this attitude promotes pride, greed, gluttony, lust, wrath, envy, and sloth, deadening and killing the spirit of wisdom, understanding, counsel, knowledge, piety, fortitude, and the fear of the Lord. If we claim to possess the attribute of love, then service should be our priority; we would accept our responsibility to humanity. In enlarging one's territory, small steps need to be taken. The more people we can help on the journey of life, the more effective our lives will become. The love mentioned in Galatians resonates. The main essence is self-sacrifice for the benefit of the one who is loved. Such love means death to self, and that means defeat of sin, which is self-will and self-gratification. The word *serves* means to render service doing that which is to the advantage of someone else without the hope of a reward or a return. This is the kind of love we are to have for one another; this is what it means when the Bible says, "By love serve one another." God's intent is that we serve out of the heart, expecting nothing in return. Having love one for another is a display of discipleship to God.

In a society of debit and credit, in which commercialism causes an increase in the debt threshold, individuals are indebted for more money than they have to spare. This way of living will continue as what is wanted takes precedence over that which is needed. During the whole process, let us remember to owe no person anything and to share in love as much as possible. Love is intertwined with obedience and purity of spirit and is without limits or boundaries except its own unconfinable confines. No reciprocation is needed. With love, in time the vilest of people will become as malleable as clay right before they embrace love. The principle of love is without feeling, yet producing without it, one feels its absence. In its presence, contentment is the essence, transcending the stratosphere as love becomes molecules of the atmosphere. Once experienced, love cannot be unexperienced, and the desire to be embodied to become one's best self is now paramount. The law exists as it was created by God, who is the law and is love. It is deceit for a person to claim to live without sharing in the experience of love, for to live is to love, and to love is to have a relationship with God.

The intra-extradimensional expository outlining of love, the chronicle of its expression, is evident in 1 Corinthians 13, which aids in the simplification. It reminds us that without love, we are nothing, in the same way that without God, nothingness exists. It is a nihility! In understanding this passage, we must draw the parallel of charity equating to love. An unwillingness to love because our love is not being returned is a reflection of love-likeness. "I cannot love him because this was done." In the expression of love, we should not seek to gain points, as that is hypocrisy and selfishness. Only the measure that you would love to receive is what you should extend to another, and that practice will only be of value if you have love. Individuals who have no connection to love or the lover will not understand the wisdom of the expression; they will have a misplaced motive to their own detriment. They will want the undesirable, thinking it is of value, not realizing that the way that seems right to them will lead them to death. Reciprocity has no leverage in the fabric of love as the self is nonexistent; hence, there is no exhausting of emotions.

It takes a supernatural response for the expression of love. After the Fall of Humankind, the value system began going down the path of decadence, which eroded more with the passing of time, and the principle became more legalistic than practical in expression. Only an external element of supreme authority can elevate a person to such a moral standing of restoration in which dominion can be expressed in harmony with the plan of the initial creating. Love takes time to develop and to mature to its full state, in which the fruit will be evident. There is no need for discontentment or resentful longing aroused by someone else's possessions, qualities, or attributes, and there is no need for love to consider itself and become consumed in the fire of pride that is kindled. It was this form of kindling which caused iniquity to enter the heart of Lucifer, which clouded his judgement as he voluntarily evicted himself from his former home. The exercising of agape love does not lose patience with people; it is friendly, generous, and considerate. To be jealous in the realm of humanity implies being displeased with the accomplishments and successes of others, which conflicts with the selfless nature. There is no need for egotistical or narcissistic behaviour. Especially with the maturation of the spiritual gifts, the inferiority complex and insecurities will fail to be visible or will no long be persistent as the call to a higher power is received. Love-likeness abides for a season as it is temporal, while love endures into eternity. If the mind is not focused on the eternal, then love will never be expressed, causing the vicious cycle of ephemeral instant gratification which intoxicates the mind, clouds the judgement, and lowers inhibition while living in the cycle of justification of the irrational decisions.

Plausible deniability fails to find a place in the presence of love. For such a reason, the person who expresses love is upright and without blame. These people behave with dignity, understanding the responsibility set upon them to be reflective ambassadors of heaven. Unseemly behaviour speaks to a loss of direction in which acts are inappropriate and misrepresentations are observed or displayed without extending respect as a courtesy to authority. It is for each individual to determine which path is more important, to love or be loved, and if it is to love or be loved, the ideal is the existence of a heterozygote situation with reciprocity. There is no reason for love to seek its own agenda; it is transparent while putting the interests of others above self. Outside the confines of marriage, the act of deliberately arousing sexual desire or interest will be absent. The action of love does not speak in an intentional effort to make someone angry, upset, or uneasy.

It is evident that the dimensions of love can only be displayed with the elevation of the spiritual person. Love bears, hopes, believes, and endures all things; it never fails or vanishes. In bearing all things, it speaks to the flexibility of love to remain constant and be adaptable to life's variability as it directs our attention towards its ability to outlive sorrows, disappointments, cruelty, distortions, and indifference, displaying the ability to protect, cover, and guard. It is not interested in indecent exposure, an exhibition of shortcomings, faults, and flaws. It believes all things, hopes for all things, and does not exploit gullibility. Instead it has a trustful attitude, seeing the good while giving the benefit of the doubt until proven otherwise. It is more on the side of believing the best while valuing others' worth. While grounded in God, hope is expressed, even the hope of the prodigal son's returning home, while in the process persevering. Love's ability to survive under extraneous circumstances is remarkable as patience is displayed. The love we have been exposed to shows one who is indispensable and invincible. As we move further, love's immortal nature is revealed.

The eternal nature of love, never failing, indicates the perpetuating nature of existence, likened unto the Creator. Things will come and go; vanity will exist and then disappear. Prophecies will be fulfilled and will pass away; tongues will pass and then they will cease; knowledge will be evident, and then that too shall pass. But one thing that will remain is love. Parents' presentation of the idea of love usually involves love-likeness. Now with our eyes and our understanding open, knowing the truth, we can celebrate, saying that now that we are more mature, we are able to acclimate to the requirements. Indeed we could only but look through a stained glass had we not been allowed to explore love's phenomenal origins; now we see clearly.

Love Dynamics

John 21:16–17 reads, "He saith to him again the second time, Simon, son of Jonas, lovest thou me? He saith unto him, Yea, Lord; thou knowest that I love thee. He saith unto him, Feed my sheep. He saith unto him the third time, Simon, son of Jonas, lovest thou me? Peter was grieved because he said unto him the third time, Lovest thou me? And he said unto him, Lord, thou knowest all things; thou knowest that I love thee. Jesus saith unto him, Feed my sheep." The word *love* expressed in the conversation between Simon and Jesus has two different meanings. When the Lord said, "Lovest thou me?" the Greek translation is *agape*;

however, in answering, Simon used the Greek word *philo*, which displays two dynamics. The distinction between the two shows that agape love is more intimate and deep in relation, speaking to affection. The misinterpretation of the expressed love caused Peter to change the dynamics to what he thought would be more appropriate. Other dynamics of this expression exist, which will be explored.

Love-Likeness Dynamics Classification

Love-likeness is the objectification of a subject while adulterating the purity of expression of love with or without the use of discriminatory vices, appreciating the part(s) while ignoring the whole for personal satisfaction without the expressed concept of a connection to the Source for purification, which leads into idolatry.

Epithumia

The word is of Greek origin and indicates affection based on strong desires for intimacy and passion. It is composed of the preposition *epi*, "upon", and the root *thumos*, "heat". The word connotes "heat upon heat" and suggests the notion of being hot after something. It can be tied to lust based on the nature of objectification. The expression has the ability to draw people together; however, it is the wrong foundation to erect a building for the lasting effect intended. This is a strong bond displayed with a mutual desire for sexual expression inside and out. Those who engage in this type of love engross themselves in the passion, which is the driving force of the asseveration of the selfishness of inappropriately and illusively pleasing each other.

Philautia

The Greek translation describes this type of expression of love as purely selfish and pleasure-seeking, in which fame, wealth, and other vanities are the aspirations, utilizing narcissistic approaches. This expression takes the form of egotism. The expression is unhealthy as it is arrogant in nature and will do whatever is needed to please self, neglecting the effect on others, the impact on others, and the possible devastation of others. This facilitates the treating of humanity as a commodity for exchange, use and refusal, in an effort to reach a higher echelon in the social hierarchy.

Eros

Eros is the experience many people are drawn towards, having been sold on the feeling and not the principle. This is what the storybooks and love novels portray, presenting an illusion for our hallucination, which eventually entraps the masses in the fixation on that which is dangerous both in this time and in eternity. Romance is the common association, which convention indicates is contrary to marriage. This expression, as seen on the big screen, is not an expression of love; it presents something that the neophyte might mistake for the real. This expression in such a manner as portrayed by society will lead to many new and emerging diseases, unnecessary exposure, the damaging of goods and services, increased rates of abortion, and eventually the destruction of marriage before it has a chance to start. Eros can be tied to lust, infatuation, and obsession. Eros in this form is wholly emotional and cannot be summoned; its estimated duration may be up to twenty-four months, which is insufficient for a lasting relationship. This ill-advised approach to love is one reason provided by individuals who have multiple partners.

Love Dynamics Classification

Eros

The expression of romantic intimacy is of absolute importance and should be exercised within the confines of the marriage bed. Hebrews 13:4 reads, "Marriage is honourable in all, and the bed undefiled." Eros is actually romantic sexual love displayed between a husband and a wife; this is not lust or infatuation. This love form was designed to be the pinnacle of physical pleasure when expressed in marriage. "Husbands, love your wives, and be not bitter against them" (Colossians 3:19).

Storge

This love expression is associated with the love that parents have for their child or children. This natural affection and a sense of belonging, along with effortless love, which is known to extend forgiveness, acceptance, and sacrifice, provides a safe space for the involved parties. Though rooted in friendship, understanding, and deep emotional connection, this love will not be expressed by persons who are not connected to the Source. If it appears to be expressed without roots, it is love-likeness. If the gift is lacking, it is necessary to ask the Lord to intervene in our lives.

Philia

The word for this New Testament love is rooted in the word *Philadelphia*, meaning brotherly love. It cherishes and has tender affection for belonging, manifested in comradeship, sharing, and communication between brothers and sisters and/or friends. Parents and children, siblings, and close friends all share this type of love in their relationships. Eros consummates marriage and keeps the fire burning, while philia creates companionship and the sharing of thoughts, feelings, attitudes, plans, and dreams. "A friend loveth at all times, and a brother is born for adversity" (Proverbs 17:17).

Agape

This is the highest level of love which can be reached; the achievement of love to this degree is the total annihilation of self. "I protest by your rejoicing which I have in Christ Jesus our Lord, I die daily" (1 Corinthians 15:31). Agape is not exclusively feeling, although it can involve various feelings. This is a conscious, controlled way of thinking, elevating the human being to the highest spiritual level. John 15:13 reads, "Greater love hath no man than this, that a man lay down his life for his friends." The nature of this love is self-sacrificing and unconditional; it is not confined or held for ransom by its environment or someone's perception. Agape is able to soar like an eagle as it is based on principle, commitment, dedication, and loyalty, facilitating the making of decisions in a logical way and a conscious state. It perfectly describes the kind of love Jesus Christ has for His Father and for His followers.

Agape defines God's immeasurable, incomparable love for humanity. It is perpetual and self-sacrificing, concerning itself greatly in the loss of the fallen human in the Garden of Eden. Those who love Jesus will do what is commanded and taught. This type of love is the most spiritually rewarding; however, without spiritual eyes, from the outside it will appear like madness. We read in 1 Corinthians 2:14, "But the natural man receiveth not the things of the Spirit of God: for they are foolishness unto him: neither can he know them, because they are spiritually discerned."

Slavery did not begin when we were programmed to think. It actually began at the Fall of Humankind; this was the first time human beings sold out not one another but themselves because of selfish desires, wanting to become as gods, desiring their eyes to be open, knowing good and evil. It was in this moment that iniquity was allowed to reveal its head and that humankind walked into slavery. In an effort rescue us from this devastating situation, God had to initiate the provisions that were made from the foundation of the earth. The Saviour had to become directly involved with humanity and the salvation of humankind. As it was with slaves, beaten, bruised, and humiliated, it is for us; this is the cost of our sins. In order for us to be redeemed, we needed to be repurchased after we sold ourselves. Indeed, Jesus Christ was the One who paid the price for our sins. "For ye are bought with a price: therefore glorify God in your body, and in your spirit, which is God's" (1 Corinthians 6:20).

An exceptional display of the agape form of love was seen when, knowing that humankind had sinned, God, who was sinless, sent His only Son to pay our price. This was an extension of selfless sacrifice to save the human race. Despite the choice presented, the decision without hesitation was for God the Son to leave the splendour of heaven in the form of a man to pay the price of our transgression, taking on the feeble mortality of humanity. Likewise, we should be ready to make the sacrifice for others and be our brother's or sister's keeper. We read in 1 John 3:17, "But whoso hath this world's good, and seeth his brother have need, and shutteth up his bowels of compassion from him, how dwelleth the love of God in him?" Love is the complete fundamental display of God's perfect essence.

When a seed is planted there is a natural expectancy for the fruit of the planting to be revealed. So it is with the seed of love. By the fruit, it shall become evident if it is love-likeness or love. Galatians 5:22–23 reads, "But the fruit of the Spirit is love, joy, peace, longsuffering, gentleness, goodness, faith, Meekness, temperance: against such there is no law." If the fruit is absent, there is no law, meaning there is no love. This fruit is one, just as God is One, and He desires us as individuals to be one. The expression of a part is not equated with the whole and is equal to none. You have been positioned to enjoy the fruit that love brings, consuming only of that fruit and no substitute. Let us live love!

SEVENTH GEAR

Dating ≠ Courting

Be Ye Perfect

It Is Finished

DATING ≠ COURTING

People are confused with what the world purports as being acceptable with irrepressible consequences. Amidst the chaos of determining who you are, navigating your life's direction with its whirlwinds and with friends present only for a season, things should be simple enough. Then comes the point of selecting someone to have a meaningful experience with. The question of dating and courting develops for those claiming liberation in the Western culture or joining the family in Eastern culture. The society has placed the young in a vulnerable position to be scammed, robbed, and snuffed of their future, bombarding them with high sexual content, preventing them from developing the character required to enjoy the best relationships, and ushering them into quagmire-like relationships they are incapable of conducting. If the process of partner selection is done with naivety, it will not only create broken individuals but also transfer that broken spirit into the family—and before long there will be a social epidemic of dysfunctional relationships. This is the time in which the selection process is made for your future. If the processes leading up to the selection are not undertaken in accordance with sound principles, then the rate of separation will continue to increase. It is possible to go through the process of selection once while having a family structure. This is better than what the world purports based on principles and moral purity.

The destructive normative profession of the alleged modern society has caused a great deal of pain, struggle, turmoil, and devastation while destroying our values and our regard for fellow humans, all based on unfounded principles of family structure. In today's world, more people than ever have separated themselves from relationships which had the commitment clause "until death", because the culture has promoted devaluation of the foundational principles for building a relationship. Selfishness and desires have overridden the consciousness to become societal norms. Understanding the principles of a happy and healthy relationship, you will become the exception in society as you will be equipped to function at a higher level of consciousness, elevated above "sensationalistic stimulation". As it relates to your future, nothing can be taken for granted; there is no going with the flow or things falling into place. You must make a diligent effort to reap value from the seed that is planted. Depending on the seeds that have been planted, the best thing that could happen is crop failure; even if the seeds planted in the pass are compromised, the future can be shaped from the perspective of the initially intended purpose. Joyousness, bliss, solemnity, contentment, and holiness are some of the intentioned experiences that will be enjoyed when the principles are invested.

Building

On your quest to develop meaningful relationships, you must know that whatever you invest in will be a reflection of the possible return. This is similar to a cause-and-effect relationship. If you start with polygamy, it would be entirely unreasonable to expect a sudden change to monogamy within an instant; hence, people end up cheating in relationships and having other families outside their primary relationship. The foundation of a building gives an idea as to the structural integrity, allowing us to anticipate the strain the building will be able to manage and under what pressure it will crumble. The question is, what type of house do you desire to be built? It is submitted to you to build your home upon the Rock. Any relationship that is engaged in while on the journey of life should develop and bring you closer to being in conformity with the Originator; defaulting from this means the relationship is not one that should be allowed to advance beyond the scope of control lest you step in sinking sand.

Dating

Dating, as is practised today, could be linked to the depravity of the society and to social and relational problems, leading to criminal behaviour and health problems and eventually mental and emotional damage, coupled with the acceptance of physical abuse, as humanity crashes on a downwards trajectory. The word *dating* was invented in the 18th century; prior, marriages were arranged and had direct parental involvement and support. Contrary to our practice, there was the negligible open practice of trial marriages or concubinage. These practices are encouraged by the world's standards of dating. The word *courtship* has been used to describe a model which is acceptable and should be used to safeguard against the snares of the world. The word *dating* to the innocent eyes would mean simply to go out at a particular time and date as a specific activity. Many will justify the practice by saying they can go on dates with their family members, their friends, and strangers without any wrong implications, not realizing that the presentation of dating gives rise to an illusion of its consequences as most dates are unsupervised, are without boundaries, and appeal to sexuality. Regardless of your personal feelings about dating, you should question if romantic dating as the world presents it is the most efficient utilization of your time and if it is the directional tangent your life is worth following.

In the Western world, the twenty-first-century census records reveal that 50–66 per cent of marriages have at least one partner who has committed or is committing fornication/adultery; more than 50 per cent of marriages will end in divorce. Research has shown that in dysfunctional families, there is an increased rate for children dropping out of school or class, having low self-esteem, and having an earlier introduction to sexual activity with less value placed on their relationships. Marriage rates have declined in the Western world as it is socially acceptable to be a concubine and cohabit. This downwards spiral is signalling that the generation is in a lost state, yet only a few are looking to deal with the situation from the root. With the encouragement of dating by the world's standard, it is acceptable to lust after a woman or man and have a relationship without the attachment. This encourages individuals to be unmarried and sexually active. Dating places a grossly low figure on the value of marriage, with people not realizing that these malpractices are fertilizing the destruction of individuals and society. People everywhere are carrying the burden of "daddy and mummy issues", complaining about who left and who stayed, destroying their future of marriage as intended because they are filled with premarital sex, sexually transmitted diseases and infection, and emotional damage and scars, all because it dating not done in accordance to God's constitution.

A person who understands his or her origin, worth, and purpose will seek to exercise the will of the Originator in all aspects of his or her life. Unnecessary attention is placed on the consequence of action, while people fail to understand the process of the result. The relationships developed along the ageing cycle are a defining factor as to the quality of life and any regrets that exist and persist. In following a manual and learning from the miscalculation of others, one is poised for regret minimization. In everything that is meant with good intention, there is an antagonistic spirit. The quality of the life humans are afforded to live can only be grasped if they remain diligent in enacting the truth. The Devil, since the first deception in the garden, has always mixed good and evil and truth and error, presenting evil and error as gospel. This strategic method of presenting the information has caused many to become confused with lingering confusion of what is right and wrong, what is acceptable sexuality, how to select sexual orientation, what the correct value system is, what their identity is, what their purpose is, and what two lives joined to the end of death means. The confusion causes forgeries that are almost indistinguishable from that which is real. Operating on the feelings, likes, and general taste of the individual, the sweet mixture of truth and error is consumed like honey in a cup, but the end only brings destruction. Enjoying life in all its glory can only be done under spiritual direction to secure the future afterlife.

Synonymous with dating is fornication, sexual immorality, and lust in the culture, which so many embrace. Most only go on dates for sexual release or to fulfil a fantasy. Going on dates with persons who are unknown who have less than pure intentions can be a dangerous venture. The modern atmosphere encourages people to present a false impression with a plan to deceive the other party as to their identity. Whether this is done in private between two individuals or among multiple peers, it can be destructive. Many interaction styles exist within the scope of dating, and one such style is group dating. This type of system, where multiple persons of varying morality, standards, and boundaries exist, can lead to a parent's nightmare or to childhood exposure to orgiastic behaviour or the sex act. Numerous reports of the ills manifested when dating is engaged in according to the world's standard and on the world's territory, and treated as a game, include individuals who have been violated, drugged, assaulted, kidnapped, damaged, raped, or robbed of purity, or who have even lost their lives. The vileness of the world has made it much more challenging to control all the variables when engaging. The human heart is deceitful and desperately wicked. You cannot know it; only God knows it. Allow Him to do His work.

The shortfall of dating is observed most graphically in the transition to marriage and is seen in a broken and destructive relationship. The sacredness of intimacy is not maintained; the final selected partner will only experience a piece of the whole as the other partner goes on a quest for variety, shared things that were not meant to be shared. The experience of intimate hugging and kissing; sexual exploration; physical, emotional, and spiritual bonding; the bringing up of a child or children; and even cohabitation should be reserved for the marriage union without reconnaissance in the dating–mating season.

Three Areas of Dating Failure

Culture

Most persons, young or old, engage in dating because it appears to be the normative way to enjoy partnership or company for a short to medium term. Given the direction of the culture and media, it is indicated that multiple partnerships are acceptable, especially when one is already in an intimate relationship, which is an error.

Sex

The predominant confrontation with amorality has inflated our sexual appetite. Individuals are bombarded with sex, sexuality, and other divisive sensual allures, which plays on emotions and compromises judgement, impeding one's inhibitions to engage in the fantasy. This aspect is in direct contradiction to the Master's will, admonishing us to flee youthful lusts and to flee fornication, which seeks self-satisfaction, apart from the responsibilities of marriage.

Relational

The current generation has been influenced to believe that urgent is the need for interaction with the opposite sex, and engaging in a dating relationship is considered the most ideal. The expressed need for someone to keep company, filling the void of loneliness, causes many to believe the remedy is dating; however, this is a display of a broken family system and structure, which causes the alienation of individual members. The insecurities manifested by way of exclusion have pushed the envelope on dating, making it a substitute for expression. As a family and group, we must remember 1 Corinthians 12:12: "For as the body is one, and hath many members, and all the members of that one body, being many, are one body: so also is Christ." From this we learn we should be able to get support from the various groups that are available to meet the basic needs for relationship development such as family or a church group.

Courting

In engineering the architecture of the most important relationships you will choose to forge, the foundation must be aligned with the purpose of the grand picture. Your future is a subtotal of the choices made by you and on your behalf. Prior to the starting of construction, the expected outcomes and objectives need to be indicated and clearly outlined. The more specific the blueprint, the easier it is to identify deviations. Billions of people fail to apply these simple principles to their lives, hence the reason for the enormous levels of bewailing and inexorable feelings, causing the human race to be deranged. It is going on dates and engaging in courtship that is the principal foundation of a marriage relationship. Without a genuine intention to participate in a romantic relationship to lead to marriage, people express the idea of courtship or even passionate affection when on dates.

The momentary impulse towards emotional miscarriage, psychological depravity, and physical blindness should be avoided as your feeling has no logical place in the process. This volatile combination should be subjected to the will of authority and transported in the designated containment system to prevent the explosive destruction from overtaking the relationships. Relationships are expressed in layers and thus require time for the delicate revelation. In starting a relationship, lust and infatuation can be debilitating to its success. In this relationship, the acceleration is exponential, but ultimately the relationships fails to endure through the test. Wisdom should be exercised in relationship endeavours to safeguard both parties from hurt. Relationships started outside the principles of God will eventually lead to despair. If one believes one has the prerequisite maturity to engage in developing partnerships for the future, it should be outlined that the interaction is either a giving relationship or a receiving relationship. The worldly participants will focus on the sensual nature to receive all that can be acquired in the shortest possible period. For this reason, people move towards the home run on the first encounter, which is outside the parameters on the covenant indicated by the Originator. The correct principle of execution is to make deposits with consistency while building trust. A systematic approach to information extraction and divulging is necessary for mutuality. A desire to *get* is based on sensuality; the spirit God desires is to *give*, which requires a spiritual connection. The main ingredients in the recipe of exceptional relationships are God, you, and the other.

At the process initiation, in which a suitable partner is selected with whom to spend time, the stage of seeking is paramount. The searching should begin with a godly conversation. This means that purity in communication and deportment should be the springboard of the relationship so as to avoid corruptible desires. One should develop the prerequisite maturity to be able to consider not only oneself but also the needs of others. Reasonability needs to be exercised when selecting a partner for the future; it would be unwise to conceive the idea of taking a stone and expecting it to be something else. The principle of instant gratification is not an accurate display of character, as it indicates a lack of patience and the ability to exercise self-control. The spirit of discernment is necessary when contemplating such a course of action, and it is imperative that both parties possess similar ideals in order to mitigate future challenges and concerns.

One fundamental recommendation is to understand that there is no one who knows the product better than the manufacturer. The product can only have a guarantee and warranty if it is used in accordance with the specifications and if the necessary maintenance protocols are enforced. If this principle is observed and each individual becomes one with the Maker, only the expected outcome will be seen; hence, love is fundamental. We read in 1 John 4:8, "He that loveth not knoweth not God; for God is love." It is in the reciprocation of the love that has been given by God that indicates where our relationships should lead. In Exodus 20:3 we read, "Thou shalt have no other gods before me." This indicator points out that idolatry is frowned upon and is not welcome in the relationship. Any relationship that is engaged in should be one that brings the individuals closer to the Creator. If the relationship creates a break in the communication or a gap of differences, there needs to be an adjustment or discontinuation. Putting someone or something above the Originator is idolatry. If you desire the company of a particular person more than you want the company of He who made you, then a red flag rises. If you prefer fancy houses, fancy cars, and material possession more than the Creator, that is another red flag. If you are so pompous to be experiencing tunnel vision and can only see yourself, that is a red flag. If you lose control and become addicted to what pleasures your appetite, that is a red flag. Once the red flags are observed, it is time for introspection, though sometimes it is more difficult to see what is in your own eyes.

In keeping the commandments of God, we display our love and affection. With human interactions and relationships, you should ensure that yours is not perverted by the introduction of seduction, lust, or infatuation. There is no other foundation on which to build but on the Rock of all the ages. Any other foundation will be one filled with the agony of destruction.

General Relationship

In spite of society's imposition on our consciousness with misinformation and wrong thinking, it is time that all the information be excreted and regurgitated as appropriate in order to save ourselves from the slow poisoning. Our society, which claims to have all the correct answers, has been the major contributor with a destructive force that has damaged and broken families and people. While it promotes and lauds promiscuity, it benefits from the demise of the race. These subtle deviations and the normalization of questionable practices will eventually seem reasonable; however, that does not make them the truth. It is necessary for our society to demonstrate social interaction practices with love and respect for all parties involved. This practice of social interaction can be deemed as dating as it meets a social obligation. The repetitive meeting may create unexpected interest, more than just a casual friendship. Upon arrival at this interval, both parties must determine the goals and objectives. This will clear the air as to expectations and reduce the likelihood of disappointment. This progression will move the couple into a general exclusive relationship phase. In this phase, each person will continue to amass friends; however, none of the other relationships will be within the same class as the one expressed by the two. In the previous phases of development in which there was social interaction, it would be considered a general relationship as the interaction is on the lines of regular friendship.

General Exclusive Relationship

In the general exclusive relationship, the two individuals share a similar set of ideals, which are the driving force in merging the parties. There is an intention to develop the relationship into a union. During the stage of general exclusivity, it is encouraged that only a one-to-one relationship be maintained. A one-to-many situation is grounded in supporting infidelity. It is ideal that only one partner be engaged and that monogamy be practised exclusively. Polygamous relationships tend to create bonds and ties which are onerous to break and sometimes are the same factors which cause the destruction of the relationship as it is ushered to the final stage. This one-on-one experience generally leads to marriage as the individuals following the principles have already established each other as the candidate with whom to spend a lifetime. The idea of going steady should not be encouraged for persons who are not mature or who have a different mindset as to objectives and projections. Objectives, dreams, and aspirations should be outlined for an assessment of the compatibility between both parties. Where there are irreconcilable incompatibilities of fundamental importance, it is acceptable to discontinue the relationship amicably. It would be better to choose to suffer affliction with the people of God than to enjoy seasonal sinful pleasures. During the development of this type of relationship, care must be taken to ensure a limit on the emotional attachment that will compromise better judgement, which can be inhospitable to letting go. The same care should be taken in the safeguarding of inhibition, preventing its lowering, which could possibly compromise sexuality, virtue, and purity or lead to any form of immorality. During this period, self-development should not be neglected; study in communication, manners, etiquette, deportment, dancing, domestication, and other social ventures should be engaged in. In this phase, extreme care should be taken to listen. This will allow for better understanding and the determination of any inconsistencies that may be derived.

Exclusive Relationship

When one has reached the exclusive zone, it indicates that both parties have agreed and seen it fitting to take the final step and make a public declaration of commitment. This usually is referred to as the engagement. It is advised that the engagement should last no more than a year to prevent defilement, as more time will be spent together and inhibitions are considered to reach their lowest level. This is an exclusive stage, and it is almost absolute that you will be married, but things can still go sideways. Though temptations may overwhelm you, be advised that heavy kissing (French and other similar variants) and petting should not be engaged in prior to marriage. Kissing to that degree is a form of caressing. This act will generally stimulate and eventually take the upstairs business downstairs. Petting and fondling of the genitals have no place outside of marriage. This practice will defile the purity of the persons engaging. It is not our right to give to another that which is not ours. These acts are a manifestation of selfish lustful desires and should not be entertained. Temptations are eminent when one becomes drawn away by one's own lust. It is this lust that conceives and give birth to sin, and after it is finished, death. The couple must not explore their sexual compatibility as doing so defiles people and positions them for catastrophe. It will place you in a compromising position, in which you now are the subject of an experiment. In an effort to bring about a meaningful outcome, you must exercise your faith in the promises of God.

Marriage

Marriage should be the end product of all the invested effort after overcoming various trials and temptations. That which was desired has been acquired. Now this is the most crucial stage because it lasts typically the longest. It is in this phase that going on a date is incredibly welcome, or even engaging in courting practices in an effort to remind yourself of the investment that is now bearing fruit.

If the integrity of the process is maintained, then the marriage will be as expected and not something which society has subjected the populous to believe. All relationships should have God as the chief controller. It is not for us to choose and then ask God to approve. You should seek after the leading of the Master, and then upon observing His will, you will know the appropriate selection. Marriage is honourable, and the bed should be undefiled. Now for the moment for which you have been waiting so patiently: you are authorized to engage sexually as you drink from your own cistern and let your fountains flow freely.

Notes

The world's standard is of the flesh, but the standard of God is of the spirit. The flesh is carnal, but the spirit is of God.

Things to avoid:

- The lust of the eyes
- Pride of life
- Idolatry

Simplified process:

1. Know your Originator.
2. Understand yourself (who you are, whose you are, where you were derived, and your purpose and focus).
3. Become one in love as you become whole.
4. Prayerfully seek after that which is required.
5. Verify approval.
6. Allow principles to take precedence.
7. Unite and become one in spirit under God's authority.

With this template, there is no need to have complicated relationships. Invest in ventures that are aligned with your purpose.

BE YE PERFECT

Be ye therefore perfect, even as your Father
which is in heaven is perfect.
—Matthew 5:48

The first rule of perfection is that you exhibit obedience mixed with faithfulness. It is possible to be perfect as the scriptures admonish. Perfection can only be achieved through God and with God. In order to serve God, we need God, hence the need for total commitment and purposeful faithfulness. "Be ye perfect" can be equated to "Be ye faithful" as faithfulness is required in order to reach perfection, while perfection will not be attained until one exhibits faithfulness. During the process of faithfulness, we will become transformed as perfection is achieved.

| Obedience/faithfulness | Transformation | Perfection |
| Be ye faithful | Be ye transformed | Be ye perfect |

Be Ye Faithful

To us has been given a glimpse of the awful scrutiny that awaits us, mainly because the majority are incapable in their current state to see what is in the spiritual as most people dwell in the physical. In overcoming, one must earnestly purpose within one's heart to remain diligent, sincere, and faithful to the cause of righteousness. While Daniel was taken in captivity, it was his intention to remain faithful to his customs and God. Without this predetermined objective, he would have become defiled as fitting in among the people of darkness was customary. In remaining faithful to his God, he was granted favour while shining his light in the midst of the people of darkness. This characteristic is a spiritual fruit that is developed from a real relationship of commitment to God. It is the fibre of our morality, stretched throughout our being, sealing our commitments while giving us the power and authority to have dominion. In having faith, there must be a foundation of belief; it is submitted to you that such a foundation is Jesus Christ. Only God is deserving of faith to be placed in Him. Foolish are the thoughts of people who consistently set themselves up for disappointment in misappropriating in whom they place their faith: in a mere mortal with limited control and reliance. The only One worth relying on is the God who has the power to uphold you with His hand of righteousness.

On our quest to master faithfulness, we need to understand what faith entails. The world describes faith as complete trust or confidence in someone or something; it may refer to hope or belief, rational or irrational, in a certain end. Referring to it as simply a belief is not based on proof or evidence. This is a very erroneous faith conception. In summation, faith is actually, according to Hebrews 11:1, "the substance of things hoped for, the evidence of things not seen". Faith is the foundation on which our relationship with God is based. The word *substance* in Greek translates to *hypostasis*, literally "a standing under". Hypostasis can be considered as the unseen support of what is obvious. The evidence is derived from the Greek word *elengchos*, meaning "a proof, or that by which a thing is proved or tested; conviction". The manifestation of faith was observed in the creation of the world; God spoke, and it was so. If we examine physical nature, we can see the creation of a child. There is not a child, yet two agree, and a child comes forward. The husband is carrying the child in the substance (scrotum) he was given by God, which will be made manifest when it meets his wife's ovaries, the combining partner. In this case, the thought of having a child would be made flesh as the child develops and is born and lives in the world. Because the child is not seen does not mean there is not a child. It is the faith that manifests the child. So too the faith of a barren woman allows her to give birth. To have faith is to operate on the premise of that which is not yet seen but will be seen through the wisdom of God. That which is rooted in hope will flourish the substance, making manifest that which is not yet seen. Seeing is not believing, but believing is seeing. This is an expression of faith.

Faith should not be placed in a person or thing; things cannot manifest anything. Having faith in the inanimate is idolatry, likened unto the worship of gods. Faith is the first step on the journey to perfection, and if we are not taking steps, we will not move from where we current stand. The expression of faith in believing the Word of God allows us to live a quality life. It was by faith that Abel offered unto God a more excellent sacrifice than Cain, giving what was requested and nothing else. It was by faith that Enoch was translated as he walked with God; it was by faith that Noah, not seeing rain, built the ark as God instructed; it was by faith that Abraham moved away from his home under the instruction of God. It is by this same faith that we are required to serve the Lord wholeheartedly. When we have this faith, it needs to be exercised, which will manifest in faithfulness. As the relationship with God develops, it becomes easier to have confidence in the word *guarantee* and to claim the promises outlined for humanity's benefit. Without faith, humanity becomes paralysed and impotent in exercising authority over the world.

In the exercise of faith, it is imperative to acknowledge the deity of Christ, knowing that there is a power and authority which can release the demon-possessed and bring healing and restoration to humanity while saving lives. Salvation comes through the grace of God; this salvation comes through Jesus Christ alone. We must believe that Christ rose from the grave as an expression of faith. If that is the case, then we must believe and preach the gospel of the kingdom of heaven, understanding there is only one God. Though God exists as one, we must acknowledge that there are three coeternal beings existing as one. "Go ye therefore, and teach all nations, baptizing them in the name of the Father, and of the Son, and of the Holy Ghost" (Matthew 28:19).

Be Ye Transformed

Romans 12:2 reads, "And be not conformed to this world: but be ye transformed by the renewing of your mind, that ye may prove what is that good, and acceptable, and perfect, will of God."

Transformation speaks to the process of making a marked change in form. In nature, it is similar to metamorphosing, becoming new. The transformation will be exhibited when there is a shift in the conformity of error, moving in the direction of light. When faith has been clutched and one becomes a believer in the things that have not yet come, the individual is ready to become more than he or she was when wondering purposelessly. The mind, being the seat of consciousness, is the area for the attack of the enemy. An improperly guided mind will lead to the destruction of the person. In order to become the person intended, you must allow the Architect to be in control, allowing God's perfect will to materialize.

The divine power of God has given us everything needed to live a life of godliness through our knowledge of Him who has called us by His own glory. These precious promises have been given to us so we may participate in the divine nature and escape the corruption in the world mounted by evil desires. An understanding of life and godliness is a transformative by-product of knowing and abiding in accordance with the Word of God, and this is why the mind needs to be whole: to transfer the completion of the human. John 17:17 reads, "Sanctify them through thy truth: thy word is truth." The word *transformed* is also seen in Matthew 17:12 and Mark 9:2 and is translated "transfiguration". When this transfiguration occurs, it presents a new view and perspective. That which was before or expected will no longer align; the process does not speak only to the physical or external, but also to the spiritual or internal. The transformative righteousness cannot be missed as it radiates the glory of God, making sight restoration possible for the blind.

The service that is rendered is not for self; it is for the benefit of others. In performing such service in a selfless way, we present actions of sacrifice. God's mercy is the only avenue which can help us to consciously take this approach as our inclinations are not of God but of humans. We were deceived, and we have been fooling ourselves with regard to the things of former times. In ignorance, we were children of disobedience lusting, but with Jesus Christ, we become sober with hope and grace, being children of obedience.

When we are exposed to truth, it means we have been entrusted with the responsibility to live accordingly. The world and its philosophies have inundated the mind with the poisonous injections, creating a challenge in escaping the corruption while blocking a godly vantage point. Through the knowledge of Him, escape is imminent as living is based on principles. "Sanctify them through thy truth: thy word is truth" (John 17:17). This is the process of becoming holy; we acquire this attribute base in our relationship from the generator of holiness, derived through knowledge of Him. There is a need for a distinction between people of light and people of darkness. The only way for the distinction to be made is for the mind to experience a renewal of the truth of God's Word. What the mind is fed upon is what the being becomes; it is now upon each individual to choose for themselves what it is that they desire to become, either a wondering formality or a mental specific.

In becoming transformed, the individual must know and accept God as sovereign, exercising obedience to this sovereign nature while exhibiting total reliance on His wisdom and authority. When one has reached the ideal, one will have a greater inclination to do that which needs to be done and not that which one wants to be done. This is the expression of freedom; humanity has been set free through Jesus Christ. If we love to do what we ought to do, that is a revelation of freedom. When one becomes free, one should restrain oneself and not become bound by the same bondage which once before held one captive. Failure to transform could indicate one of two situations, either ignorance or suppression of God's truth. It is a misrepresentation or even defamation of character to remain as we are and in the same breath claim transformation. By beholding His glory we become changed, renewed, and transformed.

When Moses was commissioned by the Lord to visit Mount Sinai for the delivery of the commandments, it is evident by the account that Moses was transformed after being in the presence of God. The only appropriate thing to be done in the presence of God is to worship, and that was what Moses did. Moses was there forty days and forty nights; he did not eat bread or drink water. The glory of

God was transferred just by the essence of His presence. God being holy caused a transfiguration of Moses to a state of holiness, from which the people had to be shielded. This is the power of being in direct connection with the Lord; this glory is attainable by any who desire to follow God's righteousness.

Be Ye Perfect

One of the manufactured challenges that exists is knowing what needs to be done, but doing what appears easiest is normally selected to accomplish a temporal experience. This disparity has created a gaping hole in the quest towards perfection. Many find themselves snared by their own actions and their indulgence in free will. When restraint is lacking, patience is absent, and the walls of inhibition break down. The concept of the foundation is missing. It behoves anyone who thinks that slavery to sin will bring this state of actualization which Jesus Christ commissioned. Reconciliation to the Father's will is of great importance. He alone can eradicate our deformities so that our character may become perfected. An example was set for us so that we may understand that amidst the deception cultivated, individuals are allowed to find comfort in indulging the appetite and imaginary contractions to their own detriment, while capitalism becomes the driving force of the era. The souls of human beings are severed, to be consumed in a cannibalistic orgy, in part because of the deformity, numbing, and clouding of the frontal lobe. In contradiction to what should be done, this is what is done.

The literal translation of the word *perfect* is "to be complete, finished, whole, one or mature"; anything else is incomplete and is performance below one's potential while glorying mediocrity. The man or woman created of God must be upright in all their ways, and He will be their guide. No one needs to be trapped by evil desires. There is only one way, and it is God's way. His truth resounds in His Word, and His life is the example to be emulated. People of faith must grow in the Spirit of God with maturity developing over time as they display spiritual integrity. Our heavenly Father is the author of perfection and completeness; He is the self-existing, the Alpha and Omega, the Beginning and End. In order to achieve this state of consciousness, we must understand that God needs to be the guide on the journey. Imperfection alone cannot produce perfection; imperfection in the hands of perfection will result in the ultimate expression of perfection and completeness. It is possible for humans to be upright and perfect as biblically outlined. There are measures in place for this achievement.

Humanity, though fallen, still has the hope the Lord presents for their development and elevation. Many wish for you not to reach or even know your full potential, but it is the desire of the Lord that you be edified with the illumination of His Word as you travel through life's vapour. The principle expressed by God is not merely a proposed theory; it is practical and applicable to our existence today just as it was in the days of old. The goal for us is not to condemn or investigate others. The intent is that we become the best people we can possibly be, one, complete, and perfect.

In order to reach perfection, you must stop striving towards it on your own strength and admit that self has no place while seeking after the perfect way. John 14:6 reads, "Jesus saith unto him, I am the way, the truth, and the life: no man cometh unto the Father, but by me." Though attainable perfection is, many will never reach it or even consider to reach it because they have no faith in the Word and they lack belief in their Maker and King. Therefore they try to accomplish the feat on their own merit. We need to start by acknowledging our humanity and then confess our sins to the One who created us.

In every period in history, God's people have experienced perfection; they have claimed it by faith, committing wholly to the service of their God with willing minds. Those who have died in such a faith relationship are beyond the hands of Satan. John experienced death for righteousness, and Stephen experienced his end and beginning for the sake of uprightness, being full of the Holy Spirit. Even when Stephen was receiving a stoning, he had compassion on those who were doing this evil against him. There are many more who completed their journey and lived perfect, dying for the cause of righteousness. They have lived, to live again. They all died in faith, not receiving the promises but seeing them afar off. Though some of those who have gone before us died in a perfect state after completing their assigned purpose, some were taken before death was able to reach them, whereas One laid down His life so that He might take it up again to remind us that He has the control over death and the grave. Three such persons are Enoch, Elijah, and Jesus Christ.

Enoch

Enoch was the seventh from Adam, the son of Jared and the father of Methuselah. While Jared lived eight hundred years after he had Enoch, he died at 962 years of age. Enoch lived sixty-five years, and begat Methuselah. The process of Enoch's life indicated the development of a more serious relationship with God than his son Methuselah had. Enoch *walked with God* for three hundred years after he'd had Methuselah. Now having a more in-depth understanding, friendship, partnership, and companionship wrapped in one relationship, Enoch had been set aside from others within his time. Truly our lives can be transformed in order for our purpose to be fulfilled, but we must seek in order to find. Enoch was at this time in one of the highest states of consciousness possible to humankind; his eyes were open to the point he realized that to become trapped by the vanity of life would have been a waste of his experience. He was a man who was upright, godly, righteous, and sober-minded, endowed with the wisdom of God. Enoch walked with God, and he was taken. This walk showed an expression of godliness and reconciliation to God. The walking with God displayed that Enoch had set himself aside to allow the excellent work of the Master to be done within him. With consistent effort and humility, he went about his duties with the utmost care, always acting as in the sight of God, pleasing God in all things.

The Holy Spirit, instead of saying that Enoch lived, says that Enoch walked with God. This drives home the point that one who lives a life without God has not yet started on the journey. The words were crafted with detailed precision. It is true that most persons will exist without choosing to live, which prevents their elevation to the higher call of walking with God. Enoch and God became such close friends that God took him. We read in Genesis 5:23–24, "And all the days of Enoch were three hundred sixty and five years: And Enoch walked with God: and he was not; for God took him." Enoch experienced the joy and love of God and was taken out of this world without death. He could not be found in the land because God had taken Him. Hebrews 11:5 tells us, "By faith Enoch was translated that he should not see death; and was not found, because God had translated him: for before his translation he had this testimony, that he pleased God." With the idea riveted in your mind that it was *by faith* that Enoch walked with God, what does this say about your faith? Do you believe that such a thing is possible? It all begins in the head. Living only 365 years, which was a man's age at that time, is possible. To lose the earth is to gain much, as we have a great promise to be fulfilled.

Elijah

Many are mystified by the transformation of Enoch, and much thought was given to the movement of Elijah to another dimension in flaming glory. Elijah can be translated "My God is Yahu/Jah". Elijah was a prophet and a miracle worker. God performed many works through him, including but not limited to the resurrection, bringing fire from the sky, and even entering heaven alive. We read in 2 Kings 2:1, "And it came to pass, when the Lord would take up Elijah into heaven by a whirlwind, that Elijah went with Elisha from Gilgal." While in preparation to be taken from the earth, Elijah was walking with God, performing miracles and working wonders, even unto the very moment of departure. In the time leading up to the departure, progression planning was in place as he trained the one who was positioned to continue with the cause of righteousness. After understanding the thing, Elisha requested a double portion of Elijah's spirit to be upon him, and Elijah agreed, providing Elisha saw him going up in the chariot to glory.

While they were living and doing the will of the Master, the time came for the departing, and in the same instant, there was the handing over and a transition ceremony. It came to pass, behold, there appeared a chariot and horse of fire that separated the trainer from the trainee, taking Elijah up by a whirlwind into heaven in the sight of Elisha. Once again, it is revealed that walking perfect and upright in accordance with the Master's will creates a transformation in the person. It is possible to walk how the Lord commands.

Jesus Christ

The incarnate, God the Son, took the form of Jesus Christ. He was sent to rescue those who strayed from His infallible counsel. "For God so loved the world, that he gave his only begotten Son, that whosoever believeth in him should not perish, but have everlasting life. Though God, He became man for the sake of humanity; loving us in spite" (John 3:16). We read in 1 John 4:9, "In this was manifested the love of God toward us, because that God sent his only begotten Son into the world, that we might live through him." With the entry of iniquity, manifesting sin, there was a severing of humankind from the Source of life, which results in death in the world today. There was a plan for humankind's redemption should the choice of dissidence be selected.

The sin of humankind came with consequences. Separation and damage were inevitable. Enmity existed. As it was outlined, the Saviour bruised Satan's head, and Satan bruised his heel. With the advent of sin, animal sacrifice was instituted to illustrate the mission of the Saviour. The penalty of sin is death, and for that reason things are as they are. "But of the tree of the knowledge of good and evil, thou shalt not eat of it: for in the day that thou eatest thereof thou shalt surely die" (Genesis 2:17).

Jesus's entry into humanity was by miraculous means; He was from a virgin conception. He was conceived of the Holy Ghost to save His people, and they called Him Immanuel, which is interpreted as "God with us". In the same way that by one man sin entered into this world, it needed one man to die to give the world a chance at redemption. A parallel is drawn between Adam and Christ; Adam could be considered the first man and Christ the last, the first made a living soul and the last a quickening spirit.

Jesus Christ, while in the human form, had the choice, as did Adam in Eden, to sin; however, the account of His life indicates that He is an overcomer. And we are reminded that we can be overcomers through Jesus. While on earth, He existed in both the divine and human nature. His birth being supernatural, He lived and experienced temptation as a human while perfectly exemplifying righteousness, reminding us that all things can be done through Christ who strengthens.

The life of Jesus was laid down for a moment before it was taken back up unto Himself. The wages of sin are death. Jesus never sinned, so He did not qualify to die. He actually laid His life down so humanity could be restored. When Lazarus was dead and Martha enquired, Jesus indicated that He is the resurrection and the life and that whosoever believes in Him shall never die. Trusting in Christ will make it possible to have life and have it more abundantly. After Jesus, there was no more need for sacrifice. Many have lived perfect lives, and in today's world it is possible just the same, but only if we hold on to Jesus and exercise our faith.

IT IS FINISHED

It is finished.
—John 19:30

The thought on many people's minds is, after this life has come to its end, is there a next destination? Immortality has always been a quest for humankind; this state is one which death has no grounds to hold subject. Jesus Christ's immortal nature was revealed at the resurrection. He desires our praise, adoration, and worship. "Now unto the King eternal, immortal, invisible, the only wise God, be honour and glory for ever and ever. Amen" (1 Timothy 1:17). Though God is immortal, humankind has no such claim in its current state; at creation, human beings were in a perfect state, in which they could have enjoyed immortality. Immortality only exists through God, as humankind needs His breath for life because it was God breathing into the man that created the living soul. A human does not have a soul; he or she is a soul. This wondering state need not perplex the mind any longer; it is true that those who are faithful to Christ will experience life again.

The breath that humankind now possesses does not belong to the human but comes from God. The soul, in accordance with the will of God, should have no fear of the end's beginning. When a human dies, all consciousness ceases and the person enters a state of sleep, during which the natural protocols of decomposition will be initiated. The dead have no authority or power to return to life on their own; neither can they visit people, communicate, or create animosity. Those manifestations are impersonations by fallen angels, taking the form and attributes of the dead to deceive you in believing the dead are in a conscious state, but it is not the dead.

Every person perishes at death. One thing is for sure: during this life that is appointed unto humans, everyone will die, after which the judgement will come, and each person will need to give an account for any inconsistencies or deviations in character. The living can find it a joy, knowing that they will die and their memories will be forgotten—in death, there is no remembrance. It is time to realize that the dead are dead and the boogeyman does not exist, though demonic influences are probable.

Close to the end of the sojourn of Jesus, He experienced many ordeals and much agony, including hatred, heartache, betrayal, denial, unjust judgement, exchange for another, bearing humanity's burden, and crucifixion. When Jesus was on the cross, towards the end, before giving up the ghost, He said, "It is finished." This statement shows completion and displays the perfect will of God. His obedience was perfect, as the prophecies were fulfilled in their exactness. As stated, the suffering was completed and finished. The price for each individual's sin was paid on that cross. "Moreover the law entered, that the offence might abound. But where sin abounded, grace did much more abound" (Romans 5:20). Salvation was made accessible to all humankind by this ultimate sacrifice on the cross, and a new covenant was established whereby animal sacrifice was required no more. Jesus's responsibility was complete. And where His responsibility ends, ours begins with the mission of telling others of His love and favour. So anyone who desires the promises of Jesus is welcome to go unto Him, and in receiving God the Son, one accepts God the Father, which acceptance is streamlined through the Holy Spirit.

When Jesus knew that all things were accomplished and the scripture had been fulfilled, He said, "I thirst." A vessel full of vinegar was given to Him, placed upon hyssop and put to His mouth. Upon receiving the vinegar, He said, "It is finished." At that moment He gave up the ghost. That chapter of living like mortals do came to its end in the fullness of time as the Messiah was cut off in the middle of the week, which was in relation to Jesus's crucifixion. He had to be the one to give up the Spirit, as it could not have been taken away from Him. John 10:18 reads, "No man taketh it from me, but I lay it down of myself. I have power to lay it down, and I have power to take it again. This commandment have I received of my Father." Jesus was speaking with authority in line with His Father's will, giving us a foretaste of what was to come. He would lay His life down only to take it unto Himself again. It was on the first day of the week that Mary Magdalene went to the sepulchre seeking after Jesus her Lord. The only thing she saw was the clothing that Jesus once wore neatly placed. Mary stood and wept, knowing not where they had taken her Lord. Two angels sitting, one at the head and the other at the feet where the body of Jesus had lain, enquired as to why she was crying, and she told them. Once she had told her story, she turned back and saw Jesus standing. Not knowing it was Jesus, she was asked why she was crying again; she thought thinking He was the gardener. She asked if the gardener knew where they had taken Him.

Jesus called her name, saying "Mary", and at that moment she knew who it was. She replied, "Rabboni", which is to say, "Master". Mary's interaction with Jesus made her a witness of the resurrection; she went and told the disciples. On the same day, during the evening, Jesus went in to them, bringing them peace and showing them His hands. They were in jubilant spirit, but it was time for the mantle to be passed on to the disciples in the same manner the Father had commissioned the Son. After saying all of this, He breathed on them and told them to receive the Holy Ghost. In that same moment, Jesus Christ reminded them of the Father's will while leaving the Holy Spirit; this completed the Godhead (God the Father, God the Son, and God the Holy Spirit). Thomas was doubtful of the report of the disciples' seeing Jesus, so he did not believe. On the eighth day, Jesus appeared to the disciples with Thomas in the midst, allowing him to see the scarring upon Him inflicted by the crucifixion.

After tarrying a little while, Jesus ascended into heaven, being received by a cloud which took him out of sight. In the same way He was taken away, He shall return to His people on the Day of Judgement. Indeed the words of Jesus were completed, and He did depart, in order to fulfil the promises as He committed to come back and receive us unto Himself. A life lived without Christ is a life of existence and is truly not yet lived; it is time to walk with God.

In a time to come, the Son of Man shall return as John saw in his vision: the Son of Man was seen clothed in a garment down to the foot. His head and hair were white as wool, His eyes were as flames of fire, His feet were like brass burnt in a furnace, and His voice was as the sound of the thundering of many waters. Though this is John's account, each individual can choose to enjoy that acquaintance as their reality. He will be coming back to receive you unto Himself, changing your mortality into immortality. All you need to do is to be faithful unto your Creator in oneness, singleness, wholeness, and completeness. Anticipate the transformation of the new heaven and new earth as former things are passed away.

Let go and let God. It is finished.

EPILOGUE

Living should be a rewarding, exciting, and fulfilling experience. You can enjoy the life you desire and have all the things you need to be satisfied. You can find the person of the opposite gender who is perfect for you. Do what is hard today to facilitate the enjoyment of that which is easy tomorrow. Your Originator extended His love towards you and completed you before you were created. I believe in you. For this reason, I have transmitted these perspectives. It is my hope that you love yourself enough to believe in your dreams and visions. Everything you can become is already within you, in the same way a seed possesses within it a tree. In order for the tree to come forth, the seed must be planted. Similarly, in order for you to become your best self, you must remember to think, assimilate the information, and move your practice into results. Envision yourself as the person you intend to become today, and in moments you will no longer be able to recognize the person you were before you began. Thank you for investing in your future. Follow these principles and your life will be equivocal to your imaginings. Extract the wealth from within your mind.

King or Queen, remind yourself, *Billionaire—I am one.*

ABOUT THE AUTHOR

Kareem Ainsley has been endowed with phenomenal intellectual acumens of philosophy and visionary projections under the leadership of the Holy Spirit, which has embodied him with wisdom and the spirit of leadership. Under this authority, he has been privileged to sit and counsel with kings, leaders and world changers in policy development and sustainable executions. His specialized expertise in the area of Medical-Clinical-Health Consultation in which is extraordinary skills in human interaction has made him a renowned relationship and life coach expert. Because of his passion towards the young he has been developing the next generation of citizens who are being positioned to develop the world and extract the greatness from within themselves and others. It is the author's intention that you journey with him and follow the guide as you become one with yourself, as you deserve to be wealthy. It is time; remind yourself: "Billionaire, I am One"